Code Napoleon

Code Napoleon

OR

The French Civil Code

BY

A BARRISTER OF THE INNER TEMPLE

Literally Translated from the Original and Official Edition,

Published at Paris in 1804

Reprinted 1999 Beard Books, Washington, D.C.

Printed in the United States of America

ISBN 1-893122-21-2

CONTENTS.

PRELIMINARY TITLE.

BOOK I.

Of Persons.

TITLE I.

TITLE II.

TITLE VI.

TITLE VII.

TITLE VIII.

TITLE IX.

TITLE X.

TITLE XI.

BOOK II.

Of Property, and the different Modifications of Property.

TITLE I.

TITLE II.

TITLE III.

TITLE IV.

BOOK III.

Of the different Modes of acquiring Property.

TITLE I.

TITLE II.

TITLE III.

TITLE VI.

TITLE VII.

TITLE VIII.

TITLE IX.

TITLE X.

TITLE XI.

TITLE XII.

TITLE XIII.

TITLE XIV.

TITLE XV.

TITLE XVI.

TITLE XVII.

TITLE XVIII.

TITLE XIX.

TITLE XX.

FRENCH CIVIL CODE.

PRELIMINARY TITLE.

OF THE PUBLICATION, EFFECT, AND APPLICATION OF THE LAWS IN GENERAL.

Decreed 5th of March, 1803. *Promulgated* 15*th of the same Month*

ARTICLE 1.

The laws are executory throughout the whole French territory, by virtue of the promulgation thereof made by the first consul.

They shall be executed in every part of the republic, from the moment at which their promulgation can have been known.

The pomulgation made by the first consul shall be taken to be known in the department which shall be the seat of government, one day after the promulgation; and in each of the other departments, after the expiration of the same interval augmented by one day for every ten myriameters (about twenty ancient leagues) between the town in which the promulgation shall have been made, and the chief place of each department.

2.

The law ordains for the future only; it has no retrospective operation.

3.

The laws of police and public security bind all the inhabitants of the territory.

Immoveable property, although in the possession of foreigners, is governed by the French law.

The laws relating to the condition and privileges of persons govern Frenchmen, although residing in a foreign country.

4.

The judge who shall refuse to determine under pretext of the silence, obscurity, or insufficiency of the law, shall be liable to be proceeded against as guilty of a refusal of justice.

5.

The judges are forbidden to pronounce, by way of general and legislative determination, on the causes submitted to them.

6.

Private agreements must not contravene the laws which concern public order and good morals.

BOOK I.

OF PERSONS.

Decreed 8*th of March*, 1803. *Promulgated* 18*th of the same Month.*

TITLE I.

OF THE ENJOYMENT AND PRIVATION OF CIVIL RIGHTS.

CHAPTER I.

Of the Enjoyment of Civil Rights.

7.

The exercise of civil rights is independent of the quality of citizen, which is only acquired and preserved conformably to the constitutional law.

8.

Every Frenchman shall enjoy civil rights.

9.

Every individual born in France of a foreigner, may, during the year which shall succeed the period of his majority, claim the quality of Frenchman; provided, that if he shall reside in France he declares his intention to fix his domicil in that country, and that in case he shall reside in a foreign country, he give security to become domiciled in France and establish himself there within a year, to be computed from the date of that undertaking.

10.

Every child born of a Frenchman in a foreign country is French. Every child born in a foreign country of a Frenchman who shall have lost the quality of a Frenchman, may at any time recover this quality by complying with the formalities prescribed in the ninth article.

11.

A foreigner shall enjoy in France the same civil rights as are or shall be accorded to Frenchmen by the treaties of that nation to which such foreigner shall belong.

12.

The foreigner who shall have married a Frenchman, shall follow the condition of her husband.

13.

The foreigner who shall have been permitted by the government to establish his domicil in France, shall enjoy in that country all civil rights so long as he shall continue to reside there.

14.

A foreigner, although not resident in France, may be cited before the French courts, to enforce the execution of engagements contracted by him in France with a Frenchman; he may be summoned before the tribunals of France, on account of engagements entered into by him with Frenchmen in a foreign country.

15.

A Frenchman may be summoned before a French court, for engagements contracted by him in a foreign country, though with a foreigner.

16.

In all causes, except commercial ones, in which a foreigner shall be plantiff, he shall be required to give security for the payment of the costs and damages incident to the suit, unless he possess in France immoveable property of value sufficient to guarantee such payment.

CHAPTER II.

Of the Privation of Civil Rights.

SECTION I.

Of the Privation of Civil Rights by the Loss of the Quality of Frenchman.

17.

The quality of Frenchman shall be lost, 1st, by naturalization in a foreign country; 2d, by accepting, without the authority of government, public employments bestowed by a foreign power; 3dly, by adoption into any foreign corporation which shall require distinctions of birth; 4thly, in short, by any settlement made in a foreign country, without intention of return.

Commercial establishments shall never be considered as having been made without intention of return.

18.

A Frenchman, who shall have lost his quality of Frenchman, may at any time recover it by returning to France with the sanction of government, declaring at the same time his intention to settle there, and his renunciation of every distinction inconsistent with the law of France.

19.

A Frenchwoman, who shall espouse a foreigner, shall follow the condition of her husband.

If she become a widow, she shall recover the quality of Frenchwoman, provided she already reside in France, or that she return thither under the sanction of government, and declare at the same time her intention to fix there.

20.

The individuals who shall recover the quality of Frenchman or Frenchwoman in the cases provided for by Articles 10, 18, and 19, shall not be permitted to avail themselves of it until they have fulfilled the conditions imposed upon them by those articles, and only for the exercise of rights open to their advantage after that period.

21.

The Frenchman who, without the authority of the government, shall engage in military service with a foreign power, or shall enrol himself in any foreign military association, shall lose his quality of Frenchman.

He shall not be permitted to re-enter France without the permission of the government, nor to recover the quality of Frenchman except by complying with the conditions required of a foreigner in order to become a citizen; and this without affecting the punishments denounced by the criminal law against Frenchmen who have borne or shall bear arms against their country.

SECTION II.

Of the Privation of Civil Rights in consequence of Judicial Proceedings.

22.

Sentences to punishments, the effect of which is to deprive the party condemned of all participation in the civil rights hereafter mentioned, shall imply civil death.

23.

Sentence to natural death shall imply civil death.

24.

Other perpetual afflictive punishments shall not imply civil death, except so far as the law shall have attached that consequence to them.

25.

By civil death, the party condemned loses his property in all the goods which he possessed; and the succession is open for the benefit of his heirs, on whom his estate devolves, in the same manner as if he were naturally dead and intestate.

He can no longer inherit any estate, nor transmit, by this title, the property which he has acquired in consequence.

He is no longer capable of disposing of his property, in whole or in part, either by way of gift during his life, or by will, nor of receiving by similar title, except for the purpose of subsistence. He cannot be nominated guardian, nor concur in any act relative to guardianship.

He cannot be a witness in any solemn public act, nor be admitted to give evidence in any court. He cannot engage in any suit, whether as defendant or plaintiff, except in the name and by the intervention of a special curator appointed for him by the court in which the action is brought.

He is incapable of contracting a marriage attended by any civil consequences.

If he have previously contracted marriage, it is dissolved, as respects all civil effects. His wife and his heirs shall respectively exercise those rights and demands to which his natural death would have given rise.

26.

Peremptory sentences only import civil death, reckoning from the day of their execution, whether real or by representation.

27.

Condemnations for contumacy shall not import civil death until after five years from the execution of the sentence by representation, and during which the condemned party may make his appearance.

28.

Those condemned for contumacy shall, during five years, or until they shall make appearance, or until their arrest during that period, be deprived of the exercise of civil rights. Their estate shall be administered and their rights exercised in the same manner as those of absent persons.

29.

When the party under sentence for contumacy shall appear voluntarily during the five years, to be reckoned from the day of the execution, or when he shall have been seized and made prisoner during that interval, the judgment shall be entirely reversed; the accused shall be restored to the possession of his property; he shall be tried afresh; and if by the new judgment he is condemned to the same punishment or a different punishment equally drawing after it civil death, it shall only take place from the date of the execution of the second judgment.

30.

When a party condemned for contumacy, who shall not have appeared, or who shall not have been made prisoner until the expiration of the five years, shall be acquitted by this new judgment, or shall only be sentenced to a punishment that does not carry with it civil death, he shall be reinstated in the full enjoyment of his civil rights for the future, reckoning from the day on which he shall have re-appeared in court; but the first judgment shall extend, as regards the past, to all consequences produced by civil death during the interval which elapsed between the period of the expiration of the five years and the day of appearance in court.

31.

If the party under sentence for contumacy dies during the five years interval of grace without having appeared, or without having been seized or arrested, he shall be deemed dead as to the entirety of his rights; judgment of contumacy shall be reversed entirely without prejudice nevertheless to the action of any civil plaintiff, which shall only be entered against the heirs of the party condemned according to the civil form.

32.

In no case shall efflux of time (prescription) after sentence restore a party condemned to his civil rights for the future.

33.

Property acquired by an outlawed person, after incurring civil death, and of which he shall be found possessed at the date of his natural death, shall belong to the nation by right of disherison. Nevertheless the government shall be allowed to make for the benefit of the widow, children, or relations of the party condemned, such disposition respecting it as humanity shall suggest.

TITLE II.

OF ACTS BEFORE THE CIVIL AUTHORITIES.

Decreed 12*th of March*, 1803. *Promulgated* 21*st of the same Month.*

CHAPTER I.

General Ordinance.

34.

The records of the civil power shall declare the year, the day, and hour, at which they shall be received; the Christian name, surname, age, profession, and domicil of all those who shall be therein mentioned.

35.

The officers of the civil courts shall insert nothing in the acts which they shall receive, either by way of note or of any explanation whatsoever, other than what is declared by the parties.

36.

In those cases in which parties interested are not bound to appear in person, it shall be allowed them to make appearance by means of a special and authentic warrant of attorney.

37.

Witnesses brought to attest documents in the civil courts shall be of the male sex only, of the age of 21 years at the least, relations or others, and shall be chosen by the parties interested.

38.

The officers of the civil court shall read over their acts to the parties appearing or to their attorneys, and also to the witnesses.

The performance of this formality shall be mentioned therein.

39.

These documents shall be signed by the officer of the civil court, by the parties appearing, and by the witnesses; or mention shall be made of the cause which prevents the parties and the witnesses from signing.

40.

The records of the civil courts shall be enrolled, in every commune, in one or more registers kept in duplicate.

41.

The registers shall be endorsed from first to last, and marked on each page, by the president of the court of first instance, or by the judge who shall supply his place.

42.

The acts shall be inscribed on the registers in succession without any blank. Rasures and references shall be approved and signed in the same manner as the body of the act. No abbreviations shall be used nor any date inserted in figures.

43.

The registers shall be closed and bound up by the officer of the civil court, at the end of every year; and within the month, one of the duplicates shall be deposited among the archives of the commune, the other among the rolls of the court of first instance.

44.

The warrants of attorney and other papers which ought to continue annexed to the records of the civil courts, shall be deposited, after being marked by the person who shall have produced them and by the officer of the court, among the rolls of the tribunal with the duplicate of the registers which shall be deposited among the said rolls.

45.

Every person shall be allowed to obtain from the depositories of the registers of the civil courts extracts from those registers; and extracts so obtained, corresponding with the registers and authenticated by the president of the court of first instance, or by the judge who shall supply his place, shall be evidence until proved false.

46.

Where no registers exist, or where they shall be lost, proof of them shall be received, as well by written documents as by witnesses; and in such cases marriages, births, and deaths, may be proved as well by registers and papers coming from the possession of fathers and mothers deceased, as by witnesses.

47.

Every act done in a civil court of a foreign country, either by Frenchmen or foreigners, shall be deemed valid, if reduced to writing according to the forms used in such country.

48.

Every act done in a civil court, in a foreign country by Frenchmen, shall be valid, if it has been acknowledged conformably to the French laws by the diplomatic agents, or by the commissioners of the republic for commercial relations.

49.

In all cases where mention of an act relating to a civil court ought to be made on the margin of another act already enrolled, it shall be done, at the request of the parties interested, by the officer of the civil court, on the current registers, or on those which have been deposited among the archives of the commune, and by the keeper of the rolls of the tribunal of first instance, on the registers deposited among the rolls ; to which end the officer of the civil court shall give notice within three days to the commissioner of government in the said court, who shall take care that such mention is made in a similar manner on both registers.

50.

Every offence against the preceding articles committed by any of the officers therein named, shall be prosecuted before the tribunal of first instance, and punished with a fine not exceeding 100 francs.

51.

Every officer entrusted with the registers shall be answerable civilly for any alterations made therein, saving his remedy, as the case may be, against the authors of such alterations.

52.

Every alteration, every falsification of the acts of the civil courts, every enrolment made upon a loose sheet and otherwise than on the registers designed for this purpose, shall give a right of action for damages to the parties, over and above the punishments contained in the penal code.

53.

The commissioner of government at the court of first instance shall be bound to verify the state of the registers at the time of their being deposited among the rolls of the court ; he shall draw up a concise statement of such verification, he shall certify all offences and crimes committed by the officers of the civil courts, and shall demand sentence of fine against them.

54.

In all cases where a tribunal of first instance shall take cognizance of acts relating to the civil courts, the parties interested may appeal against the judgment.

CHAPTER II.

Of Acts of Birth.

55.

Declarations of birth shall be made, within three days after delivery, to the civil officer of the place: the child shall be shown to him.

56.

The birth of the child shall be declared by the father, or, in his default, by the doctors in physic or surgery, the midwives, the officers of health, or other persons who shall have attended at the birth; and where the mother shall have been delivered out of her own house, by the party at whose house such delivery took place.

The act of birth shall be immediately reduced to writing, in the presence of two witnesses.

57.

The act of birth shall set forth the day, the hour, and the place of birth, the sex of the infant, and the Christian names which shall be given it, the Christian and surnames, profession, and domicil of the parents, and those of the witnesses.

58.

Every person who shall have found a new-born infant is required to carry it to the civil officer, as well as the clothes and other effects found with the infant, and to declare all the circumstances of the time and place when and where found; a particular statement of which shall be drawn up, containing moreover the apparent age of the child, its sex, the names which shall be given to it, and the civil authority to which it shall be committed. This statement shall be inscribed upon the registers.

59.

If a child is born at sea, the act of birth shall be drawn up within twenty-four hours, in presence of the father, if at hand, and of two witnesses selected from the officers of the vessel, or for want of them from the ship's crew. This act shall be reduced to writing, that is to say, on board the ships of the state, by the officer for the administration of the marine; and on board vessels belonging to a privateer or merchant, by the captain, master, or commander of the ship. The act of birth shall be inserted at the end of the roll of the ship's crew.

60.

At the first port at which the vessel shall touch, whether to refit or for any other purpose, except laying up, the officers for the administration of the marine, the captain, master, or commander, are required to deposit two authentic copies of the acts of birth, which they shall have reduced to writing, that is to say, in a French port at the office of the prefect of maritime inscription, and in a foreign port in the hands of the commissioners for commercial relations. One of these copies shall remain deposited in the office of maritime inscription, or in the chancery of the commissariat; the other shall be sent to the minister of marine, who shall cause a copy of each of the said acts, certified by himself, to be transmitted to the civil officer for the domicil of the father of the child, or of its mother, if the father is unknown: this copy shall immediately be inscribed on the registers.

61.

On the arrival of the ship at its port of discharge, the roll of the ship's crew shall be deposited in the office of the prefect of maritime inscription, who shall send a copy of the act of birth, with his signature, to the civil officer at the domicil of the child's father, or of its mother, if the father is unknown: this copy shall then be inscribed on the registers.

62.

The act of acknowledgment of a child shall be inscribed on the registers, at its date; and mention shall be made of this in the margin of the act of birth, if one exists.

CHAPTER III.

Of Acts of Marriage.

63.

Before the celebration of a marriage, the civil officer shall make two publications, with an interval of eight days between them, one being on a Sunday, before the gate of the town-hall. These publications, and the act which shall be drawn up relating to them, shall set forth the Christian names, surnames, professions, and domicils of the parties about to be married, the circumstance of their majority or minority, and the Christian names, surnames, professions, and domicils of their fathers and mothers. This act shall set forth, moreover, the days, places, and hours at which the publications shall have been made ; it shall be inscribed on one single register, which shall be endorsed and marked as directed in article 41, and deposited at the end of every year among the rolls of the court of the circle.

64.

An extract from the act of publication shall be affixed to the door of the town-hall, and remain so during the interval of eight days between the one and the other publication. The marriage shall not be celebrated until the third day exclusive after that of the second publication.

65.

Where a marriage has not been celebrated within a year, to be computed from the expiration of the interval between the publications, it shall not be celebrated until new publications have been made according to the forms hereinbefore prescribed.

66.

Acts of opposition to a marriage shall be signed, both original and copy, by the parties opposing, or by their attornies, specially and authentically appointed; they shall be communicated, with a copy of the appointment, to the party, or delivered at the domicil of the parties, and to the civil officer, who shall put his visa on the original.

67.

The civil officer shall, without delay, make mention concisely of the oppositions on the register of the publications; he shall likewise make mention, on the margin of the copy of the said oppositions, of the judgments or acts of renunciation which shall have been sent to him.

68.

Where opposition has been made, the civil officer shall not be at liberty to celebrate a marriage, until he shall have had a renunciation transmitted to him, upon pain of a fine of 300 francs, together with all costs.

69.

If there has been no opposition, a memorandum thereof shall be made in the act of marriage; and where publications have been made in several communes, the parties shall transmit a certificate from the civil officer of each commune, certifying that there is no opposition.

70.

The civil officer shall cause to be transmitted to him the act of birth of each party about to be married. Where either party shall be unable to produce it to him, its place may be supplied by showing an act of notoriety delivered by the magistrate at the parties' place of birth, or at that of his domicil.

71.

The act of notoriety shall contain the declaration of seven witnesses of either sex, relations or otherwise, the Christian names, surnames, profession, and domicil of the future husband or wife, and those of the father and mother, if they are known; the place, and as nearly as possible, the date of birth, and the causes which prevent the producing of the act of birth. The witnesses shall sign the act of notoriety with the magistrate; and if there are any witnesses who are unable or too ignorant to sign their names, mention shall be made of that circumstance.

72.

The act of notoriety shall be presented to the court of first instance in the place where the marriage is to be celebrated. The court, after having heard the commissioner of the government, shall give or refuse its approval accordingly, as it shall find the declarations of the witnesses, and the causes which prevent the production of the act of birth sufficient or insufficient.

73.

The authentic act of the consent of fathers and mothers, or of grandfathers and grandmothers, or in defect of these; that of the family, shall contain the Christian names, the surnames, the professions, and domicils of the future husband, or wife; and of all those who shall have concurred in the act, together with their degree of relationship.

74.

The marriage shall be celebrated in the commune in which one or other of the parties shall be domiciled. This domicil, as regards the marriage, shall be established by six months' continued habitation within the same commune.

75.

On the day appointed by the parties after the interval for the publications, the civil officer in the town hall, in the presence of four witnesses, relations, or otherwise, shall read to the parties the before-mentioned documents, relating to their condition and to the formalities of the marriage, and from cap. 6. title "*Of marriage*:" "*On the respective rights and duties of married persons.*" He shall receive from each party, in succession, a declaration that they are willing to take each other for husband and wife; he shall pronounce, in the name of the law, that they are united in marriage, and he shall forthwith draw up an act to that effect.

76.

In the act of marriage shall be set forth,

1st. The Christian names, surnames, professions, age, place of birth, and domicils of the married persons;

2nd. If they are of full age or minors;

3rd. The Christian names, surnames, professions, and domicils of the fathers and mothers;

4th. The consent of the fathers and mothers, grandfathers and grandmothers, and that of the family, in the cases in which they are requisi te;

5th. The respectful acts, if any have been made;

6th. The publications within the different places of domicil;

7th. The oppositions, if any have been made; the relinquishment of them, or the memorandum that no opposition has been made.

8th. The consent of the contracting parties to take each other as husband and wife, and the declaration of their union by the public officer;

9th. The Christian names, surnames, age, professions, and domicils of the witnesses, and their declaration whether they are relations or allied to the parties, on which side and in what degree.

CHAPTER IV.

Of Acts of Decease.

77.

No interment shall take place without an authority on paper, free of all expense, from the officer of the civil power, who is forbidden to deliver it until he shall have been conducted to the deceased person to assure himself of the death, and that not earlier than twenty-four hours after decease, except in cases otherwise provided for by the regulations of the police.

78.

The act of death shall be drawn up by the officer of the civil power on the declaration of two witnesses. These witnesses shall, if possible, be the two nearest relations or neighbors; or where a party shall die out of his own domicil, the person at whose house the decease shall take place, and a relation or other person.

79.

The act of death shall contain the Christian names, surname, age, profession, and domicil of the deceased person; the Christian name and surname of the consort, if any, of the deceased, whether living or dead; the Christian names, surnames, age, profession, and residence of the deponents; and if they are relations their degree of affinity.

The same act shall contain, moreover, as far as can

be ascertained, the Christian names, surnames, profession, and domicil of the father and mother of the deceased and the place of his birth.

80.

In cases of death in the military hospitals, civil or other public edifices, the governors, directors, managers, and masters of such edifices, are required to notify the same, within 24 hours, to the officer of the civil power, who shall repair to the place to satisfy himself of the death, and thereupon draw up an act conformably to the preceding article, upon the declarations which shall have been given him, and upon the observations he shall then make.

Registers shall moreover be kept in the aforesaid hospitals and edifices for the purpose of inserting such depositions and observations.

The officer of the civil power shall transmit the act of death to the officer at the last domicil of the deceased, who shall insert it in the registers.

81.

When any signs or marks of violent death, or of other circumstances which give rise to suspicion, shall appear, interment shall not take place until an officer of the police, assisted by a doctor in physic or surgery, shall have drawn up a statement of the condition of the body, and of the circumstances relative thereto, as well as the information he shall have been able to collect respecting the Christian name, surname, age, profession, place of birth, and domicil of the deceased.

82.

The officer of police is required to transmit forthwith to the civil power, at the place where the party died, all the informations set forth in his statement, after which the act of death shall be reduced to writing. The officer of the civil power shall transmit a copy thereof to the officer at the domicil of the deceased, if known: this copy shall be inserted in the registers.

83.

The keepers of the criminal records are required, within 24 hours after the execution of judgments inflicting the punishment of death, to transmit to the officer of the civil power at the place where the condemned party shall have been executed, all the informations enumerated in the 79th article, after which the act of death shall be reduced to writing.

84.

In case of death in prisons or houses of seclusion and detention, intimation thereof shall immediately be given, by the gaolers and keepers, to the officer of the civil power, who shall repair thither as directed in article 80, and shall reduce to writing the act of death.

85.

In all cases of death, by violence, or in prisons and houses of seclusion, or by execution, no mention shall be made in the registers of these circumstances, but the acts of death shall be drawn up simply in the form prescribed by article 79.

86.

In case of death during a sea-voyage, an act shall be drawn up within 24 hours, in presence of two witnesses selected from the officers of the vessel, or in defect of them, from among the ship's crew. This act shall be engrossed, in manner following, on board government ships, by the officer for the administration of the marine, and on board vessels belonging to a merchant or privateers, by the captain, master, or commander of the vessel. The act of death shall be inserted at the end of the roll of the ship's crew.

87.

At the first port where a vessel shall touch, whether to refit, or for any other cause except to unload, the officers for the administration of the marine, the captain, master, or commander, who shall have committed to writing the acts of death, are required to deposit two copies thereof conformably to article 60. On the arrival of a vessel at her unloading port, the roll of the ship's crew shall be deposited in the office of the prefect of maritime inscription; he shall transmit one copy, with his signature, to the officer of the civil power at the domicil of the deceased person: this copy shall be forthwith inserted in the registers.

CHAPTER V.

Of Acts of the Civil Power regarding the Military out of the Territory of the Republic.

88.

Acts of a civil nature done out of the territory of the republic, concerning the military or other persons attached to the army, shall be committed to writing in the forms prescribed by the preceding regulations; saving the exceptions contained in the following articles.

89.

The quarter-master in every corps, consisting of one or more battalions or squadrons, and the captain-commandant in other corps, shall discharge the functions of the officers of the civil power; the same functions shall be discharged for officers without troops, and for persons attached to the army, by the inspector at reviews belonging to the army, or to a division of the army.

90.

With every body of troops, a register shall be kept of acts of a civil nature relative to individuals of the corps, and another with the staff-officer of the army, or division of the army, for acts of a civil nature relative to officers without troops, and all others attached to the army; these registers shall be preserved in the same manner as other registers of the corps and staff, and deposited among the archives of the war, on the re-entrance of such corps or army into the territory of the republic.

91.

The register shall be endorsed and marked, in every corps, by the commanding officer; and among the staff by the chief officer of the staff.

92.

Declarations of birth in the army shall be made within 10 days succeeding the delivery.

93.

The officer charged with the custody of the civil register must, within 10 days following the inserting of an act of birth in the said register, address an extract from it to the civil officer at the last domicil of the father of the child, or of its mother, if the father is unknown.

94.

Publications of marriage among the military and those employed in the pursuit of arms, shall be made at their last domicil: they shall be put, moreover, 25 days before the celebration of the marriage, upon the order of the day of the corps, in the case of individuals who belong to such corps; and as regards officers without troops, and the employes attached to them, upon that of the army or division of the army.

95.

Immediately after the insertion in the register of the act of celebration of marriage, the officer charged with the custody of such register shall transmit a copy thereof to the civil officer at the last domicil of the married persons.

96

The acts of death shall be drawn up, in every corps, by the quarter-master; and in case of officers without troops, and their employes, by the inspector at reviews of the army on the attestation of three witnesses; and an extract from these registers shall be transmitted, within ten days, to the civil officer at the deceased's last domicil.

97.

In case of death in military hospitals, removable or stationary, the act thereof shall be drawn up by the director of the said hospitals, and sent to the quarter-master of the corps, or to the inspector at reviews of the army or division of the army of which the deceased formed part; these officers shall forward a copy thereof to the civil officer at the last domicil of the deceased.

98.

The civil officer to whom a copy of any act of a civil nature shall have been transmitted from the army, is required forthwith to inscribe it on the registers.

CHAPTER VI.

Of the Amendments of Acts of a Civil Nature.

99.

When the amendment of an act of a civil nature shall be demanded, it shall be decreed accordingly, saving an appeal, by a competent tribunal, and on the request of the commissioner of government. Parties interested shall be summoned, if there be ground.

100.

A judgment of amendment shall not at any time be objected to parties interested who shall not have demanded it, or who shall not have been summoned thereto.

101.

Judgments of amendment shall be inscribed upon the registers by the civil officer, as soon as they shall have been transmitted to him; and mention thereof shall be made on the margin of the amended act.

TITLE III.

OF DOMICIL.

Decreed 14*th March*, 1803. *Promulgated* 24*th of the same month.*

102.

The domicil of every Frenchman is, as far as regards the exercise of his civil rights, in that place where he has his principal establishment.

103.

The change of domicil shall be effected by the circumstance of a real habitation in another place, accompanied by an intention of fixing a principal establishment in such latter place.

104.

Proof of such intention shall be collected from an express declaration, made as well to the magistrates of the place which the party shall quit, as to those of the place to which he shall have transferred his domicil.

105

In default of express declaration, proof of intention shall depend on circumstances.

106.

A citizen called to a public office, temporary or revocable, shall preserve his former domicil, unless he has manifested a contrary intention.

107.

The acceptance of offices, bestowed for life, shall import an immediate removal of the functionary's domicil to the place where he is to exercise his office.

108.

A married woman has no domicil but that of her husband. A minor not emancipated shall have his domicil with his father, mother, or guardian; one of full age, placed under restraint, shall have his with his legal committee.

109.

Persons of full age who constantly serve or labor at the houses of others, shall have the same domicil as the persons with whom they serve or labor, provided they lodge also under the same roof.

110.

The place where an inheritance shall open, is to be determined by the domicil.

111.

When an act shall contain, on behalf of the parties, or one of them, an election of domicil for the execution of the same act in a different place from that of the real domicil, the notifications, demands, and proceedings, relative to such act, may be made at the domicil agreed on, and before the judge of that place.

TITLE IV.

OF ABSENT PERSONS.

Decreed 15*th of March,* 1803. *Promulgated* 25*th of the same Month.*

CHAPTER I.

Of Presumption of Absence.

112.

If there be necessity to provide for the administration of the whole or part of the effects, left by a person presumed absent, or who has no accredited agent, a decree shall be therefore made by a court of first instance, on the petition of the parties interested.

113.

The court, on the request of the most diligent party, shall appoint a notary to represent the presumed absentees as to inventories, accounts, distribution, and payments, in which they shall be interested.

114.

The public ministry is specially charged to watch over the interests of persons presumed absent; and shall be heard upon all actions which concern them.

CHAPTER II.

Of the Declaration of Absence.

115.

Wherever a person shall have ceased to appear at the place of his domicil or residence, and where no tidings shall have been heard of him during four years; the parties interested may make application to a court of first instance in order that his absence may be declared.

116.

In order to verify the absence, the court shall, after the production of papers and documents, give order that an inquiry be made peremptorily with the commissioner of the government, in the circle of the domicil or actual residence, if they are distinct from each other.

117.

The court, in adjudging upon such application, shall moreover have regard to the motives of absence, and to the causes which may have prevented the reception of tidings respecting the individual presumed absent.

118.

The commissioner of the government shall, immediately upon their being given, transmit all judgments, as well interlocutory as final, to the chief judge, the minister of justice, who shall make them public.

119.

The judgment, declaratory of absence, shall not be given until the expiration of a year after that directing an inquiry.

CHAPTER III.

Of the Effects of Absence.

SECTION I.

Of the Effects of Absence, as respects the Property possessed by the Absentee at the Date of his Disappearance.

120.

In cases where an absent person shall not have left a procuration for the administration of his property, his heirs presumptive at the date of his disappearance, or at the date of the last tidings respecting him, are empowered, by virtue of a definitive judgment declaring his absence, to take upon themselves provisional possession of the property which belonged to the absentee at the date of his departure, or of the last tidings respecting him, on condition of giving security for the fidelity of their administration.

121.

If the absentee have left behind him a procuration, his heirs presumptive shall not be at liberty to prosecute a declaration of absence, or to enter upon provisional possession, until after the lapse of ten years from the disappearance, or the last tidings respecting him,

122.

The same rule shall prevail where the procuration is extinguished; and, in such case, provision shall be made for the administration of the property of the absentee, as directed in the 1st chapter of the present title.

123.

When the heirs presumptive shall have obtained provisional possession, the will, if any exists, shall be opened on the requisition of the parties interested, or of the commissioner of government in the court; and the legatees, donees, as well as all those who have any claims upon the property of the absentee, contingent upon his death, are empowered to exercise such claims provisionally, on condition of giving security.

124.

The married party in community desirous of the continuance thereof, may prevent the provisional possession and the provisional exercise of all rights subject to the contingency of the death of the absentee, and take, or retain by preference, the administration of the property of the absentee. If the spouse demand provisional dissolution of the community, he shall exercise his claims, and all his legal and conventional rights, on condition of giving security for things susceptible of restitution. The wife, after exercising an option for the continuance of community, may still renounce it subsequently.

125.

Provisional possession shall only be regarded as a trust which shall confer on those who obtain it the administration of the property of the absentee, and which shall render them accountable to him, in case of his re-appearance, or the receipt of tidings respecting him.

126.

The parties obtaining provisional possession, or the spouse who shall have elected a continuance of community, must cause an inventory to be made of the moveable effects and papers of the absentee, in presence of the commissioner of the government of the court of first instance, or of a justice of the peace required by the said commissioner.

The court shall order, if there be foundation for doing so, a sale of the whole or part of the moveable effects. In case of sale, the produce shall be employed, as of goods fallen to the party.

Those who obtain provisional possession are empowered to demand, for their own security, that the proceeding be conducted by a man of skill, nominated by the court, to view the immoveable property, in order to verify its condition. This report shall be allowed in presence of the commissioner of the government, the costs of which shall be paid from the property of the absentee.

127.

They who, by means of provisional possession, or of legal administration, shall have obtained the property of the absentee, shall only be bound to render to him the fifth part of his revenues, in case he shall re-appear within fifteen complete years from the day of his disappearance ; and the tenth part, in case he shall not re-appear until after fifteen years.

After thirty years' absence, the whole of his revenues shall belong to them.

128.

None of those who shall have obtained property only by virtue of provisional possession, shall be at liberty to alienate or pledge the immoveable property of the absentee.

129

Where the absence has continued during thirty years from the provisional possession, or from the date at which the spouse in community shall have taken upon him the administration of the property of the absentee, or where a hundred years shall have elapsed since the birth of the absentee, the securities shall be discharged : all those who have claim may demand a distribution of the property of the absentee, and have the provisional possession pronounced final, by the court of first instance.

130.

A succession to the absentee shall be opened from the day of his decease proved, for the benefit of his next heirs at that date ; and they who shall have obtained the goods of the absentee, are required to restore them, with reservation of the fruits acquired by them, by virtue of article 127.

131.

If the absentee re-appears, or if his existence is proved during provisional possession, the effects of the judgment which shall have declared his absence shall cease: without prejudice if there be ground to the precautionary measures prescribed in the first chapter of the present title for the administration of his goods.

132.

If the absentee re-appears, or if his existence is proved, even after final possession, he shall recover his property in the state in which it shall then be, the price of that part of it which shall have been sold, or the profits accruing from the employment which shall have been made of the price of his property sold.

133.

The children and direct descendants of the absentee are empowered equally, within thirty years to be computed from final possession, to demand restitution of his property, as is mentioned in the preceding article.

134.

After the judgment declaratory of absence, every person who shall have claims to exercise against the absentee shall prosecute them against those only who shall have been part in possession of his property, or who shall have the legal administration thereof.

SECTION II.

Of the Effects of Absence, with regard to eventual Rights which may belong to the Absentee.

135.

Whoever shall claim a right fallen to an individual whose existence shall not be known, must prove that the said individual was alive when the right was open: until such proof, he shall be declared incapable of being admitted to sue for it.

136.

If a succession opens to which an individual shall be called whose existence is not known; it shall devolve exclusively upon those with whom he would have had a right to put in his claim, or upon those who shall be entitled to the succession in his default.

137.

The regulations of the two preceding articles shall take place without prejudice to the suits or petition of inheritance and other rights which shall belong to the absentee or to his representatives or assigns, and shall only be extinguished by the lapse of time established for prescription.

138.

As long as the absentee shall fail to appear, or that actions shall fail to be brought in his right, those who shall have gained the succession, shall enjoy the fruits bona fide received by them.

SECTION III.

Of the Effects of Absence, as they relate to Marriage.

139.

The absent spouse whose consort shall have contracted a new union, shall alone be admissible to impeach such marriage in person or by attorney furnished with proof of his existence.

140.

If the absent spouse has not left relations capable of succeeding to him, the consort may petition to be put into provisional possession of his property.

CHAPTER IV.

Of the Superintendence of Minors whose Father has disappeared.

141.

If a father has disappeared leaving children minors the issue of a common marriage, the mother shall have the superintendence of them, and she shall exercise all the rights of her husband, as regards their education and the administration of their property.

142.

Six months after the father's disappearance, if the mother were dead at the time of such disappearance, or if she shall die before the absence of the father is declared, the superintendence of the children shall be yielded up by the family council, to the nearest relation in the ascending line, and in their default to a provisional guardian.

143.

The same shall be done in the case where one of the spouses who shall have disappeared, shall leave children under age the issue of a former marriage.

TITLE V.

OF MARRIAGE.

Decreed 17th March, 1803. *Promulgated 24th of the same Month.*

CHAPTER I.

Of the Qualities and Conditions required in order to be able to contract Marriage.

144.

A man before the age of 18, and a woman before 15 complete, are incapable of contracting marriage.

145.

The government shall be at liberty, nevertheless, upon weighty reasons, to grant dispensations of age.

146.

There can be no marriage where consent is wanting.

147.

A second marriage cannot be contracted previously to the dissolution of the first.

148.

The son who has not attained the full age of 25 years, the daughter who has not attained the full age of 21 years, cannot contract marriage without the consent of their father and mother; in case of disagreement, the consent of the father is sufficient.

149.

If one of the two be dead, or under an incapacity of manifesting his or her will, the consent of the other is sufficient.

150.

If the father and mother are dead, or if they are under an incapacity of manifesting their will, the grandfathers and grandmothers shall supply their place; if there be a disagreement between the grandfather and grandmother of the same line, the consent of the grandfather shall suffice.

If the disagreement be between the two lines, this division shall import consent.

151.

Where the children of a family have attained the majority fixed by article 148, they are required, previously to contracting marriage, to demand, by a respectful and formal act, the advice of their father and mother, or that of their grandfathers and grandmothers when their father and mother are dead, or under an incapacity of manifesting their will.

Articles 152, 3, 4, 5, 6, *and* 7, *decreed* 12*th of March*, 1824. *Promulgated* 22*d of the same Month.*

152.

From the majority fixed by article 148 to the age of 30 years completed for sons, and until the age of 25 years completed for daughters, the respectful act required by the preceding article and on which consent to marriage shall not have been obtained, shall be renewed two several times, from month to month; and one month after the third act it shall be lawful to pass on to the celebration of the marriage.

153.

After the age of 30 years, it shall be lawful, in default of consent, upon a respectful act, to pass on, after the expiration of a month, to the celebration of the marriage.

154.

The respectful act shall be notified to such person or persons of the ascending line as are pointed out in article 151, by two notaries, or by one notary and two witnesses; and in the statement which shall be drawn up thereof, mention shall be made of the answer.

155.

In case of the absence of the ancestor to whom the respectful act ought to have been made, the celebration of the marriage may be proceeded in, on producing a judgment given declaring absence, or in default of such judgment that which shall have directed an inquiry, or if such latter judgment shall not yet have been pronounced, an act of notoriety delivered by the justice of the peace of the place where the ancestor had his last known domicil. This act shall contain the deposition or four witnesses officially summoned by the justice of the peace.

156.

The officers of the civil power who shall have proceeded to the celebration of marriages contracted by sons not having attained the full age of twenty-five years, or by daughters not having attained the full age of twenty-one years, without having the consent of the fathers and mothers, that of the grandfathers and grandmothers, and that of the family, in a case requiring them, declared in the act of marriage, shall, on the prosecution of the parties interested, and of the government commissioner in the tribunal of first instance of the place where the marriage shall have been celebrated, be condemned to the fine inflicted by article 192, and further to an imprisonment, whose duration shall not be less than six months.

157.

Where respectful acts shall have been omitted to be made in cases in which they are prescribed, the civil officer who shall have celebrated the marriage, shall be condemned to the same fine, and to an imprisonment of not less than one month.

158.

The regulations contained in articles 148 and 149, and those of articles 151, 152, 153, 154, and 155, relative to the respectful act required to be made to the father and mother in the case contemplated by those articles, are applicable to natural children legally recognized.

159.

The natural child who has not been acknowledged, and the child who after having been so, has lost his father and mother, or whose father and mother are unable to manifest their will, shall not be at liberty, before the full age of twenty-one years, to marry without the consent of a guardian ad hoc, who shall be nominated for him.

160.

If there is neither father nor mother, neither grandfathers nor grandmothers, or if they are all found to be under an incapacity of manifesting their will, male or female children under the age of twenty-one years cannot contract marriage without the consent of a family council.

161.

In a direct line, marriage is prohibited between all the ascending and descending branches legitimate or natural, and the kindred in the same line.

162.

In the collateral line, marriage is prohibited between brother and sister, legitimate or natural, and the kindred of the same degree.

163.

Marriage is further prohibited between the uncle and the niece, the aunt and the nephew.

164.

It shall be lawful, nevertheless, for the government, on weighty grounds, to remove the prohibitions contained in the preceding article.

CHAPTER II.

Of the Formalities relative to the Celebration of Marriage.

165.

The marriage shall be celebrated publicly, before the civil officer of the domicil of one of the two parties.

166.

The two publications directed by article 63, under the title "*Of the acts of the civil power,*" shall be made to the municipality of the place where each of the contracting parties shall have his domicil.

167.

Nevertheless, where the actual domicil is only established by six months' residence, the publication shall be further made to the muncipality of the last domicil.

168.

If the contracting parties, or one of them, is or are, as regards the marriage, under the power of others, the publications shall besides be made to the municipality of the domicil of those, under whose power they are found to be.

169.

The government, or those to whom it shall give charge to this effect, shall be at liberty, on weighty reasons, to dispense with the second publication.

170.

A marriage contracted in a foreign county between natives of France, and between a native of France and a foreigner, shall be valid, if celebrated according to the forms used in that country, provided that it has been preceded by the publications prescribed in article 63, under the title "*Of acts of the civil power,*" and that the Frenchman has not infringed the regulations contained in the preceding chapter.

171.

Within three months after the return of a Frenchman into the territory of the republic, the act of the celebration of marriage contracted in a foreign country, shall be transcribed into the public register of marriages, at the place of his domicil.

CHAPTER III.

Of Oppositions to Marriage.

172.

The right of opposing the celebration of marriage belongs to the person connected by marriage with one of the two contracting parties.

173.

The father, and in default of the father, the mother, and in default of the father and mother, the grandfathers and grandmothers, may oppose the marriage of their children and descendants, although they have accomplished twenty-five years.

174.

In default of ancestors, the brother or sister, the uncle or aunt, cousin or cousins german, being of age, can make no opposition except in the two following cases :

1st. Where the consent of the family-council, required by article 160, has not been obtained.

2nd. Where the opposition is founded on a state of insanity in the future spouse : This opposition, of which the court is empowered to pronounce the pure and simple abrogation, shall never be received except on condition by the opponent of urging the interdiction, and causing a decree to be made thereon, within the interval which shall be fixed by judgment.

175.

In the two cases contemplated by the preceding article, the guardian or curator shall not, during the continuance of the guardianship or curatorship, make opposition, except so far as he shall have been authorized by a family-council, which he is at liberty to convoke.

176.

Every act of opposition shall set forth the quality which gives to the opponent the right to make it;

it shall contain the election of domicil in the place where the marriage is to be celebrated; it shall, in like manner, unless it is made at the request of an ancestor, contain the motives of opposition: the whole on pain of nullity, and of suspension of the ministerial officer, who shall have signed the act containing the opposition.

177.

The tribunal of first instance shall pronounce within ten days, on the petition for revocation.

178.

If an appeal be made, a decision shall be made thereon within ten days from the citation.

179.

If the opposition be rejected, the opponents, other nevertheless than ancestors, may be sentenced to damages.

CHAPTER IV.

Of Petitions for Nullity of Marriage.

180.

A marriage contracted without the free consent of the married persons, or of one of them, can only be impeached by the married persons, or such one of them whose consent has not been free.

Where a mistake has occurred in the person, the marriage shall only be impeached by such one of the married persons as may have been led into the error.

181.

In the case mentioned in the preceding article, the petition of nullity is no longer admissible, where-ever there has been cohabitation continued during six months after the married person has acquired full liberty, or after discovery made of the error.

182.

A marriage contracted without the consent of the father and mother, of the ancestors, or of the family council, in cases where such consent was necessary, can only be impeached by those whose consent was requisite, or by such of the two married persons as stood in need of that consent.

183.

A suit for nullity is no longer maintainable either by the married persons, or by the relations whose consent was required, in those cases where the marriage has been approved, either expressly or tacitly, by those whose consent was necessary; or when a year has elapsed without complaint on their part, subsequently to their knowledge of the marriage. Such suit is no longer maintainable by a spouse, after the lapse of a year without complaint on his part, subsequently to his having attained the competent age for consenting to the marriage in his own person.

184.

Every marriage contracted in contravention of the regulations contained in articles 144, 147, 161,

2 and 3, may be impeached either by the married parties themselves, or by those who have an interest therein, or by the public authorities.

185.

Nevertheless a marriage contracted by parties who have not yet reached the required age, or of whom one has not attained that age, is no longer liable to be impeached, 1st, where six months have expired since the married person or persons have attained the competent age; 2d, where the woman not having reached that age has conceived before the expiration of six months.

186.

The father, the mother, the ancestors, and the family having consented to a marriage contracted under the circumstances mentioned in the preceding article, are inadmissible as plaintiffs in a suit for nullity.

187.

In all those cases where, conformably to article 184, a suit for nullity may be instituted by all those who have an interest therein, such suit shall not be maintained by collateral relations, or the children born of another marriage of the survivor of the parties, but only where they have an actual and existing interest therein.

188.

The married party, to the prejudice of whom a second marriage has been contracted, may demand the nullity thereof, even during the life of the party who was engaged with him.

189.

If the new married parties oppose the nullity of the first marriage, the validity or nullity of such marriage must be decided previously.

190.

The commissioner of government may and shall, in all cases to which article 184 can be applied, and subject to the modifications contained in article 185, demand the nullity of the marriage, living the two married persons, and cause them to be sentenced to separation.

191.

Every marriage not publicly contracted, and not celebrated before the competent public officer, may be impeached by the married parties themselves, by the father and mother, by the ancestors, and by all those who have an actual and existing interest therein, as well as by the public authorities.

192.

If the marriage has not been preceded by the two publications required, or if the dispensations permitted by the law have not been obtained, or if the intervals prescribed between the publications and celebrations have not been observed, the commissioner shall cause a fine to be awarded against the public officer, which shall not exceed 300 francs; and against the contracting parties, or those under whose control they have acted, a fine proportioned to their fortune.

193.

The punishments awarded in the preceding article shall be inflicted on the persons designated therein, for every contravention of the rules prescribed by article 165, even though such contraventions shall not be adjudged sufficient, whereon to pronounce a nullity of the marriage.

194.

No person shall be at liberty to claim the title of spouse, and the civil consequences of marriage, unless upon the production of an act of celebration inscribed upon the register of the civil power, saving the cases provided for by article 46, under the title "*Of acts before the civil authorities.*"

195.

The actual existence of marriage shall not discharge the pretended spouses, who shall respectively claim to be such, from producing the act of celebration of marriage before the officer of the civil power.

196.

Where there is an actual marriage, and the act of celebration of marriage before the officer of the civil power is produced, the married parties are respectively incapable of suing for a nullity of this act.

197.

Where, nevertheless, in the cases of articles 194 and 195, there are children, the issue of two individuals who have lived publicly together as husband and wife, and who are both deceased, the legitimacy of such children cannot be contested on the single ground of the non-production of the act of celebration, whenever such legitimacy is proved by an actual marriage uncontradicted by the act of birth.

198.

When the proof of a legal celebration of marriage is acquired by the result of a criminal procedure, the insertion of the judgment on the registers of the civil power confirms to the marriage, computing from the day of its celebration, all its civil consequences, as well as regards the married parties as the children the issue of such marriage.

199.

If the married parties are dead, or one of them, without having discovered the fraud, the criminal suit may be instituted by all those who have interest in causing the marriage to be declared valid, and by the commissioner of government.

200.

If the public officer is dead at the time of the discovery of the fraud, the action shall be carried on in a civil form against his heirs by the commissioner of government, in the presence of the parties interested and on their accusation.

201.

A marriage which has been declared null draws after it, nevertheless, civil consequences, as well with regard to the married parties as to their children, where the marriage has been contracted in good faith.

202.

Where good faith exists only on the part of one of the married persons, the marriage is only attended by civil consequences in favor of such persons, and the children of the marriage.

CHAPTER V.

Of the Obligations accruing from Marriage.

203.

Married persons contract together, by the single act of marriage, the obligation of nourishing, supporting, and bringing up their children.

204.

A child has no action against his father and mother for an establishment in marriage or otherwise.

205.

Children owe a maintenance to their fathers and mothers, and other ancestors who are in want thereof.

206.

Sons and daughters-in-law owe equally, under the same circumstances, a maintenance to their fathers and mothers-in-law; but this obligation ceases, 1st, when the mother-in-law has married again; 2nd, when such of the married parties as produced the affinity, and the children, the issue of the union with the other party, are dead.

207.

The obligations resulting from these regulations are reciprocal.

208.

Maintenance is only accorded in proportion to the necessity of the party who claims it, and to the fortune of the party who owes it.

209.

When he who supplies or he who receives maintenance is placed in such a situation, that the one can no longer give, or the other has no longer a need thereof, in whole or in part, a discharge or reduction thereof may be dmanded.

210.

If the person who is bound to supply maintenance can show that he is unable to pay an alimentary pension, the court shall, on being made acquainted with the cause, give order that he shall receive into his house, and there nourish and support, the party to whom he owes maintenance.

211.

The court shall, in like manner, adjudge, whether a father or mother who shall offer to receive, nourish, and support within the house, a child to whom they owe maintenance, ought in this case to be discharged from paying an alimentary pension.

CHAPTER VI.

Of the respective Rights and Duties of Married Persons.

212.

Married persons owe to each other fidelity, succour, assistance.

213.

The husband owes protection to his wife, the wife obedience to her husband.

214.

The wife is obliged to live with her husband, and to follow him to every place where he may judge it convenient to reside: the husband is obliged to receive her, and to furnish her with every thing necessary for the wants of life, according to his means and station.

215.

The wife cannot plead in her own name, without the authority of her husband, even though she should be a public trader, or non-communicant, or separate in property.

216.

The authority of the husband is not necessary when the wife is prosecuted in a criminal matter, or relating to police.

217.

A wife, although non-communicant or separate in property, cannot give, alienate, pledge, or acquire by free or chargeable title, without the concurrence of her husband in the act, or his consent in writing.

218.

If the husband refuse to authorize his wife to plead in her own name, the judge may give her authority.

219.

If the husband refuse to authorize his wife to pass an act, the wife may cause her husband to be cited directly before the court of first instance, of the circle of their common domicil, which may give or refuse its authority, after the husband shall have been heard, or duly summoned before the chamber of council.

220.

The wife, if she is a public trader, may, without the authority of her husband, bind herself for that which concerns her trade; and in the said case she binds also her husband, if there be a community between them.

She is not reputed a public trader, if she merely retail goods in her husband's trade, but only when she carries on a separate business.

221.

When the husband is subjected to a condemnation, carrying with it an afflictive or infamous punishment, although it may have been pronounced merely for contumacy, the wife, though of age, cannot, during the continuance of such punishment, plead in her own name or contract, until after authority given by the judge, who may in such case give his authority, without hearing or summoning the husband.

222.

If the husband is interdicted or absent, the judge, on cognizance of the cause, may authorize his wife either to plead in her own name or to contract.

223.

Every general authority, though stipulated by the contract of marriage, is invalid, except as respects the administration of the property of the wife.

224.

If the husband is a minor, the authority of the judge is necessary for his wife, either to appear in court, or to contract.

225.

A nullity, founded on defect of authority, can only be opposed by the wife, by the husband, or by their heirs.

226.

The wife may make a will without the authority of her husband.

CHAPTER VII.

Of the Dissolution of Marriage.

227.

Marriage is dissolved,

1st. By the death of one of the parties;

2d. By divorce lawfully pronounced;

3d. By condemnation become final of one of the married parties to a punishment implying civil death.

CHAPTER VIII.

Of second Marriages.

228.

A woman cannot contract a new marriage until ten months have elapsed from the dissolution of the preceding marriage.

TITLE VI.

OF DIVORCE.

Decreed 21*st March*, 1803. *Promulgated* 31*st of the same Month.*

CHAPTER I.

Of the Causes of Divorce.

229.

The husband may demand a divorce on the ground of his wife's adultery.

230.

The wife may demand divorce on the ground of adultery in her husband, when he shall have brought his concubine into their common residence.

231.

The married parties may reciprocally demand divorce for outrageous conduct, ill-usage, or grevious injuries, exercised by one of them towards the other.

232.

The condemnation of one of the married parties to an infamous punishment, shall be to the other a ground of divorce.

233.

The mutual and unwavering consent of the married parties, expressed in the manner prescribed by law, under the conditions, and after the proofs which it points out, shall prove sufficiently that their common life is insupportable to them; and that there exists, in reference to them, a peremptory cause of divorce.

CHAPTER II.

Of the Divorce for Cause determinate.

SECTION I.

Of the Forms of the Divorce for Cause determinate.

234.

Whatever may be the nature of the facts or offences which afford ground for a demand of divorce for cause determinate, such demand shall only be made to the court of the circle within which the married persons shall have their domicil.

235.

If any of the facts alleged by the married party demandant give ground for a criminal prosecution on the part of the public officers, the action for divorce shall remain suspended until after the judgment of the criminal tribunal; it may then be resumed, without permitting any objection or exception at law to be drawn from the criminal judgment prejudicial to the married party demandant.

236.

Every petition for divorce shall detail the facts; it shall be sent back, with the corroborating documents, if there are any, to the president of the court, or to the judge who shall perform his functions, by the married party demandant in person, unless prevented by illness ; in which case, on his request, and the certificate of two doctors of physic or surgery, or of two officers of health, the magistrate shall repair to the residence of the demandant there, to receive his petition.

237.

The judge after having heard the petitioner, and having made to him such observations as he shall deem suitable, shall mark the petition and the documents, and draw up a statement that the whole has been placed in his hands. This statement shall be signed by the judge and by the petitioner, unless the latter is ignorant or unable to write, in which case mention shall be made thereof.

238.

The judge shall make order, at the foot of his statement, that the parties shall appear in person before him, at the day and hour that he shall point out; and to this end, a copy of his order shall be addressed by him to the party against whom the divorce is demanded.

239.

On the day appointed, the judge shall make to the two married parties, if both present themselves, or to the petitioner, if appearing alone, snch representations as he shall deem likely to effect a reconciliation : if he is unable to accomplish this, he shall draw up a statement thereof, and shall set forth the communication of the petition and of the documents to the commissioner of government, and the report of the whole to the tribunal.

240.

Within the three following days, the court, on the report of the president or of the judge who shall have exercised his functions, and on the motion of the commissioner of the government, shall award or suspend the permission of citation. The suspension shall not exceed the term of twenty days.

241.

The petitioner may, by virtue of the permission of the court, cause the defendant to be summoned, in the ordinary form, to appear in person at a private hearing, within the interval prescribed by law; he shall cause a copy to be delivered at the head of his summons, of the petition of divorce, and of the documents produced in its support.

242.

At the expiration of the interval, whether the defendant appear or not, the petitioner in person, assisted by a counsel, if he shall deem it expedient, shall unfold, or cause to be unfolded, the grounds of his petition; he shall produce the documents which support it, and shall name the witnesses whom he proposes to have heard.

243.

If the defendant appear in person or by an authorized agent, he may make his observations, or cause them to be made, as well upon the grounds of the petition as upon the documents produced by the petitioner and on the witnesses named by him. The defendant shall name, on his part, the witnesses whom he proposes to have heard, and on them the petitioner in turn shall make his observations.

244.

A statement shall be drawn up of the appearance, depositions and observations of the parties, as well as of the confessions which either may make. The statement shall be read over to the aforesaid parties, who shall be required to sign it; and express mention shall be made of their signature, or of their declaration of inability or unwillingness to sign.

245.

The court shall send the parties to a public hearing of which it shall appoint the day and hour; it shall direct a communication of the proceeding to the commissioner of government, and shall appoint a judge to report. In case the defendent shall not appear, the petitioner shall be bound to signify to him the order of the court, within the interval which it shall appoint.

246.

At the day and hour appointed, on the report of the judge nominated, the commissioner of government being heard, the court shall decree first upon the exceptions of law, if any have been propounded. In case they shall be found conclusive, the petition for divorce shall be rejected: in the opposite case, or if exceptions of law have not been offered, the petition for divorce shall be admitted.

247.

Immediately after the admission of the petition for divorce, on the report of the judge appointed, the commissioner of government being heard, the court shall adjudge fully. It shall give judgment on the petition, if it appear in a state to be decided on; if not, it shall admit the petitioner to proof of pertinent facts alleged by him and the defendant to contrary proof.

248.

At every stage of the cause, the parties shall be at liberty, after the reports of the judge, and before the commissioner of the government shall have begun to speak, to propose, or cause to be proposed, their respective arguments, first upon exceptions at law and afterwards upon the merits; but in no case shall the counsel of the petitioner be heard, unless the petitioner be present in person.

249.

Immediately after pronouncing the judgment which shall direct the inquiries, the registrar of the court shall read that part of the statement which contains the nomination already made of the witnesses whom the parties propose to have heard. They shall be warned by the president that as yet they are at liberty to mention others, but that after this moment no more can be received.

250.

The parties shall propose at once their respective exceptions against the witnesses of whom they desire to get rid. The court shall decide on these exceptions after having heard the commissioner of the government.

251.

The relations of the parties, with the exception of their children aud descendants, cannot be excepted to on the ground of their affinity, nor can the domestics of the parties by reason of such quality; but the court shall have such regard as reason requires to the depositions of relations and servants.

252.

Every judgment which shall admit a proof by witnesses shall mention by name the witnesses who shall be heard, and shall fix the day and hour at which the parties are to present themselves.

253.

The depositions of the witnesses shall be received by the court sitting with closed doors, in the presence of the commissioner of government, of the parties, and of their counsel or friends to the number of three on each side.

254.

The parties by themselves or by their counsel may make to the witnesses such observations and examinations as they shall judge suitable, without being allowed nevertheless to interrupt them in the course of their depositions.

255.

Every deposition shall be reduced to writing, as well as the remarks and observations to which it shall have given rise. The statement of inquiry shall be read as well to the witnesses as to the parties: both shall be required to sign it; and mention shall be made of their signature, or of their declaration of inability or refusal to sign.

256.

After the close of the two inquiries or of that of the petitioner, if the defendant has not produced witnesses, the court shall send the parties to a public hearing, for which it shall point out the day and hour; it shall order the communication of the proceeding to the commissioner of government, and shall appoint a reporter. This order shall be signified to the defendant at the request of the petitioner, within the interval appointed therein.

257.

On the day fixed for final judgment, a report shall be made by the judge commissioned: the parties shall be at liberty afterwards to make by themselves or by the instrumentality of their counsel, such observations as they shall judge useful to their cause; after which the commissioner of government shall give his arguments.

258.

Final judgment shall be pronounced publicly; when it shall establish the divorce, the petitioner shall be authorized to go before the civil officer, and cause him to pronounce it.

259.

When the petition for divorce shall have been founded on causes of excess, cruelty, or grievous injury, although they shall be well established, the judges shall be at liberty not to allow the divorce immediately. In such case, before judgment is given, they shall authorize the woman to quit the society of her husband, without being bound to receive him, unless she judges it expedient; and they shall sentence the husband to pay her an alimentary pension proportioned to his means, if the wife has not herself sufficient funds to supply her wants.

260.

After a year of trial, if the parties are not reunited, the married person petitioning shall cause the other to be cited to appear before the court, within the intervals prescribed by law, there to hear final judgment pronounced, which shall then allow the divorce.

261.

When the divorce shall be demanded by reason that one of the married persons is condemned to an infamous punishment, the only formalities to be observed shall consist of producing before the civil court a copy in correct form of the judgment of condemnation, with a certificate from the criminal court, importing that the said judgment is no longer liable to be reviewed in any legal way.

262.

In case of appeal from the judgment of admission, or from the final judgment, given by the court of first instance in a cause of divorce, the cause shall be prepared for hearing and decided by the court of appeal, as an urgent affair.

263.

The appeal shall not be receivable except where it shall have been lodged within three months, to be reckoned from the day of intimation given of the judgment rendered on the hearing or by default. The interval for making application to the court of cassation against a judgment in the last resort shall also be one of three months, computing from the intimation. The application shall be suspensory.

264.

By virtue of every judgment given in the last resort, or passed with the force of a matter decided, which shall authorize a divorce, the married person who shall have obtained it, shall be obliged to present himself, within an interval of two months, before the civil officer, the other party being duly summoned, in order to cause him to pronounce the divorce.

265.

These two months shall not begin to run, with regard to the judgments of first instance, until after the expiration of the interval for the appeal; with regard to judgments given for default in matters of appeal not until after the expiration of the interval for opposition; and with regard to peremptory judgments in the last resort, not until after the expiration of the interval for application for cassation.

266.

The married party petitioner who shall have suffered the interval of two months hereinbefore determined to pass by, without summoning the other party before the civil officer, shall forfeit the benefit of the judgment which has been obtained, and shall not be permitted to resume his suit for divorce, except for new cause; in which case the ancient causes may be insisted on.

SECTION II.

Of the Provisional Measures to which the Petition for Divorce for Cause determinate may give rise.

267.

The provisional management of the children shall rest with the husband, petitioner, or defendant, in the suit for divorce, unless it be otherwise ordered by the court for the greater advantage of the children, on petition either of the mother, or the family, or the government commissioner.

268.

The wife, petitioner, or defendant in divorce, shall be at liberty to quit the residence of her husband during the prosecution, and demand an alimentary pension proportioned to the means of the husband. The court shall point out the house in which the wife shall be bound to reside, and shall fix, if there be ground, the alimentary provision which the husband shall be obliged to pay her.

269.

The wife shall be bound to prove her residence in the house appointed, as often as she shall be thereto required ; in default of such proof, the husband may refuse the alimentary pension, and if the wife is the petitioner for divorce, may cause her to be declared incapable of continuing her prosecution.

270.

The wife having community of goods, plaintiff or defendant in divorce shall be at liberty, in every stage of the cause, commencing with the date of the order mentioned in article 238, to require, for the preservation of her rights, that seals should be affixed to the moveable goods in community. These seals shall not be taken off until an inventory and appraisement is made, and on the undertaking of the husband to produce the articles contained in the inventory, or to answer for their value, as their legal keeper.

271.

Every obligation contracted by the husband at the expense of the community, every alienation made by him of immoveable property dependent upon it, subsequently to the date of the order mentioned in article 238, shall be declared void, if proof be given moreover, that it has been made or contracted in fraud of the rights of the wife.

SECTION III.

Of Exceptions at Law against the Suit for Divorce for Cause determinate.

272.

The suit for divorce shall be extinguished by the reconciliation of the parties, whether occurring subsequently to the facts which might have authorized such suit, or subsequently to the petition for divorce.

273.

In either case the petitioner shall be declared incapable of pursuing the action; a new one may, nevertheless, be instituted for cause accruing subsequently to the reconciliation, and the ancient causes may then be employed in support of such new petition.

274.

If the petitioner for divorce deny that a reconciliation has taken place, the defendant shall make proof thereof, either in writing or by witnesses, in the form prescribed in the first section of the present chapter.

CHAPTER III.

Of Divorce by Mutual Consent,

275.

The mutual consent of married persons shall not be admitted, if the husband have not reached twenty-five years, or if the wife be under twenty-one.

276.

The mutual consent shall not be received until two years from the marriage.

277.

It shall no longer be admissible after twenty years of marriage, nor where the wife shall have attained the age of forty-five years.

278.

In no case shall the mutual consent of married persons be sufficient, unless authorized by their fathers and mothers, or by their other living ancestors, according to the rules prescribed in article 150, under the title "*of Marriage.*"

279.

Married persons determined to effect a divorce by mutual consent, shall be bound to make previously an inventory and estimate of all their property moveable and immoveable, and to adjust their respective rights, on which notwithstanding it shall be free to them to enter into arrangements.

280.

They shall be bound in like manner to establish in writing their agreement on the three points following:

1st. To whom the children, the fruit of their union, shall be intrusted, as well during the period of the suit, as after divorce pronounced;

2d. To what house the wife is to retire and reside in during the period of the suit;

3d. What sum the husband is to pay to his wife during she same period, if she has not an income sufficient to supply her wants.

281.

The married parties shall present themselves together and in person, before the president of the civil court of their circle, or before the judge who shall discharge his functions, and make to him a declaration of their desire, in presence of two notaries brought by themselves.

282.

The judge shall make to both the married parties together, and to each of them apart, in the presence of the two notaries, such representations and exhortations as he shall deem suitable: he shall read to them the fourth chapter of the present title, which regulates "*The Effects of Divorce,*" and shall disclose to them all the consequences of the step they are taking.

283.

If the married parties persist in their resolution, an act shall be given them, by the judge setting forth that they demand a divorce and mutually consent to it; and they shall be required to produce and deposit on the instant, in the hands of the notaries, besides the acts mentioned in articles 279 and 280—

1st. The acts of their birth and that of their marriage;

2d. The acts of birth and of death, of all the children the fruit of their union;

3d. An authenticated declaration of their father and mother or other living ancestors, to the effect, that for causes to them known, they authorize him or her, their son or daughter, grandson or grandaughter married to such or such a person, to demand divorce and to consent thereto. The fathers, mothers, grandfathers and grandmothers of the married parties shall be presumed living until the production of the acts verify their decease.

284.

The notaries shall draw up at length a detailed statement of all that shall have been said or done in execution of the preceding articles; the minute thereof shall remain with the elder of the two notaries, as well as the documents produced, which shall be annexed to the statement, in which mention shall be made of intimation which shall be given to the wife to retire within twenty-four hours to the house agreed on between her and her husband, and to reside there until divorce pronounced.

285.

The declaration thus made shall be renewed within the first fortnight of the 4th, 7th, and 10th month following, observing the same formalities. The parties shall be bound each time to bring proof, by public act, that their fathers, mothers, or other living ancestors, persist in their first determination; but they shall not be bound to repeat the production of any other act.

286.

Within a fortnight from the day on which a year shall have expired, computing from the first declaration, the married parties, attended each by two friends, persons of credit within the circle, of the age of fifty years at the least, shall present themselves together, and in person, before the president of the court, or the judge who shall discharge his functions; they shall hand to him copies in correct form, of the four statements, containing their mutual consent, and of all the acts which shall have been annexed to it, and shall require of the magistrate, each separately, in the presence nevertheless of each other, and of the four persons of credit, sentence of divorce.

287.

After the judge and the attending parties shall have made their observations to the married persons, if they persevere, an act shall be delivered to them of their request and of the presentation made by them of the documents in its support: the registrar of the court shall draw up a statement which shall be signed as well by the parties (unless they shall declare they know not how or are incapable of writing, in which case mention shall thereof be made) as by the four attending persons, the judge and the registrar.

288.

The judge shall then annex to this statement, his decree that within three days, a report shall by him be made to the court in the council-chamber, upon the conclusions in writing by the commissioner of government, to whom the documents shall be, for this purpose, communicated by the registrar.

289.

If the commissioner of government finds in the documents proof that the married parties were of the age the husband of 25 years, the wife of 21 years, when they made their first declaration; that at this period they had been married during two years, and that their marriage had not subsisted more than 20 years, that the wife was under the age of 45 years, that the mutual consent had been expressed four times in the course of the year, after the preliminaries hereinbefore prescribed, and with all the formalities required in the present chapter, more especially with the authority of the fathers and mothers of the married persons, or with that of their other living ancestors in case of the previous decease of their fathers and mothers:—he shall give his conclusions in these terms, "the law permits;" in a contrary case, his conclusion shall be in these terms, "the law forbids."

290.

The court shall not upon the report enter into any other examinations than those pointed out in the preceding article. If the result shall be that, in the opinion of the court, the parties have satisfied the conditions and complied with the formalities appointed by the law, it shall admit the divorce, and send the parties before the civil officer, to have it pronounced: in the opposite case, the court shall declare that the divorce cannot be admitted, and shall set forth the grounds of their decision.

291.

The appeal against the judgment, declaring that there is no ground for directing a divorce, shall only be admissible where it is lodged by the two parties, but by separate acts, within ten days at the soonest, and at the latest within twenty days, from the date of the judgment of first instance.

292.

The acts of appeal shall be mutually signified as well to the other married party as to the commissioner of the government of the court of first instance.

293.

Within ten days, to be computed from the intimation given to him of the second act of appeal, the commissioner of government in the court of first instance shall cause to be passed to the general commissioner of government in the court of appeal a copy of the judgment, and the documents on which it has been founded. The commissioner-general in the court of appeal shall give his conclusions in writing, within ten days following the receipt of the documents: the president, or the judge officiating for him, shall make his report to the court of appeal, in the chamber of council, and judgment shall be finally given within ten days following the remission of the conclusions of the commissioner.

294.

In pursuance of the sentence establishing the divorce, and within twenty days from its date, the parties shall present themselves together and in person before the officer of the civil power, in order to cause him to pronounce the divorce. This interval exceeded, the judgment shall be as though it had never occurred.

CHAPTER IV.

Of the Effects of Divorce.

295.

Married parties who shall be divorced, for any cause whatsoever, shall never be permitted to be united again.

296.

In a case of divorce pronounced for cause determinate, the wife divorced shall not be permitted to marry for ten months after divorce pronounced.

297.

In case of divorce by mutual consent, neither of the parties shall be allowed to contract a new marriage until the expiration of three years from the pronunciation of the divorce.

298.

In the case of divorce admitted by law for cause of adultery, the guilty party shall never be permitted to marry with his accomplice. The wife adulteress shall be condemned in the same judgment; and, on the request of the public minister, to confinement in a house of correction, for a determinate period, which shall not be less than three months, nor exceed two years.

299.

For whatever cause a divorce shall take place, except in the case of mutual consent, the married party against whom the divorce shall have been established shall lose all the advantage conferred by the other party, whether by their contract of marriage, or since the marriage contracted.

300.

The married party who shall have obtained the divorce shall preserve the advantages conferred by the other spouse, although they may have made mutual stipulations and such reciprocity have not taken place.

301.

If the married parties shall have conferred no advantage, or if those stipulated do not appear sufficient to secure the subsistence of the married party who has obtained the divorce, the court may award to such party, from the property of the other, an alimentary pension, which shall not exceed the third part of the revenues of such other. This pension shall be revocable in a case where it shall cease to be necessary.

302.

The children shall be entrusted to the married party who has obtained the divorce, unless the court, on petition by the family, or by the commissioner of government, gives order, for the greater benefit of the children, that all or some of them shall be committed to the care either of the other married party, or of a third person.

303.

Whoever may be the person to whom the children shall be committed, their father and mother shall preserve respectively the right to watch over the maintenance and education of their children, and shall be bound to contribute thereto in proportion to their means.

304.

The dissolution of a marriage by divorce admitted by law shall not deprive children, the fruit of such marriage, of any of the benefits secured to them by the laws, or by the matrimonial covenants of their father and mother; but there shall be no admission of claims by the children except in the same manner and in the same circumstances in which they would have been admitted if the divorce had not taken place.

305.

In the case of divorce by mutual consent, a property in half the possessions of each of the two married parties shall be acquired in full right, from the day of their first declaration, by the children born of their marriage: the father and mother shall nevertheless retain the enjoyment of such moiety until their children's majority, on condition of providing for their nourishment, maintenance, and education, in a manner suitable to their fortune and condition; the whole without prejudice to the other advantages which may have been secured to the said children by the matrimonial covenants of their father and mother,

CHAPTER V.

Of the Separation of Persons.

306.

In cases where there is ground for a petition in divorce for cause determinate, it shall be free to the married parties to make petition for separation of persons.

307.

It shall be entered, carried on, and determined in the same manner as every other civil action: it shall not take place in consequence merely of the mutual consent of married parties.

308.

The wife against whom separation of persons shall be pronounced for cause of adultery, shall be condemned by the same judgment, and, on the requisition of the public minister, to confinement in a house of correction during a fixed period, which shall not be less than three months nor exceed two years.

309.

The husband shall continue empowered to arrest the effect of this sentence, by consenting to receive his wife again.

310.

When the separation of persons pronounced for any other cause than that of adultery in the wife shall have continued three years, the married party, who was originally defendant, may demand divorce of the court, which shall allow it, unless the original plaintiff, present or duly summoned, consents immediately that such separation shall cease.

311.

The separation of person shall import in every case a separation of property.

TITLE VII.

OF PATERNITY AND FILIATION.

Decreed 25th of March, 1803. *Promulgated the 2d of April.*

CHAPTER I.

Of the Filiation of legitimate Children, or those born in Marriage.

312.

An infant conceived during marriage claims the husband as his father. The latter, nevertheless, may disavow such child, on proof that during the time which has elapsed from the three hundredth to the one hundred and eightieth day previous to the birth of the infant, he was either, by reason of absence, or by the effect of some accident, under a physical incapability of cohabiting with his wife.

313.

The husband shall not disavow an infant, on allegation of his natural impotence; he shall not disavow it even for cause of adultery, unless the birth has been concealed from him, in which case he shall be permitted to bring forward all the facts proper to show that he is not the father.

314.

A child born within 180 days from the marriage shall not be disavowed by the husband in the following cases:

1st. If he had knowledge of the pregnancy before the marriage.

2d. If he assisted at the act of birth, and if this act is signed by him, or contains his declaration that he cannot sign.

3d. If the child is not declared likely to live.

315.

The legitimacy of an infant born three hundred days after dissolution of marriage may be contested.

316.

In the different cases where the husband is authorized to disclaim, he must do so within a month, if he be on the spot where the infant is born;

Within two months after his return, if he be absent at such time;

Within two months after discovery of the fraud, if the birth of the child have been concealed from him.

317.

If the husband die before having made his disclaimer, but yet being within the interval allowed for making it, the heirs shall have two months to contest the legitimacy of the child, to be reckoned from the period at which such child shall be put in possession of the property of the husband, or from the period at which the heirs shall be disturbed by the child in the possession.

318.

Every extrajudicial act containing a disavowal on the part of the husband or of his heirs shall be as though not made, unless followed within the interval of one month, by an action at law, brought against a tutor *ad hoc*, given to the child, the mother being present.

CHAPTER II.

Of the proofs of the Filiation of legitimate Children.

319.

The filiation of legitimate children is proved by the acts of birth inscribed upon the registers of the civil authorities.

320.

In default of this document, constant enjoyment of the condition of a legitimate child is sufficient.

321.

The enjoyment of this condition is established by a satisfactory combination of facts, indicating the connexion of parent and child between an individual and the family to which he claims to belong. The principal of these facts are,

That the individual has always borne the name of the father to whom he claims to belong;

That the father has treated him as his child, and in that character has provided for his education, his maintenance, and his establishment;

That he has been uniformly received as such in society;

That he has been acknowledged as such by the family.

322.

No one is at liberty to claim a condition contrary to that conferred on him by title of birth and possession, conformable to such title;

And reciprocally, no one can contest the condition of him who has a possession conformable to his title of birth.

323.

In default of title and constant enjoyment, or if the child have been registered, either under false names, or as born of father and mother unknown, the proof of filiation may be made by witnesses.

This proof, however, cannot be admitted, except when there is a commencement of proof in writing, or when the presumptions and probable evidence resulting from subsequent unquestionable facts are sufficiently grave to decide their admission.

324.

The commencement of proof in writing is gathered from the titles of the family, from registers, and private papers of the father or the mother, from public acts, and likewise private ones emanating from one party engaged in the dispute, or who would have had interest therein if living.

325.

Contrary proof may be made by all means proper to establish that the claimant is not the child of the mother he pretends to have, or even, the maternity being proved, that he is not the child of the husband of such mother.

326.

The civil courts alone shall be competent to adjudicate on claims of condition.

327.

A criminal action for an offence in concealing a condition, cannot be commenced until after final judgment on the question of condition.

328.

The action in claim of condition is imprescriptible, with regard to the child.

329.

An action cannot be brought by the heirs of a child who has not claimed, except he has died a minor, or within five years after his majority.

330.

The heirs may pursue this action where it has been commenced by the child, unless he have formally discontinued it, or that three years have passed without any step taken, reckoning from the last act of procedure.

CHAPTER III.

Of Natural Children.

SECTION I.

Of the Legitimation of Natural Children.

331.

Children born out of wedlock, other than such as are the fruit of an incestuous or adulterous intercourse, may be legitimated by the subsequent marriage of their father and mother, whenever the latter shall have legally acknowledged them before their marriage, or shall have recognized them in the act itself of celebration.

332.

The legitimation may take place, in favor even of deceased children who have left descendants; and in such case, the benefit thereof accrues to such descendants.

333.

Children legitimated by subsequent marriage shall enjoy the same rights as if they were born in wedlock.

SECTION II.

Of the Acknowledgment of Natural Children.

334.

The acknowledgment of a natural child shall be made by an authentic act, whenever it shall not have been done in its act of birth.

335.

This acknowledgment shall not take place for the benefit of children born of an incestuous or adulterous intercourse.

336.

The acknowledgment of the father, without the indication and concurrence of the mother, has no effect, except as regards the father.

337.

An acknowledgment made during marriage, by one of the parties, to the advantage of a natural child, which such party shall have had before marriage, and by a different person, shall not prejudice the other married party, nor the children born of such marriage. Neveretheless its effect shall be produced after the dissolution of the marriage, where no children remain.

338.

A natural child acknowledged cannot claim the rights of a legitimate child. The rights of natural children shall be settled under the title "*Of Successions.*"

339.

Every acknowledgment on the part of father or mother, as well as every claim on the part of the child, may be contested by all those who have interest therein.

340.

Scrutiny as to paternity is forbidden. In the case of rape, when the period of such rape shall refer to that of conception, the ravisher may be declared, on the petition of the parties interested, the father of the child.

341.

Scrutiny as to maternity is admissible.

The child who shall claim his mother, shall be bound to prove that he is identically the same child of whom she was delivered.

He shall not be permitted to make this proof by witnesses, until he shall have already made a commencement of proof in writing.

342.

A child shall in no case be admitted to search whether for paternity or maternity, in cases where, according to article 335, acknowledgment would not have been admitted.

TITLE VIII.

OF ADOPTION AND FRIENDLY GUARDIANSHIP.

Decreed 23d March, 1803. *Promulgated 2d of April.*

CHAPTER I.

Of Adoption.

SECTION I.

Of Adoption and its Effects.

343.

Adoption is not permitted to persons of either sex, except to those above the age of fifty years, and who at the period of adoption shall have neither children nor legitimate descendants, and who shall be at the least fifteen years older than the individuals whom they propose to adopt.

344.

No one can be adopted by more than one person, except by husband and wife.

Except in the case in article 366, no married person can adopt without the consent of the other conjunct.

345.

The faculty of adoption shall not be exercised except towards an individual, for whom, during minority, and for a period of at least six years, the party shall have supplied assistance, and employed uninterrupted care, or towards one who shall have saved the life of the party adopting, either in a fight, or in rescuing him from fire or water.

It shall suffice, in this latter case, that the adopter have attained majority, be older than the adopted, without children, or lawful descendants, and if married, that his conjunct consent to the adoption.

346.

Adoption shall not, in any case, take place before the majority of the adopted party. If the adopted having father and mother, or one of them, has not completed his twenty-fifth year, he shall be bound to produce the consent of his father and mother, or the survivor, to his adoption; and if he is more than twenty-five years of age, to require their counsel.

347.

The adoption shall confer the name of the adopter on the adopted, in addition to the proper name of the latter.

348.

The adopted shall continue in his own family, and shall there retain all his rights: nevertheless, marriage is prohibited,

Between the adopter, the adopted, and his descendants;

Between adopted children of the same individual;

Between the adopted, and the children who may be born to the adopter;

Between the adopted and the conjunct of the

adopter, and reciprocally between the adopter and the conjunct of the adopted.

349.

The natural obligation, which shall continue to exist between the adopted and his father and mother, to supply them with sustenance in cases determined by the law, shall be considered as common to the adopter and the adopted towards each other.

350.

The adopted shall acquire no right of succession to the property of relations of the adopter; but he shall enjoy the same rights with regard to succession to the adopter as are possessed by a child born in wedlock, even though there should be other children of this latter description, born subsequently to the adoption.

351.

If the adopted child die without lawful descendants, presents made by the adopter, or acquisitions by inheritance to him, and which shall actually exist at the decease of the adopted, shall return to the adopter or to his descendants, on condition of contributing to debts, without prejudice to third persons.

The surplus of the property of the adopted shall belong to his own relations; and these shall exclude always, for the same objects specified in the present article, all the heirs of the adopter other than his descendants.

352.

If during the life of the adopter, and after the decease of the adopted, children or descendants left by the latter, shall themselves die without issue, the adopter shall succeed to donations made by him, as is directed in the preceding article ; but this right shall be inherent in the person of the adopter and not transmissible to his heirs, even in the descending line.

SECTION II.

Of the Forms of Adoption.

353.

The party who shall propose to adopt, with the one who shall be willing to be adopted, shall present themselves before the justice of the peace at the domicil of the adopter, there to pass an act of their mutual consent.

354.

A copy of this act shall be transmitted, within ten days following, by the more diligent party, to the commissioner of government in the court of first instance, within whose jurisdiction the domicil of the adopter shall be found, in order to be submitted to the approbation of that court.

355.

The court, being assembled in the chamber of council, and having received suitable testimonials, shall certify, 1st, whether all the conditions of the law are complied with ; 2d, whether the party who proposes to adopt enjoys a good reputation.

356.

After having heard the commissioner of government, and without any other form of proceeding, the court shall pronounce without giving its reasons, in these terms : "*There is ground,*" or, "*There is no ground for adoption.*"

357.

In the month succeeding the judgment of the court of first instance, this judgment shall, on the prosecution of the more diligent party, be submitted to the court of appeal, which shall deal with it in the same forms as the court of first instance, and shall pronounce without assigning reasons : "*The judgment is confirmed,*" or "*The judgment is reversed ; in consequence there is ground,*" or "*There is no ground for adoption.*"

358.

Every judgment of the courts of appeal, which shall establish an adoption, shall be pronounced at the hearing, and posted in such places and in such a number of copies as the court shall judge expedient.

359.

Within three months after this judgment, the adoption shall be enrolled, on the requisition of one or other of the parties, on the register of the civil power of the place where the adopter shall be domiciled.

This enrolment shall not take place but upon view of a copy, in form, of the judgment of the court of appeal; and the adoption shall remain without effect unless it be enrolled within this interval.

360.

If the adopter happen to die after the act setting forth his inclination to form a contract of adoption has been received by the justice of peace and carried before the courts, and before these have finally pronounced, the procedure shall be continued and the adoption admitted if there be ground. The heirs of the adopter may, if they believe the adoption inadmissible, remit to the commissioner of government all memorials and observations on this subject.

CHAPTER II.

Of friendly Guardianship.

361.

Every individual aged above fifty years, and without children or legitimate descendants, who shall be willing, during the minority of an individual, to attach him to himself by a legal title, may become his friendly guardian, on obtaining the consent of the father and mother of the child, or of the survivor of them, or in their default, of a family council, or finally if the child have no known relatives, on obtaining the consent of the directors of the hospital into which he shall have been received, or of the municipality of the place of his residence.

362.

A married person cannot become a friendly guardian without the consent of the other conjunct.

363.

The justice of the peace at the domicil of the child shall draw up a statement of the petitions and consent relative to the friendly guardianship.

364.

This guardianship shall not have place except for the benefit of children aged at least fifteen years.

It shall carry with it, without prejudice to any private stipulations, the obligation of supporting the ward, of bringing him up, and of putting him in a situation to gain his livelihood.

365.

If the ward possess any property, and has been formerly under guardianship, the administration of his property, as well as that of his person, shall pass to the friendly guardian, who nevertheless shall not be permitted to throw the expenses of education on the funds of the ward.

366.

If the friendly guardian, after the lapse of five

years since his guardianship, and in the prospect of his decease before the majority of his pupil confers on him adoption by testamentary act, such disposition shall be valid, provided the friendly guardian does not leave children.

367.

In the case where a friendly guardian dies, either before the five years or after that time, without having adopted his ward, the latter shall be supplied with the means of subsistence of which the quantum and the kind, unless provided for by some anterior formal covenant, shall be regulated either amicably between the respective representatives of the guardian and his ward, or judicially in case of dispute.

368.

If, at the majority of the ward, his friendly guardian be willing to adopt him, and the former consent thereto, proceedings shall be taken for the adoption according to the forms prescribed in the preceding chapter, and the effects thereof shall be, in all points, the same.

369.

If, within three months following the majority of the ward, the requests made by him to his friendly guardian on the subject of adoption, remain ineffectual, and the ward shall not find himself in a condition to gain his livelihood, the friendly guardian may be sentenced to indemnify his ward for the incapacity in which the latter finds himself of providing for his own subsistence.

This indemnity shall resolve itself into support proper to procure him a trade; the whole without prejudice to stipulations which may have been made in prospect of this case.

370.

The friendly guardian who shall have had th management of any of his ward's property, shall b bound in every case to render an account thereof.

TITLE IX.

OF PATERNAL POWER.

Decreed the 24th of March, 1803. Promulgated 3rd of April.

371.

A child, at every age, owes honor and respect to his father and mother.

372.

He remains subject to their control until his majority or emancipation.

373.

The father alone exercises this control during marriage.

374.

A child cannot quit the paternal mansion without the permission of his father, unless for voluntary enlistment after the full age of eighteen years.

375.

A father who shall have cause of grievous dissatisfaction at the conduct of a child, shall have the following means of correction.

376.

If the child have not commenced his sixteenth year, the father may cause him to be confined for a period which shall not exceed one month; and to this effect the president of the court of the circle shall be bound, on his petition, to deliver an order of arrest.

377.

From the age of sixteen years commenced to the majority or emancipation, the father is only empowered to require the confinement of his child during six months at the most; he shall apply to the president of the aforesaid court, who, after having conferred thereon with the commissioner of government, shall deliver an order of arrest or refuse the same, and may in the first case abridge the time of confinement required by the father.

378.

There shall not be in either case, any writing or judicial formality, except the order itself for arrest, in which the reasons thereof shall not be set forth.

The father shall only be required to subscribe an undertaking to defray all expenses and to supply suitable support.

379.

The father is always at liberty to abridge the duration of the confinement by him ordered or required. If the child after his liberation fall into new irregularities, his confinement may be ordered anew, according to the manner prescribed in the preceding articles.

380.

If the father be remarried, he shall be bound to conform to article 377, in order to procure the confinement of his child by the first bed, though under the age of sixteen years.

381.

The mother surviving and not married again is not empowered to cause the confinement of a child, except with the concurrence of the two nearest paternal relations, and by means of requisition, conformably to article 377.

382.

When the child shall possess personal property, or when he shall exercise an office, his confinement shall not take place, even under the age of sixteen years, except by way of requisition in the form prescribed by article 377.

The child confined may address a memorial to the commissioner of government in the court of appeal. This commissioner shall cause the child to render a detail in the court of first instance, and shall make his report to the president of the court of appeal, who, after having given intimation thereof to the father, and after having collected the proofs, may revoke or modify the order delivered by the president of the court of first instance.

383.

Articles 376, 377, 378, and 379, shall be common to fathers and mothers of natural children, legally recognized.

384.

The father during marriage, and, after the dissolution of marriage, the father or mother surviving, shall have the enjoyment of the property of their children, until the full age of eighteen years, or until emancipation, which may take place before the age of eighteen years.

385.

The conditions of such enjoyment shall be—

1st. Those by which usufructuaries are bound;

2d. Nourishment, maintenance, and education of children, according to their fortune;

3d. The payment of arrears or interest on capital;

4th. Funeral expenses, and those of the last sickness.

386.

This enjoyment shall not take place for the benefit of a father or mother against whom a divorce shall have been pronounced; and it shall cease with regard to the mother in the case of a second marriage.

387.

It shall not extend to property which children may have acquired by separate labor and industry, nor to such as shall be given or bequeathed to them under the express condition that their father and mother shall not enjoy it.

TITLE X.

OF MINORITY, GUARDIANSHIP, AND EMANCIPATION.

Decreed 26th of March, 1803. *Promulgated the 5th of April.*

CHAPTER I.

Of Minority.

388.

A minor is an individual of either sex who has not yet accomplished the age of twenty-one years.

CHAPTER II.

Of Guardianship.

SECTION I.

Of the Guardianship of Father and Mother.

389.

The father is, during marriage, administrator of the personal effects of his children being minors.

He is accountable, as far as regards property and rents, for such effects as he has not the enjoyment of; and, as regards property, only for such whereof the law allows him the usufruct.

390.

After the dissolution of marriage occurring by the natural or civil death of one of the parties, the guardianship of children being minors, and not emancipated, belongs absolutely to the survivor of the father and mother.

391.

The father shall be at liberty, nevertheless, to nominate to the mother surviving and being guardian, a special council, without whose concurrence she shall not have power to do any act relative to the guardianship. If the father specify the acts for which the council shall be nominated, the guardian shall be competent to do other acts without assistance.

392.

This nomination of council shall only be made in one of the modes following:

1st. By act of last will;

2d. By a declaration made either before the justice of peace, assisted by his registrar, or before notaries

393.

If at the time of the husband's decease, his wife is with child, a curator for the unborn issue shall be named by a family council.

At the birth of the child the mother shall become guardian thereof, and the curator shall be its deputy guardian in full right.

394.

The mother is not bound to accept the guardianship; nevertheless, and in case she refuses it, she must discharge the duties thereof until she have caused a guardian to be appointed.

395.

If a mother being guardian desires to marry again, she is required before the act of marriage to convoke a family-council, who shall decide whether the guardianship ought to be continued to her.

In defect of such convocation she shall lose the guardianship entirely; and her new husband shall be jointly and severally responsible for all the consequences of the guardianship which she shall have unduly continued.

396.

When the family council, being duly convoked, shall continue the guardianship to the mother, it shall of necessity assign to her, as a conjoint guardian, her second husband, who shall with his wife become jointly and severally responsible for the administration subsequent to the marriage.

SECTION II.

Of the Guardianship appointed by the Father or Mother.

397.

The individual right of choosing as guardian a relation, or even a stranger, belongs only to the father or mother who shall last die.

398.

This right cannot be exercised except in the forms prescribed by article 392, and subject to the modifications and exceptions hereinafter mentioned.

399.

A wife remarried and not continued in her guardianship of the children of her first marriage, cannot choose them a guardian.

400.

When the mother remarried and continued in the guardianship, shall have made choice of a guardian for the children of her former marriage, such choice shall only be valid as far as it shall be confirmed by the family-council.

401.

The guardian elected by the father or the mother is not bound to accept the guardianship, if he be not in other respects within the class of persons, whom in default of such special election the family-council might have charged with it.

SECTION III.

Of the Guardianship of Ancestors.

402.

Where a guardian has not been chosen for a minor by his father or mother who died last, the guardianship belongs of right to his paternal grandfather; and in default of such to his maternal grandfather, and so ascending, in such manner as that the paternal ancestor shall, in all cases, be preferred to the maternal ancestor in the same degree.

403.

Where, in default of the paternal grandfather, and likewise of the maternal grandfather of the minor, an equal claim shall appear to be established between two ancestors of a higher degree, who shall both belong to the paternal line of the minor, the guardianship shall pass of right to such of the two as shall be found to be paternal grandfather of the father of the minor.

404.

If the same competition take place between two great-grandfathers of the maternal line, the nomination shall be made by the family-council, who shall, nevertheless, only have power to choose one of such two ancestors.

SECTION IV.

Of Guardianship appointed by the Family-Council.

405.

When a child a minor, and not emancipated, shall be without father or mother, or guardian elected by his father or mother, or without male ancestors, as also when the guardian of one of the descriptions above-mentioned, shall find himself either within the case of the exclusions hereinafter described, or validly excused, the nomination of a guardian shall be provided for by a family-council.

406.

This council shall be convoked either on the requisition and care of the relations of the minor, of his creditors, or of other parties interested, or even officially and on the prosecution of the justice of the peace at the domicil of the minor. Any person may declare before this justice of the peace, the fact which shall give occasion to the nomination of a guardian.

407.

The family-council shall be composed, exclusive of the justice of the peace, of six relations or connexions, taken as well from the commune where the guardianship shall be opened, as within the distance of two myriameters, half on the father's side, and half on the mother's side, and according to the order of proximity in each line.

The relation shall be preferred to the connexion in the same degree; and amongst relations of the same degree, the elder to the younger.

408.

The brothers-german of the minor, and the husbands of sisters-german, are alone excepted from the limitation of the number laid down in the preceding article.

If they are six, or above, they shall all be members of the family council, which they shall compose alone, with the widows of ancestors, and ancestors validly excused, if there be any.

If they are in number too few, the other relations

shall be summoned only for the purpose of completing the council.

409.

When the relations or connexions of either line shall find themselves insufficient in number on the spot, or within the distance pointed out by article 407, the justice of the peace shall summon either relations or connexions residing at greater distances, or within the same commune, citizens known as having had habitual friendly intercourse with the father or the mother of the minor.

410.

The justice of the peace is at liberty, even when there shall be on the spot a sufficient number of relations or connexions, to give permission to summon, at whatever distance they may be domiciliated, relations or connexions nearer in degree, or of the same degree as the relations and connexions present; in such manner however that it shall operate to withdraw some of the last, and without exceeding the number directed in the preceding articles.

411.

The interval for appearance shall be regulated by the justice of the peace on a day fixed, but in such manner that there shall always be an interval of three days at the least between the notification of the summons, and the day appointed for the assembling of the council, although all the parties summoned shall reside within the commune, or within the distance of two myriameters.

As often as any among the parties summoned shall be found to reside beyond that distance, the interval shall be augmented by one day for every three myriameters.

412.

The relations, connexions, or friends thus convened, shall be bound to appear in person, or cause themselves to be represented by especial proxy.

The proxy can only represent one person.

413.

Every relation, connexion, or friend convoked, and who without lawful excuse shall fail to appear, shall incur a fine not exceeding fifty francs, and which shall be awarded without appeal by the justice of the peace.

414.

If there be sufficient excuse, and it shall appear convenient either to wait for the absent member, or to supply his place; in such case, as in every other where the interest of the minor shall appear to require it, it shall be lawful for the justice of the peace to adjourn the assembly, or to postpone it.

415.

This assembly shall be held as of right at the house of the justice of the peace, unless he himself shall point out another place of meeting.

The presence of three-fourths at least of the members convoked shall be necessary in order to their deliberations.

416.

The justice of the peace shall preside over the family-council, and shall have therein a deliberative voice, and the casting vote in case of division.

417.

When a minor, residing in France, shall possess property in the colonies, or *vice versa*, special administration of his property shall be given to a supplementary guardian.

In this case the guardian and supplementary guardian shall be independent, and not responsible to each other in regard to the discharge of their respective functions.

418.

The guardian shall act and administer, in this capacity, from the day of his nomination, if it took place in his presence; if otherwise, from the day on which it was notified to him.

419.

Guardianship is a personal charge, which does not pass to the heirs of the guardian. They shall only be responsible for the conduct of their predecessor; and if they are of age, they shall be bound to continue it until the nomination of a new guardian.

SECTION V.

Of the Supplementary Guardian.

420.

In every guardianship there shall be a supplementary guardian, nominated by the family-council. His functions shall consist in acting for the interests of the minor, when they shall be in opposition to those of the guardian.

421.

When the functions of guardian shall devolve upon a person described under Section 1, 2, or 3, of the present chapter, such guardian is bound, before entering upon his functions, to convoke a family-council, composed as is pointed out in Section 4, for the purpose of nominating a supplementary guardian.

If he intermeddle with the management before he has complied with this formality, the family-council convened, either on the requisition of the relations, creditors, or other parties interested, or officially by the justice of the peace, may, if there be fraud on the part of the guardian, withdraw him from the guardianship without prejudice to the indemnities due to the minor.

422.

In other guardianships, the nomination of supplementary guardian shall have place immediately after that of guardian.

423.

In no case shall the guardian vote for the nomination of supplementary guardian, who shall be selected, except in the case of brothers-german, in that of two lines to which the guardian shall not belong.

424.

The supplementary guardian shall not supply entirely the place of the guardian, when the guardianship shall become vacant, or when it shall be abandoned by absence; but he shall be bound in such case, under pain of damages which may accrue therefrom to the minor, to urge the nomination of a new guardian.

425.

The functions of supplementary guardian shall cease at the same period as the guardianship.

426.

The regulations contained in sections 6 and 7 of the present chapter, shall apply to supplementary guardians.

Nevertheless the guardian shall not be at liberty to urge the deprivation of the supplementary guardian, nor to vote in family councils, which shall be convened for that object.

SECTION VI.

Of the Causes which excuse from Guardianship.

427.

Persons excused from guardianship are,

Members of authorities established by titles 2, 3, and 4, of the constitutional act;

The judges of the court of cassation, the commissioner-general of government, and his substitutes, in the same court;

The commissioners of the national accounts;

The prefects;

All citizens, exercising a public function in a department different from that in which the guardianship is established.

428.

Equally exempted from guardianship are,

Military men in active service, and all other citizens who are in the discharge of a commission from government beyond the territory of the republic.

429.

If the commission be unauthenticated and contested, the exemption shall not be pronounced until after the government shall have explained itself through the medium of the minister for the department within which the commission alleged as excuse shall lie.

430.

Citizens of the description contained in the preceding articles, who have accepted guardianship subsequently to the functions, services, and commissions, which exempt from it, shall not be permitted for such a cause to procure their discharge therefrom.

431.

Those, on the contrary, on whom the functions, services, and commissions, shall have been imposed, subsequently to the acceptance and exercise of guardianship, may, if unwilling to continue it, cause a family-council to be convoked within one month, and take measures therein for supplying their place.

If, at the expiration of these functions, services, and commissions, the new guardian claim his discharge, or the ancient one demand his guardianship again, it may be restored to the latter by a family-council.

432.

No citizen, not being a relation or connection, can be compelled to accept guardianship, except in the case where there shall not be, within the distance of four myriameters, relations or connexions in condition to undertake the guardianship.

433.

Every individual who has completed his sixty-fifth year may refuse to become a guardian. He who previously to this age shall have been nominated such, may, at seventy years, cause himself to be discharged from the guardianship.

434.

Every individual attacked with a grievous sickness, being duly proved, is exempted from guardianship. He may moreover cause himself to be discharged therefrom, if this infirmity has come upon him since his nomination.

435.

Two guardianships are, in the case of all persons, a sufficient excuse for not accepting a third.

The husband or father who shall be already charged with one guardianship, shall not be bound to accept a second, other than that of his children.

436.

They who have five lawful children are exempted from every guardianship other than that of such children. Children who have died in active service in the armies of the republic shall be always reckoned as operating such exemption.

Other children being dead shall not be reckoned, except so far as they shall themselves have left children in actual existence.

437.

The event of children born during guardianship shall not authorize its resignation.

438.

If the guardian nominated be present at the deliberation which imposes on him the guardianship, he shall be bound forthwith, and on pain of being excluded from all ulterior objection, to propose his excuses, on which the family-council shall deliberate.

439.

If the guardian nominated has not assisted at the deliberation which imposed upon him the guardianship, he may cause a family-council to be convoked in order to deliberate on his excuses.

His proceedings on this subject shall take place within an interval of three days, commencing with the intimation which shall have been given him of his nomination; this interval shall be augmented by one day for three myriameters of distance from the place of his domicil to that of the opening of the guardianship: this interval past, he shall not be heard.

440.

If his excuses are rejected he may make application to the courts to have them admitted; but he shall be bound, during the litigation, to act as guardian provisionally.

441.

If he succeed in causing himself to be exempted from the guardianship, they who shall have rejected his excuses shall be condemned in costs of suit.

If he fail, he shall himself be condemned therein.

SECTION VII.

Of Incapacity, Exclusion and Deprivation of Guardianship.

442.

Persons incapable of being guardians or members of family-councils are,

1st. Minors, except the father or the mother;

2d. Interdicted persons;

3d. Women, except the mother and female ancestors;

4th. All those who have, or whose father or mother has, with the minor a suit, in which the estate of such minor, his fortune, or a considerable portion of his property, is brought in question.

443.

Condemnation to an afflictive or infamous punish ment imports absolutely an exclusion from guardianship. It imports in like manner deprivation, in a case where the question is respecting a guardianship previously conferred.

444.

Excluded also from guardianship, and deprivable if already in the exercise of it are,

1st. Persons guilty of notorious misconduct;

2d. Those whose management thereof betrays incapacity or want of fidelity.

445.

No individual who shall have been excluded or deprived of a guardianship, can be a member of a family-council.

446.

As often as there shall be ground for the deprivation of a guardian, it shall be pronounced by a family council, convoked at the instance of the supplementary guardian, or officially by the justice of the peace.

Such guardian shall not be at liberty to neglect calling such convocation, when formally required thereto by one or more relations or connexions of the minor, of the degree of cousin-german or of still nearer degrees.

447.

Every resolution by a family-council which shall pronounce the expulsion or deprivation of a guardian, shall recite its motives, and shall not be made until the guardian shall have been heard or summoned.

448.

If the guardian concur in the resolution, mention shall be thereof made, and the new guardian shall enter immediately upon his functions.

If he object, the supplementary guardian shall sue for a confirmation of the resolution before the court of first instance, which shall decree, saving the right of appeal.

The guardian excluded or deprived may himself, in such case, summon the supplementary guardian in order to procure himself to be confirmed in his guardianship.

449.

The relations or connexions who shall have required the convocation, may become parties in the cause, which shall be carried on and judged as an urgent affair.

SECTION VIII.

Of the Guardian's Administration.

450.

The guardian shall have the care of the person of the minor, and shall represent him in all civil acts.

He shall deal with his property like a good father of a family, and shall answer in damages for the consequences of his mismanagement.

He must not buy the property of the minor, nor

take it on lease, unless the family-council have authorized the supplementary guardian to let it him to hire, nor accept an assignment of any claim or credit against his ward.

451.

Within ten days following that of his nomination, duly notified to him, the guardian shall require the removal of seals, if any have been affixed, and shall proceed immediately to make an inventory of the goods of the minor, in presence of the supplementary guardian.

If any thing be due to him from the minor, he must declare it in his inventory, on pain of forfeiture, and this on the requisition which the public officer shall be bound to make thereon to him, and whereof mention shall be made in the statement.

452.

Within the month following the close of the inventory, the guardian shall cause to be sold at an auction, held by a public officer in presence of the supplementary guardian, and after bills or notices, of which mention shall be made in the statement of sale, all the moveable goods other than those which the family-council shall have authorized him to preserve in kind.

453.

The father and mother, as long as they have the personal and legal enjoyment of the property of the minor, are excused from selling the moveable goods, if they prefer preserving them in order to their restoration in kind.

In this case they shall cause an estimate to be made, at their own expense, of their just value, by an experienced person named by the supplementary guardian, and who shall be sworn before the justice of the peace.

They shall render the estimated value of such of the moveable goods as they are unable to produce in kind.

454.

At the period of entering upon the exercise of every guardianship, other than that of the father and mother, the family-council shall regulate by observation, and according to the importance of the property administered, the amount of the minor's annual expense, as well as that of the administration of his property.

The same act shall specify whether the guardian is authorized to procure the assistance in his management of one or more private administrators, paid by salaries and acting under his responsibility.

455.

The council shall determine positively the sum at which the obligation on the tutor shall commence, of employing the surplus of the revenues above the expenditure ; this employment must be made within the interval of six months, which past, the guardian shall become debtor for interest in default of employing it.

456.

If the guardian have not caused the sum at which the employment shall commence to be determined by a family-council, he shall, after the interval expressed in the preceding article, become debtor for the interest of the whole sum unemployed, however small it may be.

457.

The guardian, even though father or mother, may not borrow for the minor, nor alienate, nor mortgage his immoveable property, without being authorized thereto by a family-council.

This authority shall not be accorded except in case of an absolute necessity, or an evident advantage.

In the first case the family-council shall not grant its authority, until it shall have been proved, by a succinct account presented by the guardian, that the money, personal effects, and revenues of the minor, are insufficient.

The family-council shall point out, in all cases, the immoveable property which ought to be sold by preference, and all the conditions which it shall deem useful.

458.

The resolutions of the family-council relative to this object shall not be executed until after the guardian shall have demanded and obtained confirmation thereof before the civil court of first instance, which shall decree thereon in the chamber of council, and after having heard the commissioner of government.

459.

The sale shall be made publicly, in presence of the supplementary guardian, at an auction held by a member of the civil court, or by a notary appointed for this purpose, and after the publication of three notices, in three consecutive weeks, in the usual place within the district.

460.

The formalities required by articles 457 and 458, in order to the alienation of the property of a minor, do not apply to the cases in which a judgment shall have directed an auction on the application of a co-proprietor indivisibly.

Provided only in such case that the auction do not take place except in the form prescribed by the preceding article; strangers shall, of necessity, be admitted thereto.

461.

The guardian shall not be at liberty to accept or to repudiate a succession fallen to the minor, without a previous authority from the family-council. The acceptance shall only take place under the benefit of the inventory.

462.

In a case where a succession repudiated in the name of the minor shall not have been accepted by another, it may be resumed either by the guardian, authorized to this end by a new resolution of the family-council, or by the minor himself when arrived at full age, but in the state in which it shall be found at the time of the resumption, and without power to impeach any sales and other acts which shall have legally taken place during the interval.

463.

A donation made to the minor shall not be accepted by the guardian, except with the authority of a family-council.

It shall have, with regard to the minor, the same effect as with regard to an adult.

464.

No guardian shall be at liberty to bring an action respecting real claims of the minor, nor to acquiesce in a demand relative to such claims, without the authority of a family-council.

465.

The same authority shall be necessary to a guardian in order to claim a partition; but it is competent to him without such authority to answer a claim for partition directed against the minor.

466.

In order to obtain from it the whole effect which would follow as against adults, the partition should be made by an officer of law, and should be preceded by an estimate made by experienced persons named by the civil court of the place of opening the succession.

Such experienced persons, after having taken an oath well and faithfully to fulfil their office, before the president of the same court, or another judge delegated by him, shall proceed to the division of the inheritance and the formation of lots, which shall be taken by chance, and in the presence either of a member of the court, or of a notary commissioned by him, who shall make distribution of the lots.

Every other partition shall be considered merely as provisional.

467.

The guardian shall not be at liberty to compound for the minor, until he shall be thereto authorized by the family-council, and under the direction of three jurisconsults, appointed by the commissioner of government in the court of first instance.

No composition shall be valid, except so far as it shall have been confirmed by the court of first instance, after having heard the commissioner of government.

468.

The guardian who shall have causes of grievous dissatisfaction respecting the conduct of the minor, may lay his complaints before a family-council, and if thereto authorized by such council, may claim the confinement of the minor, conformably to what has been decreed on this subject under the title "*Of Paternal Power.*"

SECTION IX.

Of the Accounts of the Guardianship.

469.

Every guardian is accountable for his management at the close of it.

470.

Every guardian other than the father and mother may be required, even during the guardianship, to submit to the supplementary guardian accounts of the situation of his charge, at such periods as the family-council shall deem it proper to fix upon, provided, nevertheless, that the guardian shall not be bound to furnish more than one of them each year.

These accounts of situation shall be drawn up and remitted free of charge on unstamped paper and without any legal formality.

471.

The final account of the guardianship shall be rendered at the expense of the minor, when he shall have reached his full age, or obtained his emancipation. The guardian shall advance the expenses.

The guardian shall be allowed therein every charge satisfactorily verified, and the object of which shall be useful.

472.

Any agreement which may happen between the guardian and the minor on his coming of age, shall be null, unless preceded by the rendering of a detailed account, and the production of vouchers; the whole verified by the receipt of the auditors, ten days at least before such agreement.

473.

If the account afford ground for disputes, they shall be prosecuted and determined like other disputes on a civil matter.

474.

The sum to which the balance of the account due from the guardian shall amount, shall carry interest without demand, to be computed from the close of the account.

The interest on what shall be due to the guardian from the minor, shall only run from the day of the demand of payment subsequent to the close of the account.

475.

Every action by a minor against his guardian, relative to the transactions of the guardianship, ceases by prescription after ten years, computing from the majority.

CHAPTER III.

Of Emancipation.

476.

The minor is emancipated to all intents and purposes by marriage.

477.

The minor, even though not married, may be emancipated by his father, or, in default of father, by his mother, when he shall have attained the full age of fifteen years.

This emancipation shall be effected by the simple declaration of the father or mother, received by the justice of the peace, assisted by his registrar.

478.

A minor left without father or mother may likewise be emancipated, if the family-council judge him capable thereof, provided only he have accomplished his eighteenth year.

In such case the emancipation shall result from the resolution which shall have authorized it, and from the declaration of the justice of the peace, as president of the family-council, made in the same act, that the minor is emancipated.

479.

When the guardian shall not have taken any measures for the emancipation of the minor, of which mention is made in the preceding article, and when one or more relations, or connexions of such minors of the degree of cousin-german, or of other nearer degrees, shall judge him capable of being emancipated, they may require the justice of the peace to convoke the family-council in order to deliberate on this subject.

The justice of the peace is bound to yield his assent to this requisition.

480.

The accounts of the guardianship shall be rendered to the minor emancipated, assisted by a curator, who shall be nominated for him by the family-council.

481.

A minor emancipated shall make leases, whose duration shall not exceed nine years; he shall receive his revenues and shall therefore give discharge, and shall do all acts consisting only of pure administration, without being liable in respect of such acts in all cases in which an adult would not be so himself.

482.

He shall not bring a real action or be defendant therein, even to receive and give discharge for a personal capital, without the assistance of a curator, who in the last case shall take charge of the employment of the capital received.

483.

A minor emancipated is not permitted to borrow, under any pretext, without a resolution of the family-council, confirmed by the civil court, after having heard the commissioner of government.

484.

He shall not be permitted to sell or alienate his immoveable property, or to do any other act than those of pure administration, without observing the forms prescribed to an unemancipated minor.

With regard to obligations contracted by him in the way of purchases or otherwise, they shall be reducible in case of excess ; the courts shall on this subject take into consideration the fortune of the minor, the good or bad faith of the persons who shall have contracted with him, the utility or inutility of the expenses.

485.

Every emancipated minor, whose engagements shall have been reduced by virtue of the preceding article, may be deprived of the benefit of emancipation, which shall be recovered by him in pursuing the same forms as those which shall have taken place in conferring it upon him.

486.

The minor shall re-enter into guardianship from the day on which his emancipation shall have been revoked, and so continue until his majority shall be accomplished.

487.

The minor emancipated, who enters into trade, is reputed an adult for the acts relative to such trading.

TITLE XI.

OF MAJORITY, INTERDICTION, AND THE JUDICIAL ADVISER.

Decreed 29*th March,* 1803. *Promulgated* 18*th of April.*

CHAPTER I.

Of Majority.

488.

Majority is fixed at twenty-one years completed; at this age a person is capable of all acts regarding civil life, saving the restriction contained under the title "*Of Marriage.*"

CHAPTER II.

Of Interdiction.

489.

An adult, who is in an habitual state of idiotcy, of insanity, or madness, must be interdicted, even though such state present some lucid intervals.

490.

Any person is competent to claim the interdiction of a relative. It is the same with one spouse with regard to the other.

491.

In the case of madness, if the interdiction is not claimed, either by the spouse or by the relatives, it must be claimed by the commissioner of government, who may also claim it in cases of idiotcy or insanity against an individual who is unmarried, and without known relatives.

492.

Every demand of interdiction shall be made before the court of first instance.

493.

Acts of idiotcy, insanity, or madness, shall be alleged in writing. They who prosecute the interdiction shall produce witnesses and documents.

494.

The court shall order that the family-council formed, according to the mode pointed out in section 4 of chap. 2, of the title "*Of Minority, Guardianship, and Emancipation,*" shall give its judgment on the state of the person whose interdiction is demanded.

495.

They who shall have claimed the interdiction shall not form part of the family-council: however the husband or wife, and the children of the person whose interdiction shall be claimed, may be admitted thereto without having a deliberative voice therein.

496.

After having received the judgment of the family-council, the court shall interrogate the defendant in the chamber of council; if he cannot be present there, he shall be interrogated at his dwelling, by one of the judges commissioned for this purpose, assisted by his registrar. In all cases the commissioner of government shall be present at the interrogation.

497.

After the first interrogatory, the court shall, if there be ground, appoint a provisional administrator, to take care of the person and goods of the defendant.

498.

Judgment on a petition for interdiction shall only be given at a public hearing, the parties being heard or summoned.

499.

In rejecting the petition for interdiction, the court shall be empowered nevertheless, if the circumstances require it, to order that the defendant shall not thenceforward plead, make agreement, borrow, receive a moveable capital, nor give discharge therefor, alienate, nor encumber his property by mortgages without the assistance of an adviser, who shall be nominated for him by the same judgment.

500.

In case of appeal from the judgment given in the first instance, the court of appeal may, if it judge necessary, interrogate anew the party whose interdiction is demanded, or cause him to be interrogated by a commissioner.

501.

Every judgment importing interdiction, or nomination of an adviser, shall, on the instance of the petitioners, be entered, signified to the party, and inscribed within ten days on the schedules, which shall be hung up in the hall of audience, and in the offices of the notaries of the circle.

502.

Interdiction on the nomination of an adviser shall have its effect from the day of the judgment. All acts past subsequently by the interdicted person, or without the assistance of the adviser, shall be void in law.

503.

Acts anterior to interdiction may be annulled, if the cause of interdiction existed notoriously at the period of making such acts.

504

After the death of an individual, acts done by him cannot be impeached for cause of insanity, except so far as his interdiction shall have been pronounced or claimed before his decease; unless the proof of insanity is derived from the very act impeached.

505.

If there be no appeal from the judgment of interdiction given in the first instance, or if it is confirmed on appeal, application shall be made for the nomination of a guardian and of a supplementary guardian for the interdicted person, according to the rules prescribed under the title, "*Of Minority, Guardianship, and Emancipation.*" The provisional administrator shall suspend his duties, and render his accounts to the guardian, unless he be such himself.

506.

The husband is of right the guardian of his wife under interdiction.

507.

The wife may be nominated guardian of her husband: in such case the family-council shall regulate the form and conditions of the administration, saving the remedy which shall be allowed in the courts to the wife, who shall conceive herself injured by the resolution of the family.

508.

No person, with the exception of the husband or wife, ancestors and descendants, shall be bound to hold the guardianship of a person interdicted beyond ten years. At the expiration of that period, the guardian may demand and shall obtain the substitution of another.

509.

A person interdicted bears likeness to a minor, as regards his person and his property; the laws on the guardianship of minors shall be applicable to the guardianship of persons under interdiction.

510.

The revenues of a person interdicted ought particularly to be employed in alleviating his misfortune and accelerating his cure. According to the symptoms of his malady, and the state of his fortune, the family-council shall be empowered to pass a resolution that he shall be attended in his own house, or that he shall be placed in a house of health, or even in an hospital.

511.

When there shall be question concerning the marriage of the child of a person under interdiction, the dowry, or the advancement of the inheritance, and the other matrimonial stipulations, shall be regulated by the opinion of the family-council, confirmed by the court on the conclusions of the commissioner of government.

512.

The interdiction ceases with the causes which produced it; nevertheless the liberation shall not be pronounced without the observation of the formalities prescribed in order to obtain the interdiction, and the party under interdiction shall not reassume the exercise of his rights until after judgment of liberation.

CHAPTER III.

Of the Judicial Adviser.

513.

Prodigals may be forbidden to implead, to settle disputes, to borrow, to receive any moveable capital, and to give a discharge therefor, to alienate, or to encumber their property by mortgages, without the assistance of an adviser, nominated to them by the court.

514.

Prohibition from proceeding without the assistance of an adviser, may be claimed by such as have a right to demand interdiction; their petition must be prosecuted and determined in the same manner.

This prohibition cannot be obtained without observing the same formalities.

515.

No judgment, in matter of interdiction, or of nomination of adviser, shall be given either in the first instance or by way of appeal, except upon the conclusions by the commissioner of government.

BOOK II.

OF PROPERTY, AND THE DIFFERENT MODIFICATIONS OF PROPERTY.

Decreed 25th of January, 1804. *Promulgated February 4th.*

TITLE I.

OF THE DISTINCTION OF PROPERTY.

516.

ALL property is moveable or immoveable.

CHAPTER I.

Of immoveable Property.

517.

Property is immoveable either by its nature, or by its destination, or by the objects to which it is applied.

518.

The soil of the earth and buildings are immoveable by their nature.

519.

Wind or watermills, fixed on pillars and forming part of a building, are also immoveable by their nature.

520.

Crops hanging by the roots, and fruits not yet gathered from the trees, are in like manner immoveable.

As soon as grain is cut and the fruits plucked, although not carried away, they become moveable.

If one part only of the crop is cut, such part alone is moveable.

521.

The cuttings of underwood of the ordinary kind, or forest trees made up in regular faggots, only become moveable in proportion as the trees are felled.

522.

The live stock which the proprietor of a farm gives up to his tenant, or farmer, for the purposes of cultivation, whether valued or not, are regarded as immoveable as long as they continue attached to the farm in pursuance of the agreement.

Such as may be given in cheptel to others than the farmer or cultivator are moveable.

523.

Pipes which serve to conduct water in a house, or other possession, are immoveable, and form part of the estate to which they are attached.

524.

Articles which the proprietor of a farm has placed thereon, for the service and management of such a farm, are immoveable by destination.

Thus immoveables by destination, having been placed by the proprietor for the use and management of his farm, are,

Beasts required for agricultural purposes;

Implements of husbandry;

Seeds given to farmers or other cultivators;

Pigeons belonging to dove-houses;

Rabbits in warrens;

Bee-hives;

Fish in ponds;

Presses, coppers, stills, vats, and tubs;

Implements necessary for the working of forges, paper-mills, and other machinery;

Straw and manure.

Immoveable also by destination are, all moveable effects which a proprietor has attached to a farm to continue so for ever.

525.

A proprietor is considered to have attached moveable effects to his estate for ever, when they are fastened thereto by plaster, lime, or cement, or when they cannot be separated without being broken and damaged, or without breaking or injuring that part of the estate to which they are attached.

The mirrors of an apartment are considered as fixed for perpetual continuance, when the frame-work on which they are fastened forms part of the body of the wainscot.

It is the same with respect to pictures and other ornaments.

As regards statues, they are immoveable when they are placed in a niche formed expressly to receive them, although they may be capable of removal without breaking or damage.

526.

Immoveable in respect of the object to which they are applied are,

The usufruct of immoveable things ;

Servitudes or agricultural services ;

Actions whose object is the recovery of immoveable property.

CHAPTER II.

Of Moveables.

527.

Property is moveable in its nature, or by the determination of the law.

528.

Moveables in their nature are bodies which may be transported from place to place, whether they move themselves like animals, or whether like inanimate things, they are incapable of changing their place, without the application of extrinsic force.

529.

Moveables by determination of law are, bonds and actions relating to sums demandable or personal effects, actions and interests in companies for objects of finance, commerce, or industry, although immoveables depending on such undertakings belong to the companies. These actions or interests are reputed moveable with respect to each individual member, as long as the society exists.

Moveable also by determination of law are perpetual or life annuities, whether granted by the republic or by private persons.

Article decreed 21*st of March,* 1804. *Promulgated the* 31*st of March.*

530.

Every annuity granted in perpetuity as the price of the sale of immoveable property, or as the condition of ceding an immoveable fund by free or chargeable title, is in its nature redeemable.

It is nevertheless allowed to the creditor to regulate the provisions and conditions of redemption.

It is also permitted him to stipulate that such annuity shall not be redeemed until after a certain term, which shall in no case exceed thirty years; every stipulation to the contrary is void.

531.

Boats, ferry-boats, vessels, mills, and floating-baths, and generally all machinery not fixed on piles and not forming part of the mansion, are moveable: the seizure of some articles of this kind may nevertheless, on account of their importance, be subject to particular forms, as shall be explained in the code of civil procedure.

532.

The materials arising from the demolition of an edifice, and those collected for the construction of a new one, are moveable until they are employed by the artificer in building.

533.

The word "*moveables*" employed alone in the regulations of law or an individual, without other addition or designation, does not comprehend ready money, jewels, credits, books, medals, instruments of science, art, and trade, body linen, horses, equipages, arms, grain, wine, hay, and other commodities; in like manner, it does not comprehend objects of commerce.

534.

The words "*goods moveable,*" only comprehend moveables destined for the use and ornament of apartments, as tapestries, beds, seats, mirrors, clocks, tables, china, and other objects of that nature.

Pictures and statues which form part of the furniture of an apartment are also comprised therein, but not collections of pictures which may be in galleries or private rooms.

It is the same with respect to pieces of porcelain: such only as form part of the decoration of an apartment are comprised under the denomination of "*goods moveable.*"

535.

The expression "*moveable goods,*" that of "*personalty,*" or of "*personal property;*" comprehend generally all that is deemed "*moveable,*" according to the rules heretofore established.

The sale or gift of a furnished house only comprehends the "*moveable goods.*"

536.

The sale or gift of a house, with all therein contained, does not comprehend cash, nor credits, and other rights of which the titles may be deposited within the house; all other personal effects are contained therein.

CHAPTER III.

Of Property, with Reference to those who are in the Possession of it.

537.

Private persons have the free disposition of the property belonging to them, subject to the modifications established by the laws.

Property not belonging to private persons is administered, and cannot be alienated except in the forms and in pursuance of the regulations peculiar to it.

538.

Highways, roads and streets at the national charge, rivers and streams which will carry floats, shores, ebb and flow of the sea, ports, harbors, roads for ships, and generally all portions of the national territory, which are not susceptible of private proprietorship, are considered as dependencies on the public domain.

539.

All property unclaimed and without owner, and that of persons who die without heirs, or of which the succession is abandoned, belongs to the nation.

540.

Gates, moats, ramparts of places of war, and fortresses, form also part of the national domain

541.

It is the same with respect to soils, fortifications, and ramparts of places which are no longer places of war; they belong to the nation unless they have been validly alienated, or unless their proprietorship has been barred by prescription.

542.

Common property is that to the ownership or produce of which the inhabitants of one or more communes have an acquired right,

543.

One may have over property either a right of ownership, or a simple right of enjoyment, or only claims for ground-services.

TITLE II.

OF PROPERTY.

Decreed the 27th of January, 1804. Promulgated the 6th of February.

544.

Property is the right of enjoying and disposing of things in the most absolute manner, provided they are not used in a way prohibited by the laws or statutes.

545.

No one can be compelled to give up his property, except for the public good, and for a just and previous indemnity.

546.

Property in a thing, whether real or personal, confers a right over all which it produces, and over all connected with it by accession, whether naturally or artificially.

This right is termed the "*right of accession.*"

CHAPTER I.

Of the Right of Accession over the Produce of any Thing.

547.

The natural or artificial fruits of the earth.
Civil advantages.

The increase of animals, belong to the proprietor by right of accession.

548.

The fruits produced by any thing only belong to the proprietor on condition of reimbursing the expenses of labor, tillage, and seed, incurred by third persons.

549.

A party simply in possession is only entitled to the fruits where he is so by good faith : in the opposite case he is bound to render the produce with the thing itself to the proprietor who claims it.

550.

He is in possession by good faith who possesses, as proprietor, by virtue of a conveyance of the defects of which he is not aware.

He ceases to be in possession by good faith from the moment wherein he discovers such defects.

CHAPTER II.

Of the Right of Accession over what is connected and incorporated with any Thing.

551.

Every thing which is connected and incorporated with any thing belongs to the proprietor, according to rules which shall be hereafter established.

SECTION I.

Of the Right of Accession relatively to Things immoveable.

552.

Property in the soil imports property above and beneath.

The proprietor may make above all kinds of plantations and buildings which he shall judge convenient, saving the exceptions established under the title "*Of Servitudes and Services relating to Land.*"

He may make beneath all buildings and excavations which he shall judge convenient, and draw from such excavations all the products which they are capable of furnishing, saving the restrictions resulting from the laws and statutes relating to mines, and from the laws and regulation of police.

553.

All buildings, plantations, and works upon the soil or beneath the surface, are presumed to have been made by the proprietor at his own expense, and to belong to him, until the contrary be shown; without prejudice to the property which a third person may have acquired or may acquire by prescription, whether it be a vault beneath the building of another, or any other part of the building.

554.

The proprietor of the soil having made buildings, plantations, and works with materials which did not belong to him, must pay the value thereof; he may also be condemned in damages, and interest if there be ground; but the owner of such materials is not allowed to remove them.

555.

When plantations, buildings, and works have been made by a third person and with his own materials, the proprietor of the soil has a right either to retain them, or to oblige such third person to remove them.

If the proprietor of the soil demand the demolition of the plantations and buildings, it must be done at his charge who made them and without any indemnity; he may moreover be condemned in damages and interest, if there be ground, for the injury which may have been sustained by the proprietor of the soil.

If the proprietor prefer preserving such plantations and buildings, he owes a reimbursement for the value of the materials and the price of the work, without regard to the greater or less augmentation of value which the soil has received. Nevertheless if the plantations, buildings, and works have been made by a third person evicted but not condemned to a restitution of profits on account of his good faith, the proprietor shall not demand the demolition of the said works, plantations, and buildings: but he shall have his election, either to repay the value of the materials and the price of workmanship, or to reimburse a sum equal to the augmented value of the estate.

556.

The accumulations and increase of mud formed successively and imperceptibly on the soil bordering on a river or other stream, is denominated "*alluvion.*"

Alluvion is for the benefit of the proprietor of the shore, whether in respect of a river, a navigable stream, or one admitting floats, or not; on condition, in the first case, of leaving a landing-place or towing-path conformably to regulations.

557.

It is the same with regard to derelictions occasioned by a running stream retiring insensibly from one of its banks, and encroaching on the other; the proprietor of the bank discovered profits by the alluvion, without giving the proprietor on the opposite side a right to reclaim the land which he has lost.

This right does not take place with regard to derelictions of the sea.

558.

Alluvion does not take place with respect to lakes and ponds, the proprietor of which preserves always the land which the water covers when it is at the pond's full height, even though the volume of water should be diminished.

In like manner the proprietor of a pond acquires no right over land bordering on his pond which may happen to be covered by an extraordinary flood.

559.

If a river or a stream, navigable or not, carries away by a sudden violence a considerable and distinguishable part of a field on its banks, and bears it to a field lower, or on its opposite bank, the owner of the part carried away may reclaim his property; but he is required to make his demand within a year: after this interval it is inadmissible, unless the proprietor of the field to which the part carried away has been united, has not yet taken possession thereof.

560.

Islands, islets, and accumulations of mud formed in the bed of rivers or streams navigable, or admitting floats, belong to the nation, if there be no title or prescription to the contrary.

561.

Islands and accumulations of mud formed in rivers and streams not navigable, and not admitting floats, belong to the proprietors of the shore on that side where the island is formed; if the island be not formed on one side only, it belongs to the proprietors of the shore on the two sides, divided by an imaginary line drawn through the middle of the river.

562.

If a river or other stream in forming itself a new arm, divide and surround a field belonging to the proprietor of the shore, and thereby form an island, such proprietor shall retain the ownership of his land, although the island be formed in a river or in a navigable stream or one admitting floats.

563.

If a river or a navigable stream, capable of admitting floats or not, form a new course, abandoning its ancient bed, the proprietors of the land newly occupied take, by title of indemnity, the ancient bed abandoned, each in proportion to the land of which he has been deprived.

564.

Pigeons, rabbits, and fish passing to another dove-house, warren, or pond, belong to the proprietors of the latter, provided they have not been attracted by fraud and artifice.

SECTION II.

Of the Right of Accession relatively to moveable Property.

565.

The right of accession having for its object two things moveable which belong to different masters, is entirely subordinate to the principles of natural equity.

The following rules shall serve as examples to guide the judge in determining, in cases not provided for, according to the peculiar circumstances.

566.

When two objects appertaining to different masters, which have been united in such a manner as to form one whole, are nevertheless separable, so that one can subsist without the other, the whole belongs to the master of that which forms the principal part, on condition of paying to the other the value of the one which was united to it.

567.

That is to be deemed the principal part to which the other was only united for the use, ornament, or completion of the first.

568.

Nevertheless, when the object united is much more valuable than the principal one, and when it has been employed unknown to the proprietor, the latter may demand that the object united shall be separated in order to be restored to him, even though it may be attended with some deterioration of that to which it was joined.

569.

If of two objects united in order to form one whole, the one cannot be regarded as accessory to the other, that shall be deemed the principal which is most considerable in value, or in size, if the value of both is nearly equal.

570.

If an artisan or any person whatsoever has employed a material which did not belong to him, in order to form something of a new description, whether the material can or cannot be restored to its original shape, the proprietor thereof has a right to claim the thing which has been formed from it, on paying the price of the workmanship.

571.

If however the workmanship were so important, that it surpassed by much, the value of the material employed, the labor shall then be deemed the principal part, and the artificer shall have a right to retain the thing wrought, on paying the price of the material to the proprietor.

572.

Where a person has made use of materials which partly belong to him and in part do not, in order to form an object of a new description, without having destroyed any of the materials, but in such a way that they cannot be separated without inconvenience, the object is common to both proprietors; by reason as respects the one of the materials belonging to him, and in regard to the other by reason at once of the material belonging to him, and the price of his workmanship.

573.

When an object has been formed by the mixture of many materials belonging to different proprietors, but of which no one can be regarded as the principal material: if such materials are capable of being separated, he without whose knowledge such materials were mingled, may demand the division thereof.

If the materials are incapable of separation without inconvenience, they acquire therein a common property proportioned to the quantity, quality, and value of the material belonging to each of them.

574.

If the material belonging to one of the proprietors were far superior in quantity or value to the other, in such case the proprietor of the material superior in value may claim the thing produced by the mixture, on paying to the other the price of his material.

575.

When an object remains in common between the proprietors of the materials of which it has been formed, it ought to be sold by auction for their mutual advantage.

576.

In all cases where a proprietor, whose material has been made use of, without his knowledge, in order to form an object of a different description, can claim a property in such object, he has the election of demanding restitution of his material, in kind, in the same quantity, weight, measure, and goodness, or its value.

577.

Persons who shall have employed materials belonging to others and without their knowledge, may also be condemned in damages and costs if there be ground, without prejudice to prosecution in an extraordinary manner if there be occasion.

TITLE III.

OF USUFRUCT, RIGHT OF COMMON, AND OF HABITATION.

Decreed the 30th of January, 1804. Promulgated the 9th of February.

CHAPTER I.

Of Usufruct.

578.

Usufruct is the right of enjoying things of which the property is in another, in the same manner as the proprietor himself, but on condition of preserving them substantially.

579.

Usufruct is established by the law, or by the consent of man.

580.

Usufruct may be established either simply, or to a certain day, or conditionally.

581.

It may be established over every species of property, moveable or immoveable.

SECTION I.

Of the Rights of the Usufructuary.

582.

The usufructuary has a right to the enjoyment of every species of benefit, whether natural, or artificial or civil, which the object of usufruct is capable of producing.

583.

Natural benefits are those which the earth produces spontaneously. The production and increase of animals are also natural fruits.

The artificial fruits of the soil are those which are obtained by cultivation.

584.

Civil fruits are rents of houses, interest on sums due, arrears of rent. The value of farms is also ranged under the class of civil fruits.

585.

Natural and artificial fruits, hanging by branches and roots at the period when the usufruct commences, belong to the usufructuary.

Those which are in a similar state at the period when the usufruct closes, belong to the proprietor, without recompense on either side for tillage and sowing, but without prejudice also to such portion of the fruits as may be acquired by the joint-cultivator, if there were one at the commencement or cessation of the usufruct.

586.

Civil fruits are reputed to accrue from day to day, and belong to the usufructuary, in proportion to the duration of his usufruct. This rule applies to the value of farming leases, as well as to rents of houses and other civil fruits.

587.

If the usufruct comprises objects which cannot be used without destroying them, as money, grain, and liquors, the usufructuary has a right to make use of them, but on condition of restoring them at the end of the usufruct in similar quantity, quality, and goodness, or their estimated value.

588.

The usufruct of an annuity confers likewise on the usufructuary, during the continuance of his usufruct, a right to the perception of the arrears, without rendering him liable to any restitution.

589.

If the usufruct comprehend things which, without being immediately consumed, are deteriorated by little and little in the using, as linen and moveable furniture, the usufructuary has a right to employ them for the purposes to which they were destined, and is only compelled to restore them at the end of his usufruct in the state in which they may then be, not being damaged by his fraud or fault.

590.

If the usufruct comprehend underwood, the usufructuary is bound to observe the order and proportionate quantity of his cuttings, conformably to the established usage and custom of proprietors, without indemnity however to be made to the usufructuary or his heirs, for ordinary cutting, whether of underwood, poles, or timber, which may have been omitted during his enjoyment.

Trees which can be removed from a nursery-ground without injuring it, do not therefore form part of the usufruct, except on the condition that the usufructuary shall conform to the usage of such places in restoring them.

591.

The usufructuary receives the benefit likewise, always conforming to the seasons and custom of the ancient proprietors, of those parts of a wood of tall trees as have been placed in regular cuts, whether such cuts are made periodically over a certain extent of ground, or whether they are made of a certain number of trees taken indiscriminately over the whole surface of the domain.

592.

In no other cases can the usufructuary touch full grown timber-trees: he can only employ trees blown down or broken by accident, for the reparations to which he is bound: he may however for that object cause some to be felled in case of necessity, but on condition of making such necessity appear to the proprietor.

593.

He may take also in the woods props for vines: he may take also from the trees, their annual or periodical produce: the whole according to the usage of the country or the custom of the proprietors.

594.

Fruit-trees which die, those likewise which are torn down or broken by accident, belong to the usufructuary, on condition of replacing them by others.

595.

The usufructuary may enjoy in his own person, let on lease to another, or even sell or transfer, his right by gratuitous title. If he lets on lease, he must conform, with regard to the seasons at which leases ought to be renewed and as respects their duration, to the regulations established relative to a husband with regard to the property of a wife, under the title "*Of the Contract of Marriage and of the respective Rights of Married Persons.*"

596.

The usufructuary is entitled to the enjoyment of the augmentation accruing by alluvion to the object of his usufruct.

597.

He enjoys the right of servitude, toll, and generally all the rights which the proprietor is capable of enjoying, and he enjoys them in the same manner as the proprietor himself.

598.

He enjoys also, in the same manner as the proprietor, such mines and quarries as are in a course of working at the commencement of the usufruct; nevertheless if there be question concerning a working which cannot be made without a grant, the usufructuary shall not have the enjoyment thereof until he shall have obtained the permission of government.

He has no right over mines and quarries not yet opened, nor over peat-bog, nor over treasure which may be discovered during the continuance of his usufruct.

599.

The proprietor cannot by his own deed, nor in any possible manner, injure the rights of the usufructuary.

The usufructuary on his part cannot at the conclusion of his usufruct claim any indemnity for improvements which he may pretend to have made, although the value of the thing may have been augmented thereby.

He or his heirs may however carry away mirrors, pictures, and other ornaments which he may have caused to be put up, but on condition of restoring their places to the original state.

SECTION II.

Of the Obligations of the Usufructuary.

600.

The usufructuary takes things in the state in which they are: but he cannot enter into the enjoyment of them, until he has caused an inventory of the moveable, and a statement of the immoveable objects of the usufruct, to be drawn up in the presence of the proprietor, or after having duly summoned him.

601.

He must give security to enjoy like a careful husbandman, unless he be dispensed therefrom by the act constituting the usufruct: nevertheless the father and mother having the legal usufruct of the property of their children, the seller or donor with a reservation of usufruct, are not bound to give security.

602.

If the usufructuary cannot find security, the immoveables are let on lease or put in sequestration;

Sums comprehended in the usufruct are placed out;

Commodities are sold, and the price received therefrom is in like manner placed out;

The interest on such sums and the prices of such leases belong in this case to the usufructuary.

603.

In default of security on the part of the usufructuary, the proprietor may require that such moveables as perish in the using should be sold, in order that the price thereof may be placed out like that of the commodities; and then the usufructuary enjoys the interest during his usufruct: the usufructuary however may demand, and the judges are empowered to order, according to circumstances, that one portion of the moveables necessary for his use should be left for him, on his simple security on oath, and on condition of producing them at the expiration of the usufruct.

604.

Delay in giving security does not deprive the usufructuary of the fruits to which he may have claim; they are his due from the moment at which the usufruct commences.

605.

The usufructuary is only bound to necessary reparations.

Substantial reparations are at the charge of the proprietor, unless they have been occasioned by the neglect of necessary repairs, since the commencement of the usufruct: in which case the usufructuary is also bound to them.

606.

Substantial repairs are those of the main walls and

vaults, the re-establishment of beams, and entire roofs;

That of ditches and of buttresses, and enclosing walls in entirety;

All other reparations are necessary repairs.

607.

Neither the proprietor, nor the usufructuary is bound to rebuild what falls down through age, or what is destroyed by mere accident.

608.

The usufructuary is bound, while his enjoyment continues, to all annual charges on the estate, such as contributions and others which by custom are considered charges on the fruits.

609.

With respect to charges which may be imposed on property during the continuance of the usufruct, the usufructuary and the proprietor contribute thereto in manner following:

The proprietor is obliged to pay them, and the usufructuary must account to him for the interest;

If they are advanced by the usufructuary, he has a right to recover them at the end of the usufruct.

610.

A legacy given by a testator, of an annuity or alimentary pension, may be acquitted by the general legatee of the usufruct in its entirety, and by the legatee having the general title of usufruct in the proportion of his enjoyment, without any second payment on their part.

611.

The usufructuary by particular title is not bound by debts for which the estate is mortgaged: if he be compelled to pay them he has his remedy against the proprietor, saving what is said in article 1020, under the title "*Of Donations during Life and of Wills.*"

612.

The usufructuary either general or by general title must contribute with the proprietor to the payment of debts in manner following;

An estimate is made of the value of the estate the subject of usufruct, a rate of contribution to debts is then fixed in proportion to such estimate.

If the usufructuary is willing to advance the sum which the estate must contribute, the capital is restored to him at the termination of the usufruct without any interest.

If the usufructuary is not willing to make such advance, the proprietor has the election, either to pay such sum, (and in this case the usufructuary must account to him for the interest during the continuance of his usufruct) or to cause a portion of the property subject to usufruct, to the required amount, to be sold.

613.

The usufructuary is only bound to the charges of

such proceedings at law as regard the enjoyment, and of other judgments to which such proceeding may give rise.

614.

If during the continuance of the usufruct a third person is guilty of any usurpation on the estate, or any other attempt against the rights of the proprietor, the usufructuary is bound to give him information against such intruder; in default thereof he is himself responsible for all damage which may result therefrom to the proprietor, as he would be with respect to injuries committed by himself.

615.

If the usufruct be established only over an animal which happens to perish without the fault of the usufructuary, the latter is not bound to restore another for it, nor to pay its value.

616.

If a flock over which an usufruct has been established perishes entirely by accident or by disease, and without the fault of the usufructuary, the latter is not bound towards the proprietor except to account for the skins or their value.

If the flock does not entirely perish, the usufructuary is bound to replace them, until the increase amounts to the number of those animals which perished.

SECTION III.

Of the Manner in which Usufruct is put an end to.

617.

Usufruct is extinguished,

By the natural and civil death of the usufructuary;

By the expiration of the time for which it has been granted;

By the consolidation or union in the same person of the two qualities of usufructuary and proprietor;

By the non-exercise of the right during thirty years;

By the total loss of the object over which usufruct was established.

618.

Usufruct may likewise cease by the abuse of which the usufructuary is guilty in his enjoyment, either by committing spoliation upon the estate, or by suffering it to fall to decay for want of repair.

The creditors of the usufructuary may interfere in controversies, for the preservation of their rights; they may offer amends for spoliation committed, and guarantee for the future.

The judges may, according to the importance of the circumstances, either pronounce the absolute extinction of the usufruct, or give order for the re-entry of the proprietor into the enjoyment of the object encumbered therewith, on condition of paying annually, to the usufructuary or his agent, a fixed sum up to the period at which the usufruct would have ceased.

619.

Usufruct which is not granted to particular persons, only lasts for thirty years.

620.

Usufruct granted until a third person has reached a fixed age, continues until such period, although such third person die before the age fixed.

621.

The sale of a thing which is the subject of usufruct makes no alteration in the right of the usufructuary ; he continues to enjoy his usufruct unless he has formally renounced it.

622.

The creditors of an usufructuary may cause a renunciation made to their prejudice to be annulled.

623.

If one part only of the thing subject to usufruct be destroyed, the usufruct is preserved over the remainder.

624.

If the usufruct be established over a building only, and such building be destroyed by a fire or other accident, or if it have fallen down through age, the usufructuary shall have no right to the enjoyment either of the soil or the materials.

If the usufruct be established over a domain of which a building forms a part, the usufructuary shall enjoy the soil and the materials.

CHAPTER II.

Of Common and Habitation.

625.

The rights of common and of habitation are established and forfeited in the same manner as those of usufruct.

626.

A person is incapable, as in the case of usufruct, of enjoying them without previously giving security, and without making lists and inventories.

627.

The commoner and he who has a right of habitation ought to enjoy them like careful husbandmen.

628.

The rights of common and of habitation are governed by the title which has established them, and receive according to its regulations, more or less extent.

629.

If this title is not explicit on the extent of these rights, they are regulated as follows.

630.

He who has commonage over the fruits of an estate, cannot exact from thence more than is necessary to him for his own wants and those of his family.

He may exact therefrom for the wants likewise of children who have come to him subsequently to the grant of commonage.

631.

The possessor of commonage cannot yield or let his right to another.

632.

He who has the right of habitation in a house, may dwell there with his family, even though he should not have been married at the period when such right was conferred upon him.

633.

The right of habitation is confined to what is necessary for the habitation of him to whom such right is conceded, and of his family.

634.

The right of habitation can neither be ceded nor hired.

635.

If the possessor of commonage absorb the whole fruits of an estate, or if he occupy the entirety of a house, he is subjected to the charges of culture, to necessary reparations, and to the payment of contributions, like an usufructuary.

636.

Commonage in woods and forests is regulated by particular laws.

TITLE IV.

OF SERVITUDES OR MANORIAL SERVICES.

Decreed the 31*st of January*, 1804. *Promulgated the* 10*th of February*.

637.

A servitude is a charge imposed upon an estate for the use and benefit of an estate belonging to another proprietor.

638.

Servitude does not establish any pre-eminence of one estate over another.

639.

It is derived either from the natural situation of places, or from obligations imposed by law, or from agreements between proprietors.

CHAPTER I.

Of Servitudes derived from the Situation of Places.

640.

Inferior lands are subjected, as regards those which lie higher, to receive the waters which flow naturally therefrom to which the hand of man has not contributed.

The proprietor of the lower ground cannot raise a bank which shall prevent such flowing.

The superior proprietor of the higher lands cannot do any thing to increase the servitude of the lower.

641.

He who possesses a spring within his field may make use of it at his pleasure, saving the right which the proprietor of a lower field may have acquired by title or by prescription.

642.

Prescription in such case can only be acquired by an uninterrupted enjoyment during the space of thirty years; to be computed from the moment at which the proprietor of the lower field has made and completed the works apparently designed to facilitate the fall and course of the water within his property.

643.

The proprietor of a spring cannot change the course thereof when it supplies the inhabitants of a commune, village, or hamlet, with water for their necessary use: but if the inhabitants have not acquired the use of it by prescription or otherwise, the proprietor may claim an indemnity, to be settled by competent persons.

644.

He whose property borders on a running water, other than that which is declared a dependency on the public domain by article 538, under the title "*Of the Distinction of Property,*" may employ it in its passage for the watering of his property.

He whose estate is intersected by such water, is at liberty to make use of it within the space through which it runs, but on condition of restoring it, at the boundaries of his field, to its ordinary course.

645.

If a dispute arise between proprietors to whom such waters may be useful, the courts, in pronouncing their judgment, must reconcile the interest of agriculture with the respect due to property; and in all cases particular and local regulations on the course and use of waters must be observed.

646.

Every proprietor may compel his neighbor to determine the boundaries of their contiguous properties. Such determining of boundaries must be at their common expense.

647.

Every proprietor may enclose his estate, saving the exception contained in article 682.

648.

The proprietor who is desirous of enclosing his land, loses his right to the free pasturage and waste land, in proportion to the land which he withdraws.

CHAPTER II.

Of Servitudes established by Law.

649.

Servitudes established by law have for their object the public benefit, or that of the commune, or of private persons.

650.

Those established for the public benefit, or that of the commune, have for their object footways by the side of navigable rivers or streams admitting floats, the construction or reparation of roads, and other public works, or those relating to the commune.

Every thing relating to this species of servitude, is determined by the laws, or by particular regulations.

651.

The law subjects proprietors to different obligations as respects each other, independently of all convention.

652.

Part of these obligations is regulated by the laws touching rural police.

Others relate to party-walls and ditches, and the cases in which supporting walls are necessary, to views over the property of the neighbor, to the dropping of water from house-eaves, to rights of way.

SECTION II.

Of the Party-Wall and Ditch.

653.

In towns and fields every wall which serves as a boundary between buildings, even to its base, or between courts and gardens, or even between enclosures in the fields, is presumed party, if there be no title or mark to the contrary.

654.

It is a mark of non-partition when the summit of the wall is straight and perpendicular with its base on one side, and presents on the other an inclined plane. Again, when there is on one side only a coping, or ridges, and shouldering-pieces of stone, which might have been placed there in building the wall.

In such cases the wall is deemed to belong exclusively to the proprietor on whose side are the eaves or corbels, and ridges of stone.

655.

The reparation and rebuilding of the party-wall are at the expense of all those who have claim thereto, and in proportion to the claim of each.

656.

Nevertheless each joint-proprietor of a party-wall may relieve himself from contributing to the reparations and rebuilding by abandoning his claim of partition, provided that the party-wall do not sustain a building belonging to him.

657.

Every joint-proprietor is at liberty to build against a party-wall, and to place beams and joists in the whole thickness of the wall, except fifty-four millimetres (two inches) without prejudice to the right which his neighbor has to cause the beam to be reduced by the chisel to half the thickness of the wall, in case the latter shall desire to fix beams in the same place, or to build a chimney against it.

658.

Every joint-proprietor may cause a party-wall to be built higher, but he must alone defray the expense of such elevation, of the necessary reparations above the height of the common enclosure, and furthermore of an indemnity against the expense in the rate of the additional building and according to the value.

659.

If the party-wall is not in condition to support the additional building, he who desires to elevate it must cause it to be entirely rebuilt at his own expense, and the excess in thickness must be taken from his own side.

660.

The neighbor who has not contributed to the elevation may acquire right of partition by paying half of the expense it has cost, and the value of one moiety of the soil furnished for the excess of thickness, if there be any.

661.

Every proprietor joining a wall has in like manner the power of rendering it common, in whole or part, by paying to the owner of the wall the half of its value, or the half of the value of that portion which he desires to make common, and the half of the value of the soil on which the wall is built.

662.

One of two neighbors must not form in the body of a party-wall any hollow, nor apply or lean any work against it without the consent of the other, or, on his refusal, without having directed, under the advice of competent persons, the necessary means for erecting such new work without injury to the rights of the other.

663.

Each inhabitant of a town or suburb can compel his neighbor to contribute to the construction and reparation of the enclosure forming the boundary of their houses, courts, and gardens situated within the said towns and suburbs: the height of the enclosure shall be fixed according to particular regulations or constant and acknowledged usages; and in defect of such usages or regulations, every boundary wall between which two neighbors shall for the future be constructed or rebuilt, must be at least thirty-two decimeters (ten feet) high, including the coping, within towns containing fifty thousand souls and upwards, and twenty-six decimeters (eight feet) in others.

664.

When the different stories of a house belong to different proprietors, if the titles to the property do not regulate the mode of reparations and reconstructions, they must be made in manner following:

The main walls and the roof are at the charge of all the proprietors, each in proportion to the value of the story belonging to him.

The proprietor of each story makes the floor belonging thereto.

The proprietor of the first story erects the staircase which conducts to it; the proprietor of the second story carries the stairs from where the former ends to his apartments; and so of the rest.

665.

On the rebuilding a partition-wall or a house, the

servitudes, active and passive, continue with respect to such new wall or house, without power nevertheless to increase them, and provided the reconstruction have taken place before a right by prescription has been acquired.

666.

All ditches between two estates are presumed common if there be no title or proof to the contrary.

667.

It is a proof that a ditch is not common when the bank or earth thrown up is found only on one side of it.

668.

The ditch is deemed to belong exclusively to him on whose side the earth is found to be thrown up.

669.

A common ditch must be maintained at the common charge.

670.

Every hedge which separates two estates is reputed common, unless there be only one of the estates in an enclosed condition, or unless there be vouchers or sufficient possession to prove the contrary.

671.

It is not allowable to plant trees of lofty trunk, but at the distance prescribed by particular regulations actually existing, or by constant and acknowledged usages; and in default of regulations and usages only at the distance of two metres from the line which separates the two estates in the case of trees of lofty trunk, and at the distance of half a metre in the case of other trees and quick hedges.

672.

A neighbor may require trees and hedges planted at a less distance to be pulled up.

He whose property is overshadowed by the branches of his neighbor's trees, may compel the latter to cut off such branches.

If it be the roots which encroach on his estate, he has a right to cut them therein himself.

673.

Trees which are found in a common hedge are common like the hedge ; each of the two proprietors has the right to require that they should be felled.

SECTION II.

Of the Distance and intermediary Works required for certain Buildings.

674.

He who causes a well or a cesspool to be dug near a wall partition or not,

He who wishes a chimney to be built there, or a hearth, a forge, or oven, or a kiln,

To build a stable against it,

Or to form against such wall a magazine of salt, or a heap of corrosive substance,

Is obliged to leave the distance prescribed by particular regulations and usages on subjects, or to form the works prescribed by the same regulations and usages, in order to avoid injury to his neighbor.

SECTION III.

Of Views over a Neighbor's Property.

675.

One of two neighbors cannot without the consent of the other form in the partition-wall any window or aperture, in any manner whatsoever, even a fan-light.

676.

The proprietor of a wall which is not common, joining immediately the estate of another, may form in such wall lights or windows of wire-lattice, and fan-lights.

These windows must be furnished with a lattice-work of iron, the meshes of which shall extend to an opening of one decimeter, (about three inches eight lines at the most) and with a dormant window.

677.

These windows or lights must not be less than twenty-six decimeters (eight feet) above the floor or base of the chamber which is desired to be lighted, if it be the ground-floor, and nineteen decimeters (six feet) above the floor for the upper stories.

24

678.

A party must not have direct views nor windows for sight, nor balconies or other similar projections over the estate enclosed or unenclosed of his neighbor, within the distance of nineteen decimeters (six feet) between the wall on which they are formed and the aforesaid estate.

679.

A party shall not have side or oblique views over the same estate within the distance of six decimeters (two feet).

680.

The distance mentioned in the two preceding articles is computed from the exterior basement of the wall in which the aperture is made, or if there be balconies or other similar projections from their exterior line to the boundary line of the two properties.

SECTION IV.

Of the Droppings of House-Eaves.

681.

Every proprietor must so form his roofs, that the rain-water shall drop upon his own land or the public way; he must not suffer it to flow upon his neighbor's land.

SECTION V.

Of the Right of Way.

682.

Every proprietor whose fields are surrounded, and who has no outlet to the *public road,* may claim a passage over the fields of his neighbors for the agricultural purposes of his estate, on condition of an indemnity proportioned to the injury which he may occasion.

683.

The road ought regularly to be taken on that side where the passage is the shortest from the *farm surrounded to the public highway.*

684.

Nevertheless it ought to be fixed in that spot where it can occasion the least injury to him over whose farm it is granted.

685.

The action for indemnity, in the case provided for in article 682, may be prescribed against; and the road must be continued though the action for indemnity be no longer admissible.

CHAPTER III.

Of Servitudes established by the Act of Man.

SECTION I.

Of the different Species of Servitudes which may be established over Property.

686.

It is allowed to proprietors to establish over their property, or in favor of their property, such servitudes as seem good to them, provided nevertheless that the services established be not imposed either on a person, or in favor of a person, but only on an estate and for the benefit of an estate, and provided moreover such services contain nothing contrary to public order.

The mode of using and extent of servitudes thus established, are governed by the document which constitutes them; in default of such document, by the rules hereafter given.

687.

Servitudes are established either for the use of buildings, or for that of landed estates.

Those of the first species are called *urbane,* whether the buildings to which they are due are situated in a town or in a field;

Those of the second species are called *rural.*

688.

Servitudes are either continual or interrupted.

Continual servitudes are those whose use is or may be continual without having a necessity for the positive act of man: such are water-pipes, house-eaves, windows, and other things of that description.

Interrupted servitudes are those which require the positive act of man for their exercise: such are rights of way, of drawing water, of pasture, and other similar ones.

689.

Servitudes are apparent or non-apparent.

Apparent servitudes are those which are manifested by external works, such as a gate, a window, or aqueduct. Non-apparent servitudes are those which have no external sign of their existence, as, for example, a prohibition to build upon a field, or against building beyond a determinate height.

SECTION II.

Of the Mode of establishing Servitudes.

690.

Continual and apparent servitudes are acquired by deed, or by possession for thirty years.

691.

Continual non-apparent servitudes, and interrupted servitudes whether apparent or not, can only be established by deeds.

Even immemorial possession does not suffice to establish them; without power nevertheless to impeach at the present time servitudes of this nature already acquired by possession in districts where they may have been acquirable in this manner.

692.

The appointment of the father of a family is equivalent to a deed as regards continual and apparent servitudes.

693.

There is no appointment by the father of a family but when it is proved that the two farms actually divided have belonged to the same proprietor, and that it is by him that things have been put into the state whence results the servitude.

694.

If the proprietor of two estates, between which there exists an apparent sign of servitude, disposes of one of these estates, without inserting in the contract any stipulation relative to the servitude, it continues to exist actively or passively in favor of the land alienated, or over the land alienated.

695.

The deed constituting servitude, as far as respects those which cannot be acquired by prescription, can only be supplied by a document acknowledging the servitude, and emanating from the proprietor of the estate subject to servitude.

696.

When a servitude is established, it is considered that every thing is granted which is necessary in order to make use of it.

Thus the servitude of drawing water at another's fountain necessarily imports a right of way.

SECTION III.

Of the Rights of the Proprietor of the Estate to which the Servitude is due.

697.

He to whom a servitude is due has a right to form all the works necessary to make use of and preserve it.

698.

These works are at his own expense, and not at that of the proprietor of the estate subjected to servitude, unless the deed establishing the servitude declare the contrary.

699.

In the case even where the proprietor of an estate subjected to servitude is charged by the deed with the construction at his own expense of works necessary for the usage or preservation of the servitude, he may always get rid of such charge, by abandoning the estate subjected to servitude to the proprietor of that estate to which the servitude is due.

700.

If the estate for the benefit of which the servitude has been established happens to be divided, the servitude remains due for each portion, provided always, nevertheless, that the burden of the estate subjected to servitude shall not be aggravated.

Thus, for example, if the case be respecting a right of way, all the joint proprietors shall be obliged to exercise it by the same path.

701.

The proprietor of an estate from which a servitude is due can do nothing which tends to diminish the usage thereof or to render it less commodious.

Thus he cannot change the condition of places, nor transport the exercise of the servitude into a place different from that in which it has been originally assigned.

Nevertheless, if this original assignment has become more burdensome to the proprietor of the estate subjected to the servitude, or if he is prevented from making there advantageous repairs, he may offer to the proprietor of the other estate a place epually commodious for the exercise of his rights, and the latter shall not be at liberty to refuse.

702.

On the other hand, he who claims the servitude, can only use it according to his title, without power to effect either in the estate which owes the servitude, in the estate to which it is due, any change which aggravates the condition of the former.

SECTION IV.

Of the Manner in which Servitudes are extinguished.

703.

Servitudes cease when things are in such a state that it is impossible any longer to make use of them.

704.

They revive if things are re-established in such a manner that they can be made use of; unless a sufficient space of time has already elapsed to raise a presumption that the servitude has been extinguished, as is described in article 707.

705.

Every servitude is extinguished when the estate to which it is due, and that which owes it, are united in the same hands.

706.

Servitude is extinguished by non-usage during thirty years.

707.

The thirty years begin to run according to the different species of servitudes, either from the day on which they have ceased to be enjoyed, when the case regards interrupted servitudes, or from the day on which an act has been made contrary to the servitude, in the case of continual servitudes.

708.

The mode of servitude is subject to prescription like the servitude itself and in the same manner.

709.

If the estate in favor of which the servitude is established belong to several coparceners, the enjoyment by one precludes prescription with regard to all.

710.

If among the joint-proprietors there be one against whom the prescription has not been able to run, as a minor, he shall have preserved the right for all the others.

BOOK III.

OF THE DIFFERENT MODES OF ACQUIRING PROPERTY.

Decreed the 19*th of April,* 1803. *Promulgated the* 29*th of the same Month.*

GENERAL DISPOSITIONS.

711.

Ownership in goods is acquired and transmitted by succession, by donation between living parties, or by will and by the effect of obligations.

712.

Ownership is acquired also by accession, by incorporation, and by prescription.

713.

Property which has no owner belongs to the nation.

714.

There are things which belong to no one, and the use whereof is common to all.

The laws of police regulate the manner of enjoying such.

715.

The right of hunting and fishing is alike regulated by particular laws.

716.

Property in a treasure discovered in a man's own field belongs to himself: if discovered in another person's field, one moiety thereof belongs to him who discovered it, and as regards the other moiety to the proprietor of the field.

Treasure is every thing concealed or hidden in the earth over which no one can prove property, and which is discovered purely by the effect of chance.

717.

Claims respecting property thrown into the sea, respecting objects which the sea casts up, of what nature soever they may be, over plants and herbage which grow on the banks of the sea, are also regulated by particular laws.

It is the same with regard to things lost whereof the owner does not appear.

TITLE I.

OF SUCCESSIONS.

Decreed the 19*th of April,* 1803. *Promulgated* 29*th of the same Month.*

CHAPTER I.

Of the opening of Successions, and of the Seisin of Heirs.

718.

Successions are opened by natural death and by civil death.

719.

A succession is opened by civil death from the moment at which that death is incurred, conformably to the regulations of chap. 2, section 2, of the title, "*Of the Enjoyment and Privation of Civil Rights.*"

720.

If several persons, respectively called to the succession of each other, perish by one and the same accident, so that it is not possible to ascertain which of them died first, the presumption of survivorship is determined by the circumstances of the event, and in defect of such, by force of age and sex.

721.

If those who perished together were under fifteen years, the eldest shall be presumed to have survived.

If they were all above sixty, the youngest shall be presumed to have survived.

If some were under fifteen years, and others more than sixty, the former shall be presumed to have survived.

722.

If those who perished together were of the age of fifteen years complete, but less than sixty, the male is always presumed to have survived, where there is equality of age, or if the difference which exists does not exceed one year.

If they were of the same sex, the presumption of survivorship which gives rise to succession according to the order of nature must be admitted; thus the younger is presumed to have survived the elder.

723.

The law regulates the order of succeeding between legitimate heirs; in defect of such, the property passes to natural children, afterwards to the father or mother surviving; and if there be neither of those, to the state.

724.

The lawful heirs are seised in full right of the property, claims, and funds of the deceased, under the obligation to discharge all the expenses of the succession: natural children, the spouse surviving, and the state, must cause themselves to be put in possession by act of law, in the forms which shall be determined.

CHAPTER II.

Of the Qualities requisite to succeed.

725.

In order to succeed, the party must of necessity be in existence at the moment at which the succession is opened.

Those incapable of succeeding are,

1st. He who is not yet conceived;

2d. The child who is not born likely to live;

3d. He who is civilly dead.

726.

A foreigner is not permitted to succeed to property which his relation, foreigner or Frenchman, possesses in the territory of the republic, except in those cases and in the manner in which a Frenchman succeeds to his relation possessing property within the country of such foreigner, conformably to the regulations of article 11, under the title "*Of the Privation and Forfeiture of Civil Rights.*"

727.

Unworthy to succeed, and as such excluded from successions, are,

1st. He who shall be condemned for having caused or attempted to cause the death of the defunct;

2d. He who has brought against the defunct a capital charge adjudged calumnious;

3d. The heir being of age, who, being informed of the murder of the defunct, shall not have denounced it to the officers of justice.

728.

This failure of denunciation cannot be objected to the ancestors and descendants of the murderer, nor to his connexions in the same degree, nor to the husband or wife, nor to his brothers or sisters, nor to his uncles and aunts, nor to his nephews and nieces.

729.

The heir excluded from the succession for cause of unworthiness, is bound to restore all the fruits and revenues of which he has had the enjoyment since the opening of the succession.

730.

The children of such unworthy person, coming to the succession in their own right, and without the aid of representation, are not excluded by the fault of their father; but the latter cannot in any case claim, over the property of such succession, the usufruct which the law allows to fathers and mothers over the property of their children.

CHAPTER III.

Of the different Orders of Succession.

SECTION I.

General Dispositions.

731.

Successions are decreed to the children and descendants of the deceased, to his ancestors and collateral relations, in the order and according to the rules hereafter determined.

732.

The law considers neither the nature nor the origin of property in order to regulate the succession thereto.

733.

Every succession which falls to ancestors or collaterals, is divided into two equal parts; one for the relations of the paternal line, the other for relations of the maternal line.

Uterine relations, or children of the same father, are not excluded by germanes; but they only take share in their own line, saving what shall be declared in article 752. Germanes take part in the two lines.

There is no devolution from one line to another, except when no ancestor or collateral can be found in one of the two lines.

734.

This first division being effected between the paternal and maternal lines, no further division is made between the different branches; but the moiety devolved upon each line belongs to the heir or heirs nearest in degree, saving the case of representation, as shall be spoken of hereafter.

735.

The proximity of relationship is established by the number of generations; every generation is called a degree.

736.

The series of degrees forms the line; the series of degrees between persons descending from each other is called the *line direct;* the *line collateral* is the series of degrees between persons who do not descend from each other, but who are descended from a common author.

The line direct is distinguished into the line direct descending and the line direct ascending.

The first is that which connects the head with those who descend from him; the second is that which connects a person with those from whom he descends.

737.

In the direct line are computed as many degrees as there are generations between the persons: thus the son is, with respect to his father, in the first degree; the grandson in the second; and in like manner the father and grandfather with respect to sons and grandsons.

738.

In the collateral line the degrees are computed by generations, from one of the relations to, but not including their common author, and from the latter to the other relations.

Thus two brothers are in the second degree; the uncle and the nephew are in the third degree; cousins-german in the fourth; and so of the rest.

SECTION II.

Of Representation.

739.

Representation is a fiction of law, of which the effect is to cause representatives to enter into the place, the degree, and the rights of the party represented.

740.

Representation takes place to infinity in the direct descending line.

It is admitted in all cases, whether the children of the deceased come in competition with the descendants of a child previously dead; or whether all the children of the deceased having died before him, the descendants of such children are found to be in equal or unequal degrees toward them.

741.

Representation does not take place in favor of ancestors; the nearest in each of the two lines always excludes the more distant.

742.

In the collateral line, representation is admitted in favor of children and descendants of brothers and sisters of the deceased, whether they come to the succession concurrently with uncles or aunts, or whether all the brothers and sisters of the deceased being previously dead, the succession is found to be devolved upon their descendants in equal or unequal degrees.

743.

In all cases where representation is admitted, the petition is effected by stocks: if one original stock have produced several branches, the subdivision is made also by stocks in each branch, and the members of the same branch make distribution between themselves by heads.

744.

There is no representation of persons living, but only of those who are civilly or naturally dead.

There can be no representation of a person the succession to whom is renounced.

SECTION III.

Of Successions devolving upon Descendants.

745.

Children or their descendants succeed to their father and mother, grandfathers, grandmothers, or other ancestors, without distinction of sex or primogeniture, and although they be the issue of different marriages.

They succeed by equal portions and by heads when they are all in the first degree and called in their own right: they succeed by stocks, when they come all or in part by representation.

SECTION IV.

Of Successions devolving upon Ancestors.

746.

If the deceased has left neither posterity, nor brother, nor sister, nor descendants from them, the succession is divided into moieties between the ancestors of the paternal line and the ancestors of the maternal line.

The ancestor who is found in the nearest degree receives the moiety allotted to his line, to the exclusion of all others.

Ancestors in the same degree succeed by heads.

747.

Ancestors succeed, to the exclusion of all others, to things by them given to their children or descendants dead without issue, when the objects given are found again in kind in the succession.

If the objects have been alienated, the ancestors receive the price which may be therefore due. They succeed also to the action for recovery which the donee may have.

748.

When the father and mother of a party dead without issue have survived him, if he has left brothers, sisters, or descendants from them, the succession is divided into two equal portions, of which a moiety only devolves upon the father and mother, who share it equally between them.

The other moiety belongs to the brothers, sisters, or decendants from them, as shall be explained in section 5 of the present chapter.

749.

In the case where a person dead without issue leaves brothers, sisters, or descendants from them, if the father or the mother be previously dead, the portion which in such case would have devolved conformably to the preceding article, is re-united to the moiety accruing to the brothers, sisters, or their representatives, as shall be explained in section 5 of the present chapter.

SECTION V.

Of collateral Successions.

750.

In case of the previous decease of the father and mother of a person dead without issue, his brothers, sisters, or their descendants are called to the succession, to the exclusion of the ancestors and other collaterals.

They succeed, either in their own right, or by representation, as has been regulated in section 2 of the present chapter.

751.

If the father and mother of the party dead without issue have survived him, his brothers, sisters, or their representatives are only called to a moiety of the succession.

If the father or the mother only has survived, they are called to the enjoyment of three-fourths.

752.

The distribution of the moiety or of the three-fourths devolved upon the brothers or sisters, according to the terms of the preceding article, is effected between them by equal portions, if they are all by the same bed; if they are by different beds, a division is made of a moiety between the two lines paternal and maternal of the deceased; the germanes take part in both lines, and the uterine relations and those on the father's side each in their own line only; if there are brothers and sisters on one side only, they succeed to the whole, to the exclusion of all the other relations of the other line.

753.

In default of brothers or sisters or descendants from them, and in default of ancestors in one or other of the lines, the succession devolves as regards one moiety on the surviving ancestors; and as regards the other moiety, on the nearest relations of the other line.

If there be a competition of collateral relations in the same degree, they share by heads.

754.

In the case of the preceding article, the father or mother surviving has the usufruct of a third of the goods to which he does not succeed in property.

755.

Relations beyond the twelfth degree do not succeed. In default of relations capable of succeeding in one line, the relations of the other line succeed as regards the whole.

CHAPTER IV.

Of irregular Successions.

SECTION I.

Of the Rights of Natural Children over the Property of their Father or Mother, and of the Succession to Natural Children dead without issue.

756.

Natural children are not heirs; the law does not grant to such any rights over the property of their father or mother deceased, except when they have been legally recognized. It does not grant to them any right over the property of relations of their father or mother.

757.

The right of the natural child over the property of the father or mother deceased, is regulated in the following manner:

If the father or mother has left lawful descendants, such right extends to one-third of the hereditary portion which the child would have had if he had been legitimate: it extends to a moiety when the father or mother does not leave descendants, but many ancestors, or brothers, or sisters; to three-fourths when the father or mother does not leave either descendants or ancestors, either brothers or sisters.

758.

The natural child has a right to the whole of the oroperty, when his father or mother does not leave relations of a degree capable of succeeding.

759.

In case of the previous decease of the natural child, his children or descendants may claim the rights fixed by the preceding articles.

760.

The natural child or his descendants are bound to deduct from what they have the right to claim, all which they have received from the father or the mother whose succession is opened, and which shall be subject to account, according to the rules established in section 2 of chapter 6 of the present title.

761.

All claim is forbidden them, when they have received in the lifetime of their father or mother, the half of what is allowed them by the preceding articles, with an express declaration on the part of their father or mother, that their intention is to reduce the natural child to the portion which they have assigned him.

In the case in which this portion shall be inferior to the half of what ought to come to the natural child, he shall not be at liberty to claim more than the additional sum necessary to complete such moiety.

762.

The regulations of articles 757 and 758 are not applicable to children who are the fruit of adulterous or incestuous intercourse.

The law awards to them a subsistence merely.

763.

This subsistence is regulated by consideration of the ability of the father or mother, the number and quality of legitimate heirs.

764.

When the father or mother of an adulterous or incestuous child shall have caused him to learn a mechanical art, or when one of them shall have secured to him a subsistence while living, the child cannot set up any claim against their succession.

765.

The succession to a natural child deceased without issue, devolves upon his father or mother who may have acknowledged him; or by moieties to both, if he has been acknowledged by both.

766.

In case of the previous decease of the father and mother of the natural child, the property which he has received from them passes to the legitimate brothers or sisters, if found in kind in the succession: actions for recovery, if any exist, on the price of such property alienated, if still due, revert equally to the legitimate brothers and sisters.

All other property passes to the natural brothers or sisters, or their descendants.

SECTION II.

Of the Rights of the surviving Conjunct and of the Republic.

767.

When the deceased leaves neither relations of a degree capable of succeeding, nor natural children, the property of his succession belongs to his conjunct not being divorced surviving him.

768.

In default of conjunct surviving, the succession is acquired by the republic.

769.

The conjunct surviving and the commissioners of public property, who claim right to the succession, are bound to cause seals to be affixed, and to preserve an inventory to be made in the forms prescribed for the acceptance of successions under privilege of inventory.

770.

They must demand provisional possession in the court of first instance within the jurisdiction of which the succession is opened. The court cannot decree on such petition until after three publications and notices in the usual forms, and after having heard the commissioner of government.

771.

The spouse surviving is also bound to make use of the personal property, or to give sufficient security to assure its restoration, in case heirs of the deceased should present themselves within the space of three years: after such delay, the security is discharged.

772.

The spouse surviving or the commissioners of public property who shall not have complied with the formalities respectively prescribed to them, may be condemned to damages and interest towards the heirs, if any such appear.

773.

The regulations of articles 769, 770, 771, and 772, are common to natural children summoned for want of relations.

CHAPTER V.

Of the Acceptance and Repudiation of Successions.

SECTION I.

Of Acceptance.

774.

A succession may be accepted simply and absolutely or under privilege of inventory.

775.

No one is bound to accept a succession which has fallen to him.

776.

Married women are incapable of a valid acceptance of a succession without the authority of their husbands or of act of law, conformably to the regulations of cap. 6, under the title "*Of Marriage.*"

Successions falling to minors and interdicted persons, cannot be validly accepted but in conformity to the regulations of the title "*Of Minority, Guardianship, and Emancipation.*"

777.

The effects of acceptance have relation back to the day of the opening of the succession.

778.

Acceptance may be express or tacit; it is express, when the title or quality of heir is assumed in an authentic or private act; it is tacit when the heir makes an act which necessarily supposes his intention of accepting, and which he would have no right to do but in his quality of heir.

779.

Acts purely conservatory, of attention and provisional administration, are not acts of entry upon heirship, if the title or quality of heir have not been assumed.

780.

Donation, sale, or conveyance of his successional rights made by one coheir, either to a stranger, or to all the other coheirs, or to some one of them, imports on his part acceptance of the succession.

It is the same 1st, with a renunciation, though gratuitous, made by one of the heirs, in favor of one or more of his coheirs:

2nd, With a renunciation made even to the advantage of all the coheirs without distinction, when he receives the price of his renunciation.

781.

When he to whom a succession has fallen is dead without having repudiated it or without having accepted it expressly or tacitly, his heirs may accept or repudiate it in his right.

782.

If the heirs cannot agree in accepting or rejecting the succession, it must be accepted under privilege of inventory.

783.

One of full age cannot impeach an express or tacit acceptance made by him of a succession, except in the case where such acceptance shall have been the consequence of a fraud practised against him: he can never disclaim it under pretext of hardship, excepting only in the case where the succession is found to be absorbed or diminished more than half, by the discovery of a will unknown at the moment of acceptance.

SECTION II.

Of the Renunciation of Successions.

784.

Renunciation of a succession is not to be presumed: moreover it cannot be made, except at the office of the court of first instance within the circle where the succession is opened, or a particular register kept for this purpose.

785.

The heir who renounces, is considered as never having been heir.

786.

The share of the party renouncing is added to his coheirs; if he be the only one, it devolves upon the next degree.

787.

Parties can never come in as representatives of an heir who renounces: if the party renouncing is the sole heir in his own degree, or if all his coheirs renounce, the children come in in their own right, and succeed by heads.

788.

The creditors of a party renouncing to the prejudice of their rights, may cause themselves to be authorized by law to accept the succession in right of their debtor, in his place and stead.

In such case, the renunciation is annulled merely in favor of the creditors, and up to the amount only of their claims; it is not so as respects the advantage of the heir who has renounced.

789.

The power of accepting or repudiating a succession, is prescribed by the lapse of time required for the longest prescription respecting claims to real property.

790.

So long as prescription of the right to accept has not been acquired against heirs who have renounced, they have the ability still of accepting the succession, if it has not been already accepted by other heirs: without prejudice nevertheless to the rights which may be acquired by third persons over the property of the succession, whether by prescription, or by acts validly made with the curator to the vacant succession.

791.

A party cannot, even by contract of marriage, renounce the succession to a living person, nor alienate the eventual claims which he may have to such succession.

792.

The heirs who shall have conveyed away or concealed the goods of a succession are deprived of the power of renouncing therein: they become heirs simply and absolutely, notwithstanding their renunciation, without power to claim any share in the objects conveyed away or concealed.

SECTION III.

Of the Privilege of Inventory, of its Effects, and of the Obligations of the Beneficiary Heir.

793.

The declaration of an heir that he does not mean to assume this quality but under the privilege of an inventory, ought to be made at the office of the civil court of first instance of the circle in which the succession is opened: it must be inscribed on the register destined to receive acts of renunciation.

794.

This declaration has no effect except as it is preceded or followed by a faithful and exact inventory of the goods of the succession, in the forms regulated by the laws upon that proceeding, and within the intervals which shall be hereafter determined.

795.

The heir has three months to form an inventory, computing from the day on which the succession is opened.

He has moreover, for the purpose of deliberating on his acceptance or renunciation, a delay of forty days, which began to run from the day on which the three months allowed for the inventory expire, or from the day of closing the inventory, if it has been finished before the three months.

796.

If, however, there are in the succession objects liable to perish, or expensive in their preservation, the heir may, in his quality of capable to succeed, and without being liable to inference of an acceptance on his part, cause himself to be authorized by act of law to proceed to a sale of such effects.

Such sale ought to be made by the public officer, after notices and publications regulated by laws relating to that procedure.

797.

During the continuance of the intervals for making the inventory and for the deliberation, the heir cannot be compelled to assume this quality, and sentence cannot be obtained against him; if he renounce when those intervals are expired, or before, the expenses legally incurred by him up to that period are to be charged upon the succession.

798.

After the expiration of the intervals above mentioned, the heir, in case of prosecution directed against him, may demand a new delay, which the court which has possession of the suit may grant or refuse according to circumstances.

799.

The expenses of prosecution, in the case of the preceding article, are at the charge of the succession, if the heir can prove, either that he had not any knowledge of the death, or that the delays were insufficient, whether by reason of the situation of the property, or by reason of disputes having arisen; if he can bring no proof thereon, the expenses remain at his personal charge.

800.

The heir preserves nevertheless, after the expiration of the delays granted by article 795, and also of those allowed by the judge conformably to article 798, the faculty of still making an inventory and of constituting himself heir beneficiary, if he has not otherwise done an act of heirship, or if there does not exist against him a judgment passed by force of a matter decided which condemns him in the quality of simple and absolute heir.

801.

The heir who is found guilty of concealing or who has omitted knowingly and of bad faith, to comprehend in the inventory some effects of the succession, is deprived of the privilege of the inventory.

802.

The effect of the privilege of the inventory is to give to the heir the advantage,

1st. Of not being bound to payment of the debts of the succession, except to the amount of the value of the goods collected by him, besides the power of discharging himself from the payment of the debts by abandoning all the goods of the succession to the creditors and legatees.

2d. Of not confounding his personal property with that of the succession, and of preserving towards it the right of claiming the payment of his own demand.

803.

The beneficiary heir is charged to administer the goods of the succession, and must render an account of his administration to the creditors and legatees.

He cannot be compelled by his own property until after he has been in arrear in rendering his account, and in default of having satisfied this obligation.

After the settling of the account, he can only be answerable in his own personal property to the amount of the sums remaining in his hands.

804.

He is only responsible for serious faults in the administration with which he is invested.

805.

He cannot sell the moveables of the succession but by the agency of a public officer, by auction, and after public notices and the accustomed publications.

If he present them in kind, he is only responsible for the depreciation or deterioration caused by his own negligence.

806.

He can only sell the immoveable property in the forms prescribed by the laws on this procedure; he is bound to pay over the price thereof to the mortgage creditors who make themselves known.

807.

He is bound, if the creditors or other persons interested require it, to give good and sufficient security for the value of the moveables comprised in the inventory, and for the portion of the price of the immoveable property not paid over to mortgage creditors.

In failure of this security to be furnished by him, the moveable property is sold, and the price is deposited, as well as the unappropriated portion of the price of the immoveable property, to be employed in the acquittance of the charges on the succession.

808.

If there are opposing creditors, the beneficiary heir can only pay in the order and in the manner directed by the judge.

If there are not opposing creditors, he pays the creditors and the legatees as soon as they present themselves.

809.

Creditors not opposing, who do not appear until after the settling of the account and the payment of the balance, have no redress to exercise except against the legatees.

In both cases such redress is prescribed by the lapse of three years, to be computed from the day of the settling of the account and from the payment of the residue.

810.

The expenses of the seals, if any have been affixed, of the inventory and of the account, are at the charge of the succession

SECTION IV.

Of vacant Successions.

811.

When after the expiration of the delays for making the inventory and for deliberating, no person appears who claims a succession, there is no heir known, or the known heirs have renounced therein, such succession is taken to be vacant.

812.

The court of first instance within the circle in

which it is opened names a curator on the petition of the persons interested, or on the requisition of the commissioner of government.

813.

The curator in a vacant succession is bound, before every thing, to certify the state thereof by an inventory: he exercises and prosecutes the rights belonging to it: he answers demands formed against it: he administers on condition of causing the money arising from the succession, as well as that produced by the sale of the moveables or immoveables, to be paid into the hands of the receiver of national revenues, for the preservation of their rights, and on condition of rendering account to whomsoever it shall belong.

814.

The regulations of section 3 of the present chapter, on the forms of the inventory, on the mode of administration, and on the account to be rendered on the part of the heir beneficiary, are furthermore common to the curators of vacant successions.

CHAPTER VI.

Of Division and Restitution.

SECTION I.

Of the Action for Division and of its Form.

815.

No one can be compelled to remain without division, and distribution may be always sued for, notwithstanding prohibitions and conventions to the contrary.

The distribution may nevertheless be suspended by agreement during a limited time; such agreement cannot be made obligatory beyond five years; but it may be renewed.

816.

The distribution may be demanded even though one of the coheirs shall have enjoyed separately a part of the goods of the succession, if there have not been an act of distribution, or sufficient possession to acquire a prescriptive right.

817.

The action for distribution, with respect to coheirs, minors, or interdicted persons, may be exercised by their guardians, specially authorized by a family-council.

With respect to absent coheirs, the action belongs to the relations put in possession.

818.

The husband may, without the concurrence of his wife, claim a distribution of objects moveable or immoveable fallen to her and which come into community: with respect to objects which do not come into community, the husband cannot claim the distribution thereof without the concurrence of his wife; he can only demand a provisional distribution in case he has a right to the enjoyment of her property.

The coheirs of the wife cannot claim final distribution without suing the husband and his wife.

819.

If all the heirs are present and of age, the affixing of the seals on the effects of the succession is not necessary, and the distribution may be made in the form and by such act as the parties interested judge convenient.

If all the heirs are not present, if there are among them minors or interdicted persons, the seal must be affixed with the least possible delay, whether at the request of the heirs, or on the prosecution of the commissary of government in the court of first instance, or officially by the justice of the peace within the circle in which the succession is opened.

820.

Creditors may also require the affixing of seals, by

virtue of an executory title or of a permission from the judge.

821.

When the seal has been affixed, all creditors may make opposition thereto, although they have neither executory title nor permission from the judge.

The formalities for the removal of the seals and the formation of the inventory are regulated by the laws on the procedure.

822.

The action for distribution and the disputes which arise in the course of the proceedings, are submitted to the court of the place where the succession is opened.

It is before this court that auctions are held, and that petitions ought to be brought relative to the warranty of lots between copartners, as well as those for rescinding of the distribution.

823.

If one of the coheirs refuse to consent to the distribution, or if disputes arise either respecting the mode of proceeding therein, or on the manner of completing it, the court pronounces as in a summary matter, or commissions, if there be ground, one of the judges for the proceedings in the distribution, on whose report it decides the dispute.

824.

The estimate of the immoveable property is made

by competent persons chosen by the parties interested, or on their refusal nominated officially.

The statement of these persons must present the basis of the estimate: it must show whether the thing estimated can be conveniently divided; in what manner; in short to fix, in case of division, each of the parts which may be formed of it and their value.

825.

The valuation of the moveables, if there have not been an appraisement made in a regular inventory, ought to be made by people conversant with these affairs, at a fair price and without increase.

826.

Each of the coheirs may demand his own share in kind of the moveables and immoveables of the succession; nevertheless, if there are seising or opposing creditors, or if the majority of the coheirs deem a sale necessary for the discharge of the debts and incumbrances on the succession, the moveables must be sold publicly in the ordinary form.

827.

If the immoveables cannot be commodiously divided, a sale by auction must be proceeded in before the court.

Nevertheless the parties, if all of age, may consent that the auction should be made before a notary, on the choice of whom they can agree.

828.

After the moveables and immoveables have been valued and sold, the judge appointed sends the parties (if there be ground for doing so) before a notary respecting whom they can agree, or one officially nominated if the parties cannot agree upon the choice.

They proceed before this officer to the accounts which the copartners may owe, to the formation of the general mass, to the composition of the lots, and to the supplies to be made to each of the copartners.

829.

Every coheir makes restitution of the estate according to rules which shall be hereafter established, of gifts he may have received, and of sums for which he is debtor.

830.

If the restitution is not made in kind, the coheirs to whom it is due may deduct a correspondent portion from the mass of the succession.

The deductions are made as far as possible, in objects of the same nature, quality, and goodness, as the objects not restored in kind.

831.

After these deductions, recourse is had on what remains in the mass, to the formation of so many equal lots as there are coheirs or stocks in coparcenary.

832.

In the formation and arrangements of the lots, parties must avoid as much as possible disjointing estates and dividing works; and it is expedient, if it can be, to dispose in each lot the same quantity of moveables and immoveables, of rights or credits of the same nature and value.

833.

The inequality of the lots in kind is balanced by a return either in rent or in money.

834.

The lots are formed by one of the coheirs, if they can agree between themselves on a choice, and if the party elected accepts the commission; in the opposite case, the lots are made by a competent person appointed by the judge-commissary.

They are afterwards drawn at hazard.

835.

Before proceeding to draw the lots, each coparcener is admitted to offer his objections against their formation.

836.

The rules established for the division of the masses to be distributed are equally observed in the subdivision to be made between the coparcenary stocks.

837.

If in the operations sent before a notary disputes should arise, the notary shall draw up a statement of the difficulties and of the respective allegations of the parties, shall send them before the commissary nominated for the distribution; and, further, the forms shall be pursued which are prescribed by the laws on that procedure.

838.

If all the coheirs are not present, or if there are amongst them interdicted persons, or minors although emancipated, the distribution must be made by act of law, conformably to the rules prescribed by article 819, aad those following up to and including the preceding one. If there are many minors who have opposing interests in the distribution, a special and particular guardian must be appointed for each.

839.

If there be ground for an auction, in the case of the preceding article, it cannot be made except by act of law with the formalities prescribed for the alienation of the property of minors. Strangers are always admitted thereto.

840.

Distributions made conformably to the rules above prescribed, whether by guardians with the authority of a family-council, or by minors emancipated, assisted by their curators, or in the name of absentees or persons not present, are final: they are only provisional, if the rules prescribed have not been observed.

841.

Every person, even a relation of the deceased, not being capable of succeeding him, and to whom a coheir shall have ceded his claim upon the succession, may be excluded from the division, either by all the coheirs, or by one only, on reimbursing him the price of such cession.

842.

After the distribution, delivery must be made to each of the coparceners, of the particular titles to the objects which may have devolved to him.

The titles to a property divided remain with him who has the greatest share, on condition of aiding therewith such of the coparceners as shall be interested therein, when it shall be required of him.

Titles common to a whole inheritance are delivered to him whom all the heirs have chosen to be the depositary thereof, on condition of aiding therewith the coparceners, on every requisition. If there be a difficulty in the choice, it is regulated by the judge.

SECTION II.

Of Restitutions.

843.

Every heir, even beneficiary, coming to a succession, must restore to his coheirs, all he has received from the deceased by donation during life directly or indirectly: he cannot retain such gift nor claim a legacy left him by the deceased, unless such gifts and legacies have been given him expressly in addition and not subject to partition, or with a dispensation of restitution.

844.

In the case even where gifts and legacies shall have been made in addition and with dispensation of restitution, the heir coming to distribution cannot retain them except to the amount of the disposable proportion: the excess is subject to restitution.

845.

The heir who renounces a succession, may nevertheless retain a donation made during life, or claim a legacy given him, to the amount of his disposable proportion.

846.

A donee who was not heir presumptive at the time of the donation, but who has become capable of succeeding on the day of opening the succession, must equally make restitution, unless the donor have dispensed therewith.

847.

Donations and legacies given to the son of him who is found to be successor at the period of opening the succession, are always taken to have been made with dispensation of restitution.

The father coming to the succession of the donor is not bound to make restitution.

848.

In like manner, the son coming in his own right to the succession of the donor, is not bound to restore a donation made to his father, even though he shall have accepted the succession to the latter: but if the son only comes by representation, he must restore a donation made to his father, even in the case where he shall have repudiated the succession.

849.

Donations and legacies made to the husband or wife of a party succeeding, are deemed to have been made with dispensation of restitution.

If the donations and legacies are made conjointly to the two married parties of whom one only is capable of succeeding, the other restores a moiety thereof; if donations are made to the married party capable of succeeding, restitution must be made of the whole.

850.

Restitution is only made to the succession of the donor.

851.

Restitution is due from him who has been employed for the establishment of one of the co-heirs, or for the payment of his debts.

852.

The expenses of nourishment, of maintenance, of

education, of apprenticeship, the ordinary expenses of equipment, those of marriage and customary presents, must not be restored.

853.

It is the same with respect to profits which the heir may have derived from contracts made with the deceased, if such contracts did not present any indirect advantage when they were made.

854.

In like manner restitution is not due in respect of paternships formed without fraud between the deceased and one of his heirs, when the conditions thereof have been regulated by an authentic act.

855.

Immoveable property which has perished by accident and without the fault of the donee is not subject to restitution.

856.

The fruits and interests of things subject to restitution are only due computing from the day on which the succession is opened.

857.

The restitution is due only from one coheir to another: it is not due to legatees nor to the creditors of ther succession.

858.

The restitution is made in kind or by taking less.

859.

It may be demanded in kind, in the case of immoveables, as often as the immoveable given has not been alienated by the donor, and there are not in the succession immoveables of the same nature, value, and goodness, of which may be formed lots nearly equal for the other co-heirs.

860.

The restitution only takes place by taking less when the donee has alienated the immoveable before the opening of the succession; it is due to the value of the immoveable at the date of the opening.

861.

In all cases reimbursements ought to be made to the donee of the expenses at which the object has been improved, regard being had to the augmented value as found at the time of distribution.

862.

Reimbursement should be made also to the donee of expenses necessarily incurred in the preservation of the object, although they have not improved the bulk.

863.

The donee on his part must give account of the injuries and deteriorations which have diminished the value of the immoveable, by his own act or through his fault and negligence.

864.

In the case where the immoveable has been alienated by the donee, the improvements or injuries caused by the purchaser must be charged conformably to the three preceding articles.

865.

When the restitution is made in kind, the property is reunited to the stock of the succession, free and quit of all charges, created by the donee; but the mortgage-creditors may intervene in the distribution for the purpose of preventing a restitution being made in fraud of their claims.

866.

When the donation of an immoveable made with dispensation of restitution to one capable of succeeding exceeds his disposable portion, restitution of the excess is made in kind, if the retrenchment of such excess can operate advantageously.

In the contrary case, if the excess is above one moiety of the value of the immoveable, the donee must restore it in entirety, saving a deduction from the stock to the amount of his disposable portion; if such portion exceed half the value of the immoveable, the donee may retain the immoveable in entirety, on condition of taking less and of recompensing the co-heirs in money or otherwise.

867.

The coheir who makes restitution in kind of an immoveable, may retain the possession thereof until he has been reimbursed the sums due to him for expenses or improvements.

868.

The restitution of moveables is only made by taking less.

It is regulated on the basis of the value of the moveables at the time of the donation, according to the estimatory statement annexed to the act; and in defect of such statement, according to a valuation by competent persons, at a fair price and without increase.

869.

The restitution of money given is made by taking less in the money of the succession.

In case of deficiency, the donee may free himself from restitution of the money by abandoning to the due amount, the moveables, or in default of moveables, the immoveables of the succession.

SECTION III.

Of Payment of Debts.

870.

The coheirs contribute among them to the payment of the debts and charges on the succession each in the proportion to what he takes therein.

871.

The legatee by general title contributes with the heirs proportionably to his emolument; but the particular heir is not bound by debts and charges, saving however a mortgage on the immoveable bequeathed.

872.

When some of the immoveables of a succession are encumbered with rents by a special mortgage, each of the coheirs may require that the rents should be redeemed, and the immoveables rendered free, before they proceed to the formation of lots. If the coheirs make distribution of the succession in the state in which they find it, the immoveable encumbered ought to be estimated at the same rate as the other immoveables; a deduction of the capital of the rent is made from the total valuation; the heir within whose lot such immoveable falls alone remains charged with the encumbrance of the rent, and he must indemnify his coheirs against it.

873.

The heirs are bound by the debts and charges on the succession, personally for their part and individual portions, and conditionally for the whole; saving the remedy either against their coheirs, or against the general legatees, in proportion to the part in which they are bound to contribute thereto.

874.

The particular legatee who has discharged the

debt with which the immoveable bequeathed was encumbered, enters by substitution into the rights of the creditor against the heirs and successors by general title.

875.

The co-heir or successor by general title, who has paid, in consequence of the mortgage, more than his share of the common debt, has no resource against the other co-heirs or successors by general title, except for such part as each of them ought personally to sustain, even in the case where the co-heir having paid the debt shall have caused himself to be substituted into the rights of the creditors ; without prejudice nevertheless to the rights of a co-heir, who, by the effect of the privilege of inventory, shall have preserved the power of claiming payment of his personal demand, like every other creditor.

876.

In case of the insolvency of one of the co-heirs or successors by general title, his share in the mortgage debt is assessed upon all the others, in their respective proportions.

877.

Executory demands against the deceased are in like manner executory against the heir personally ; but the creditors nevertheless shall not be at liberty to pursue the execution thereof until eight days after the notification of such demands in person or at the domicil of the heir.

878.

They may demand, in all cases, and against every creditor, the separation of the patrimony of the deceased from that of the heir.

879.

This right however can be no longer exercised, when there is a transfer in the claim against the deceased, by the acceptance of the heir as debtor.

880.

Prescription takes place, with reference to moveables, by the lapse of three years.

With regard to immoveables, an action may be maintained as long as they are in the hands of the heir.

881.

The creditors of the heir are not permitted to demand a separation of the patrimonies against the creditors of the succession.

882.

The creditors of one coparcener, in order to prevent the making of distribution in fraud of their rights, may oppose its being done out of their presence; they have a right of interposing therein at their own charge; but they cannot impugn a distribution completed, provided however it has not been proceeded in without them and in prejudice of an opposition formed by them.

SECTION IV.

Of the Effects of Distribution and of the Warranty of the Lots.

883.

Every coheir is deemed to have succeeded alone and immediately to all the effects comprised in his lot, or fallen to him by auction, and never to have had any property in the other effects of the succession.

884.

The coheirs are respectively sureties for each other, against those molestations and evictions only which proceed from a cause anterior to the distribution.

The guarantee does not take effect if the species of eviction suffered be excepted by a particular and express clause in the act of distribution; it ceases if it is by his own fault that the coheir suffers eviction.

885.

Each of the coheirs is personally bound, in proportion to his hereditary share, to indemnify his coheir against the loss which his eviction has caused him.

If one of the coheirs is found to be insolvent, the portion in which he is bound must be equally assessed upon the party indemnified and all the solvent coheirs.

886.

The guarantee of the solvency of one who owes a

rent cannot be made use of beyond the five years succeeding the distribution.

There is no ground for the warranty on account of the insolvency of a debtor where it has occurred subsequently to the distribution completed.

SECTION V.

Of Annulment of Distributions.

887.

Distributions may be rescinded for cause of violence or fraud.

There may also be ground for annulment where one of the coheirs establishes, to his own prejudice, a loss of more than one fourth. The simple omission of an object in the succession does not give room for an action for annulment, but merely for a supplement to the act of distribution.

888.

The action for annulment is admitted against every act which has for its object the cessation of the coparcenary of the coheirs, although it be ratified by sale, by exchange, by composition, or in any other manner.

But after the distribution, or the act which supplies its place, the action for rescision is no longer admissible against the agreement founded upon the real difficulties presented by the first act, even though there should not have been process commenced upon this subject.

889.

The action is not admitted against a sale of a successional right made without fraud to one of the coheirs, at his own risk and peril, by his other co-heirs or by one of them.

890.

In order to judge if damage have been done, a valuation is made of the objects according to their value at the period of the distribution.

891.

The defendant on a petition for annulment may arrest the progress thereof and prevent a new distribution, by tendering and furnishing to the plaintiff the supplement of his hereditary portion, either in money, or in kind.

892.

The co-heir who has alienated his lot in whole or in part, is no longer admissible to sustain an action for annulment on the ground of fraud or violence, if the alienation which he has made is subsequent to the discovery of the fraud, or to the cessation of the violence.

TITLE II.

OF DONATIONS DURING LIFE, AND OF WILLS.

Decreed the 3d of May, 1803. Promulgated the 3d of the same Month.

CHAPTER I.

General Regulations.

893.

A man shall not be allowed to dispose of his property by gratuitous title, except by donation during life or by will, in the form hereafter established.

894.

A donation during life is an act by which the donor deprives himself actually and irrevocably of the thing given, in favor of the donee who accepts it.

895.

A will is an act by which the testator disposes, for the time when he shall no longer exist, of the whole or of part of his property, and which he is at liberty to revoke.

896.

Entails are prohibited.

Every disposition by which the donee, the heir appointed or the legatee, shall be charged to preserve and render to a third person, shall be null, even with regard to the donee, the heir appointed and the legatee.

897.

Excepted from the preceding article are those dispositions permitted to fathers and mothers, to brothers and sisters, in the sixth chapter of the present title.

898.

The disposition by which a third person shall be called to receive the donation, the inheritance, or legacy, in the case where the donee, the heir appointed or the legatee, will not receive it, shall not be regarded as an entail, and shall be valid.

899.

It shall be the same with a disposition during life or by will, by which the usufruct shall be given to one, and the naked property to another.

900.

In every disposition during life or by will, impossible conditions, such as shall be contrary to the laws and to morals, shall be reputed not written.

CHAPTER II.

Of the Capability of disposing or of receiving by Donation during Life or by Will.

901.

In order to make a donation during life or by will, it is necessary to be of sane mind.

902.

All persons may dispose or receive, either by donation during life, or by will, excepting such as are declared incapable of doing so by the law.

903.

A minor under the age of sixteen years is capable of disposing in no way, saving that which is ordained in cap. 9 of the present title.

904.

A minor who has reached the age of sixteen years can make disposition by will only, and to the amount of not more than half the property of which the law permits an adult to dispose.

905.

A married woman cannot make donation during life without the assistance or the special consent of her husband, or without being thereto authorized by the law, conformably to what is prescribed by articles 217 and 219, under the title " *Of Marriage.*"

She shall not need either the consent of her husband, or the authorization of the law, in order to dispose by will.

906.

In order to be capable of receiving during life, it suffices to be conceived at the moment of the donation.

In order to be capable of receiving by will, it suffices to be conceived at the period of the testator's death.

Nevertheless the donation or the will shall not have their effect, except so far as the infant shall be born likely to live.

907.

A minor, although arrived at the age of sixteen years, shall not be permitted, even by will, to make disposition for the benefit of his guardian.

A minor shall not be permitted, on arriving at majority, to make disposition either by donation during life, or by will, for the benefit of him who was formerly his guardian, unless the final accounts of the guardianship have been previously rendered and settled.

Excepted in the two cases above mentioned are the ancestors of minors, who are or who have been their guardians.

908.

Natural children shall not be permitted, by donation during life or by will, to receive any thing beyond what is accorded to them under the title "*Of Successions.*"

909.

Doctors in physic or in surgery, officers of health and apothecaries, who shall have attended a person during the malady of which he dies, shall not be allowed to profit by donations during life or by will which such person shall have made in their favor in the progress of the disorder.

Excepted 1st, are remunerative dispositions made by particular documents, regard being had to the ability of the disposer and to the services rendered.

2d. General dispositions, in the case of relationship even to the fourth degree inclusive, provided however the deceased has not heirs in direct line; unless he to whose profit the disposition has been made shall be himself among the number of such heirs.

The same rules shall be observed with regard to the minister of religion.

910.

Dispositions during life or by will, for the benefit of hospitals, of the poor of a commune, or of establishments of public utility, shall not take effect, except so far as they shall be authorized by an ordinance of the government.

911.

Every disposition for the benefit of an incapacitated person shall be null, whether disguised under the form of a chargeable contract, or made under the name of substituted persons.

The fathers and mothers, the children and descendants, and the husband or wife of the incapacitated person shall be deemed substituted.

912.

Dispositions shall not be allowed for the benefit of a foreigner, except in a case where such foreigner might be allowed to make disposition for the benefit of a Frenchman.

CHAPTER III.

Of the disposable Portion of Goods, and of Reduction.

SECTION I.

Of the disposable Portion of Goods.

913.

Free gifts, whether by acts during life, or by will, shall not exceed the half of the property of the disposer, if he leave at his decease but one legitimate child; the third part if he leave two children; the fourth part if he leave three or more of them.

914.

Comprehended in the preceding article, under the name of children, are descendants in any degree whatsoever; nevertheless they are only reckoned for the child whom they represent in the succession of the disposer.

915.

Free gifts, by acts during life or by will, shall not exceed a moiety of the property, if in default of children, the deceased leaves one or more ancestors in both the paternal and maternal line; and three fourths if he leave ancestors only in one line.

The property thus preserved for the benefit of ancestors shall be received by them in the order in which the law calls them to succeed; they shall alone enjoy the right to this reservation, in all cases in which a distribution in competition with the collaterals shall not have given them their disposable proportion of the goods at which it is fixed.

916.

In default of ancestors and descendants, free gifts by acts during life or by will may exhaust the whole of the property.

917.

If the disposition by act during life or by will is of an usufruct or life-annuity of which the value exceeds the disposable proportion, the heirs for whose benefit the law makes a reservation, shall have the option either of executing such disposition, or of abandoning the property of the disposable proportion.

918.

The value in full property of goods alienated, either on condition of a life-annuity, or by sinking the money, or with reservation of usufruct, to one of those capable of succeeding in the direct line, shall be deducted from the disposable proportion; and the excess, if there be any, shall be carried to the mass. Such deduction and such carrying to account cannot be demanded by such of the other persons capable of succeeding in direct line as shall have consented to those alienations, nor in any case by those capable of succeeding in the collateral line.

919.

The disposable proportion may be given in whole or in part, either by act during life, or by will, to children or others, successors of the donor, without being subject to restitution by the donee or legatee coming to the succession, provided the disposition has been made expressly by gratuitous title, and not subject to distribution.

The declaration that the gift or legacy is by gratuitous title, or not subject to distribution, may be made, either by the act which shall contain the disposition, or subsequently in the form of dispositions during life, or by will.

SECTION II.

Of the Reduction of Donations and Legacies.

920.

Dispositions, either during life, or by reason of death, which shall exceed the disposable proportion, shall be reducible to such proportion at the opening of the succession.

921.

The reductions of dispositions during life shall not be demanded except by those for whose profit the law makes reservation, by their heirs or assigns; the donees, legatees, and creditors of the deceased shall not be allowed to demand such reduction nor to profit thereby.

922.

The reduction is settled by forming one mass of all the property existing at the decease of the donor or testator. By a fiction such property is added thereto as he shall have disposed of by donations during life, according to their condition at the period of such donations, and their value at the time of the donor's death. After having deducted the debts, a calculation is made upon the whole property, of what proportion, regard being had to the quality of the heirs whom he leaves, he was empowered to dispose.

923.

It shall never be allowed to reduce donations during life until after having exhausted the value of all the property comprised in the testamentary dispositions; and when there shall be room for such reduction, it shall be made by commencing with the last donation, and so returning in their order to the more distant ones.

924.

If the donation during life to be reduced has been made to one of the successors, he may retain, out of the property bestowed, the value of the portion which belongs to him as heir, in goods not disposable if they are of the same nature.

925.

When the value of the donations during life shall exceed or equal the disposable proportion, all the testamentary dispositions shall be lapsed.

926.

When the testamentary dispositions shall exceed either the disposable proportion, or the portion of such proportion which shall remain after having deducted the value of the donations during life, the reduction shall be made rateably, without any distinction between general and particular legacies.

927.

Nevertheless in all cases where the testator shall have expressly declared his intention to be that such legacy should be acquitted in preference to others, such preference shall take place; and the legacy which shall be the object thereof shall not be reduced except inasmuch as the value of the others shall fail to complete the legal reservation.

928.

The donee shall restore the fruits of that which shall exceed the disposable proportion, computing from the day of the donor's decease, if the demand for reduction has been made within the year; if not, from the day of such demand.

929.

The immoveables recovered by the effect of the reduction shall be unencumbered by the debts or mortgages of the donee.

930.

The action for reduction or reclaim may be maintained by the heirs against third persons detaining immoveables forming part of donations and alienated by the donees, in the same manner and in the same order as against the donees themselves, seizure being previously made of their property. This action ought to be maintained according to the order of the dates of the alienators, beginning with the most recent.

CHAPTER IV.

Of Donations during Life.

SECTION 1.

Of the Form of Donations during Life.

931.

All acts importing donation during life shall be passed before notaries, in the ordinary form of contracts; and a minute thereof shall be left, on pain of nullity.

932.

A donation during life shall not bind the donor, or produce any effect, except from the day on which it shall have been accepted in express terms.

The acceptance may be made, living the donor, by a subsequent and authentic act, of which a minute shall remain; but then the donation shall not have effect with regard to the donor, except from the day on which the act which shall verify such acceptance shall have been notified to him.

933.

If the donee be of age, the acceptance must be made by him or in his name, by a person holding his power of attorney importing power to accept the donation made, or a general power of accepting donations which shall have been or which may hereafter be made.

Such procuration ought to be executed before notaries; and a copy thereof must be annexed to the minute of the donation, or to the minute of acceptance if made by a separate act.

934.

A married woman shall not be allowed to accept a donation without the consent of her husband, or, in case of her husband's refusal, without the authority of the law, conformably to what is prescribed by articles 217 and 219, under the title "*Of Marriage.*"

935.

A donation made to a minor not emancipated, or to an interdicted person, must be accepted by his guardian, conformably to article 463, under the title "*Of Minority, Guardianship, and Emancipation.*"

A minor emancipated may accept with the assistance of his curator.

Nevertheless the father and mother of the minor emancipated or not emancipated, or the other ancestors, may, though neither the tutors nor curators of the minor accept from him even during the life of his father and mother.

936.

A person deaf and dumb, who knows how to write, shall be capable of accepting by himself or by attorney.

If he is unable to write, the acceptance must be made by a curator nominated for this purpose, according to the rules established under the title "*Of Minority, Guardianship, and Emancipation.*"

937.

Donations made for the benefit of hospitals, of the poor of a commune, or of establishments for public utility, shall be accepted by the managers of such communes or establishments, having been thereto duly authorized.

938.

A donation duly accepted shall be perfect by the simple consent of the parties; and the property in the objects bestowed shall be transferred to the donee without necessity of any other conveyance.

939.

When there shall be a donation of property susceptible of mortgages, the transcription of the acts containing the donation and acceptance, as well as the notification of the acceptance which shall have taken place by separate act, ought to be made at the offices for mortgages within the circle in which the property is situated.

940.

Such transcription shall be made at the instance of the husband, when the property shall have been given to his wife; and if the husband does not satisfy such formality, the wife may proceed therein without authority.

When the donation shall be made to minors, to interdicted persons, or to public establishments, the transcription shall be made at the instance of the guardians, curators, or managers.

941.

The want of transcription may be objected by all persons having interest, those however excepted whose duty it is to cause the transcription to be made, or their assigns, and the donor.

942.

Minors, interdicted persons, married women, shall not be reinstated after default of acceptance or transcription of donations; saving the remedy against their guardians or husbands, if occasion be, and without power of restitution in the case even where the said guardians and husbands shall be found insolvent.

943.

A donation during life shall only comprehend the present property of the donor; if it comprehend future property, it shall in that respect be null.

944.

Every donation during life made under conditions, the execution of which depends on the single will of the donor, shall be null.

945.

It shall be in like manner null, if it have been made under the condition of discharging other debts or encumbrances than those which existed at the period of the donation, or which shall be expressed either in the act of donation, or in the statement which ought to be thereto annexed.

946.

In a case where the donor has reserved to himself the liberty of disposing of an article comprehended in the donation, or of a fixed sum in the property bestowed; if he dies without having disposed thereof, the said sum or the said article shall belong to the heirs of the donor, notwithstanding any clauses or stipulations to the contrary.

947.

The four preceding articles do not apply to donations whereof mention is made in chapters 8 and 9 of the present title.

948.

No act of donation of personal property shall be valid, except for effects of which an estimatory statement, signed by the donor and the donee, or those who accept for him, shall have been annexed to the minute of the donation.

949.

It is permitted to the donor to make reservation for his own benefit, or to dispose for the benefit of another, of the enjoyment or usufruct of the moveable or immoveable property bestowed.

950.

When the donation of moveable effects shall have been made with reservation of usufruct, the donee shall be bound at the expiration of the usufruct, to take the effects bestowed which shall be found in kind, in the state in which they are; and he shall have an action against the donor or his heirs, by reason of articles not in existence to the amount of the value which shall have been given them in the estimatory statement.

951.

The donor may stipulate for the right of a return of the objects bestowed, either in case of the previous decease of the donee only, or in case of the previous decease of the donee and of his descendants.

This right shall not be contracted for except for the benefit of the donor only.

952.

The effect of the right of return shall be to rescind

all alienations of property bestowed, and to cause such property to revert to the donor, free and quit of all charges and mortgages, saving nevertheless the mortgage of dowry and of matrimonial conventions, if the other property of the married party donor does not suffice, and in the case only where the donation shall have been made to the party by the same contract of marriage, from which result such rights and mortgages.

SECTION II.

Of Exceptions to the Rule on the Irrevocability of Donations during Life.

953.

The donation during life shall not be revoked except for cause of the non-performance of the conditions subject to which it shall have been made, for cause of ingratitude, and by reason of the unexpected birth of children.

954.

In the case of revocation for cause of non-performance of conditions, the property shall return into the hands of the donor, free of all charges and mortgages on account of the donee; and the donor shall have, against third persons detaining immoveable property bestowed, all the rights which he would have had against the donee himself.

955.

The donation during life shall not be revoked for cause of ingratitude except in the following cases:

1st. If the donee have attempted the life of the donor;

2d. If he have become guilty of cruelty, crimes, or heinous injury towards him;

3d. If he refuses him subsistence.

956.

The revocation for non-performance of conditions, or for cause of ingratitude, shall never take place absolutely.

957.

The petitions for revocation on account of ingratitude ought to be made within the year, to be computed from the date of the crime imputed by the donor to the donee, or from the date at which the crime might have been known to the donor.

Such revocation is not allowed to be petitioned for by the donor against the heirs of the donee, nor by the heirs of the donor against the donee, unless in the last case the action have been instituted by the donor, or unless he have died within a year after the crime.

958.

The revocation for cause of ingratitude shall not prejudice either alienations made by the donee, or mortgages and other real charges which he may have imposed on the object of the donation, provided that the whole be anterior to the inscription which shall have been made of the abstract of the petition for revocation in the margin of the transcription prescribed by article 939.

In case of revocation, the donee shall be condemned to restore the value of the objects alienated, regard being had to the time of the petition and the fruits computing from the day of such petition.

959.

Donations in favor of marriage shall not be revocable on account of ingratitude.

960.

All donations during life made by persons who had no children or descendants actually living at the time of the donation, of what value soever such donations may be, and by what title soever they may have been made, and although they may have been mutual or remuneratory, except such as shall have been made in favor of marriage by others than the ancestors of the married parties, or by the married parties to each other, shall be absolutely revoked by the birth of a legitimate child to the donor, even of a posthumous one, or by the legitimation of a natural child by subsequent marriage, if it be born subsequently to the donation.

961.

Such revocation shall take place, although the

child of the donor were conceived at the time of the donation.

962.

The donation shall be in like manner revoked, even when the donee shall have entered into possession of the property bestowed, and when it shall have been ceded by the donor subsequently to the birth of the child; provided, nevertheless, that the donee shall not be bound to restore the profits received by him, of what nature soever they may be, except from the day, on which the birth of the child or his legitimation by subsequent marriage shall have been notified to him by summons or other act in regular form; and this, although the petition for re-entry into the property bestowed shall only have been formed subsequently to such notification.

963.

The property comprised in the donation absolutely revoked, shall be restored to the patrimony of the donor, free of all charges and mortgages on the part of the donee, without liability to be affected, even subsidiarily, by the restitution of the dowry of the wife of such donee, by her previous claims or other matrimonial covenants; which shall take place even though the donation shall have been made in favor of the marriage of the donee and inserted in the contract, and though the donee shall be bound by way of security, by the donor, to the execution of the contract of marriage.

964.

The donations thus revoked shall not be revived or take effect anew either by the death of the child of the donor or by any confirmatory act; and if the donor is desirous of conferring the same property on the same donee, either before or after the death of the child by whose birth the donation was revoked, he can only accomplish it by a new disposition.

965.

Every clause or covenant by which the donor shall have renounced his right to revoke a donation on account of the birth of a child, shall be regarded as null, and shall be incapable of producing any effect.

966.

The donee, his heirs or assigns, or others detaining things bestowed, shall not be allowed to object prescription in order to make valid a donation revoked by the birth of a child, until after a possession of thirty years, which shall only begin to run from the day of the birth of the last child of the donor, though posthumous; and this, without prejudice to interruptions, such as of claim.

CHAPTER V.

Of Testamentary Dispositions.

SECTION I.

Of general Rules on the Form of Wills.

967.

Every person shall be at liberty to dispose by will, either under the title of appointment of an heir, or under the title of legacy, or under any other denomination proper to manifest his will.

968.

Two or more persons shall not be permitted to make a will in the same act, either for the benefit of a third person, or under the title of a reciprocal and mutual disposition.

969.

A will may be an olographe, or made by public act or in the mystic form.

970.

An olographic will shall not be valid unless it be written throughout, dated and signed by the hand of the testator: it is not subjected to any other formality.

971.

The will by public act is that which is received by two notaries in the presence of two witnesses, or by one notary in the presence of four witnesses.

972.

If the will is received by two notaries, it is dictated to them by the testator, and it must be written by one of such notaries, as it is dictated.

If there be only one notary, it must equally be dictated by the testator, and written by such notary.

In both cases, it must be read over to the testator, in presence of the witnesses.

Express mention of the whole must be made.

973.

This will must be signed by the testator; if he declare that he knows not how or is unable to sign, express mention shall be made of his declaration in the act, as well as of the cause which prevents him from signing.

974.

The will must also be signed by the witnesses; nevertheless in the country it shall suffice that one of the two witnesses signs, if the will is received by two notaries, and that two of the four witnesses sign if it is received by one notary.

975.

Neither of the legatees by what title soever they

are so, nor their relations nor connections even to the fourth degree inclusively, nor the clerks of the notaries by whom the acts shall be taken, shall be capable of being received as witnesses of the will by public act.

976.

When the testator shall be desirous of making a mystic or secret will, he shall be bound to sign his dispositions, whether he has written them himself, or whether he has caused them to be written by another. The paper which shall contain his dispositions, or the paper which shall serve as envelope, if there be one, shall be closed and sealed. The testator shall present it thus closed and sealed to the notary and to six witnesses at the least, or he shall cause it to be closed and sealed in their presence; and he shall declare that the contents of such paper are his will, written and signed by himself, or written by another and signed by him: the notary shall thereon draw up the act of superscription, which shall be written on the paper or on the sheet which shall serve for envelope; this act shall be signed as well by the testator as by the notary, together with the witnesses. All the above shall be done immediately and without diversion to other acts; and in case the testator, by an impediment happening subsequently to the signature of the will, is rendered unable to sign the act of superscription, mention shall be made of his declaration on that subject, and it shall not be necessary, in such case, to augment the number of witnesses.

977.

If the testator knows not how to sign, or if he were unable to sign when he caused his dispositions to be written, a witness shall be called to the act of superscription in addition to the number contained in the preceding article, who shall sign the act with the other witnesses; and mention shall be made therein of the cause for which such witness was called.

978.

Those who know not how or who are unable to read, shall not be allowed to make dispositions in the form of a mystic will.

979.

In the case where a testator cannot speak but is able to write, he may make a mystic will, on condition that such will shall be written throughout, dated and signed with his own hand, that he shall present it to the notary and to the witnesses, and that at the head of the act of superscription, he shall write in their presence, that the paper which he presents is his will; after which the notary shall write the act of superscription, in which mention shall be made of the testators having written these words in presence of the notary and of the witnesses; and moreover every thing observed which is prescribed in article 976.

980.

The witnesses called to be present at wills must

be males, of age, republicans, and in the enjoyment of civil rights.

SECTION II.

Of particular Rules touching the Form of certain Wills.

981.

The wills of military men and of individuals employed in the armies may be received in any country whatsoever, by the commander of a battalion or spuadron, or by any other officer of a superior rank, in presence of two witnesses, or by two military commissaries, or by one of such commissaries in presence of two witnesses.

982.

They may moreover be received, if the testator be sick or wounded, by the chief officer of health, assisted by the military commandant charged with the police of the hospital.

983.

The regulations of the articles above shall not take place except in favour of those who shall be on a military expedition, or in quarters, or in garrison out of the territory of the republic, or prisoners in an enemy's country; but those who are in quarters or in garrison in the interior shall not have the benefit thereof unless they shall be in a place besieged or in a citadel or other place of which the gates shall be closed and the communications cut off by reason of war.

984.

The will made according to the above established form shall be null six months after the testator shall have returned into a place in which he shall have the liberty of employing the ordinary forms.

985.

Wills made in a place with which all communication shall be intercepted on account of the plague or other contagious distemper, may be made before the justice of the peace, or before one of the municipal officers of the commune in presence of two witnesses.

986.

These regulations shall take place as well with respect to those who shall be attacked by such disorders, as to those who shall be in the places infected therewith, although they be not actually sick.

987.

The wills mentioned in the two preceding articles, shall become null six months after the communications shall have been re-established in the place where the testator remains, or six months after he shall have past into a place where they shall not be interrupted.

988.

Wills made at sea, in the course of a voyage, may be received, in manner following.

On board ships and other vessels of the state, by the officer commanding the vessel, or, in his absence, by him who supplies his place in the order of the service, one or other conjointly with the officer of administration or with him who fulfils these functions:

And on board commercial vessels, by the supercargo of the ship or him who performs the functions thereof, one or other conjointly with the captain, the master or the commander, or in their absence by those who replace them.

In all cases such wills must be received in the presence of two witnesses.

989.

On board ships of the state, the will of the captain or that of the officer of administration, and on board commercial vessels, that of the captain, of the master or commander, or that of the supercargo, may be received by those who follow them in the order of service, on conforming themselves as to other points to the regulations of the preceding article.

990.

In all cases, a double original shall be made of the wills mentioned in the two preceding articles.

991.

If the vessel touch at a foreign port in which resides a commissary for the commercial relations of France, they who shall have received the will are required to deposit one of the originals closed or sealed, in the hands of such commissary, who shall cause it to be transmitted to the minister of marine; and the latter shall cause it to be deposited among the rolls of the justice of the peace at the place where the testator was domiciled.

992.

On the return of the vessel to France, whether into the port of her fitting out, or into a different port from that of her fitting out, the two originals of the will, alike closed and sealed, or the one which shall remain, if the other have been deposited during the course of the voyage in conformity with the preceding article, shall be remitted to the office of the prefect of maritime inscription; such prefect shall transmit them without delay to the minister of marine, who shall order the doposit thereof according to the directions of the preceding article.

993.

Mention shall be made on the roll of the ship, in the margin, at the name of the testator, of the disposal which shall have been made of the originals of the will, whether into the hands of a commissary for commercial relations, or to the office of a prefect of maritime inscription.

994.

The will shall not be regarded as made at sea, although it be in the course of a voyage, if at the time when it was made the ship had touched land, either foreign, or within the French dominion, where there was a French public officer; in which case it shall not be valid except so far as it shall have been drawn up according to the forms prescribed in France, or according to those usual in the countries where it shall have been made.

995.

The regulations above shall be common to passengers merely who shall not form part of the ship's crew.

996.

A will made at sea, in the form prescribed by article 988, shall only be valid where the testator shall die at sea, or within three months after he shall have landed, and in a place where he shall be able to renew it in the ordinary forms.

997.

A will made at sea shall not contain any dispositions for the benefit of the officers of the vessel, unless they are relations of the testator.

998.

The wills comprehended in the preceding articles of the present section, shall be signed by the testators and by those who shall have taken them.

If the testator declare that he cannot sign or knows not how to sign, mention of his declaration shall be made, as well as of the cause which prevents his signing.

In cases where the presence of two witnesses is requisite, the will shall be signed at least by one of them, and mention shall be made of the cause for which the other shall not have signed.

999.

A Frenchman who shall be in a foreign country, may make his testamentary dispositions by act under his private signature, as is prescribed in article 970, or by authentic act, with the forms usual in the place where such acts shall be passed.

1000.

Wills made in a foreign country shall not be allowed to be executed on property situated in France, until after they have been registered in the office of the testator's domicil, if he have preserved one, otherwise at the office of his last known domicil in France; and in case the will shall contain dispositions of immoveables which shall be situated there, it must be moreover registered at the office where such immoveables are situated, without being chargeable with a double duty for it.

1001.

The formalities to which different wills are subjected by the regulations of the present and of the preceding section, must be observed on pain of nullity.

SECTION III.

Of Appointments of Heir, and of Legacies in general.

1002.

Testamentary dispositions are either general or by general title, or by particular title.

Each of these dispositions, whether it have been made under the denomination of appointment of heir, or whether made under the denomination of legacy, shall produce its effect according to the rules hereafter established for general legacies, for legacies by general title, and for particular legacies.

SECTION IV.

Of the general Legacy.

1003.

The general legacy is the testamentary disposition by which the testator gives to one or more persons the entirety of the property which he leaves at his death.

1004.

When at the decease of the testator there are heirs to whom one portion of his property is reserved by the law, such heirs are seised absolutely, by his death, of all the property of the succession ; and the general legatee is bound to demand from them a transfer of the property comprehended in the will.

1005.

Nevertheless, in similar cases, the general legatee shall have the enjoyment of the property comprehended in the will, computing from the day of the death, if the demand of transfer were made within a year from that event; if otherwise snch enjoyment shall only commence from the day of the demand legally made, or from the day on which snch transfer shall have been voluntarily consented to.

1006.

When at the decease of the testator there shall be no heirs to whom a portion of his property shall be reserved by the law, the general legatee shall be seised absolutely by the death of the testator, without being bound to demand a transfer.

1007.

Every olographic will shall, before it is put in execution, be presented to the president of the court of first instance of the circle within which the succession is opened. Such will shall be opened, if it has been sealed. The president shall draw up a statement of the presentation, of the opening, and of the state of the will, which he shall order to be deposited in the hands of a notary appointed by himself.

If the will is in the mystic form, its presentation, its opening, its description, and its deposit, shall be made in the same manner; but the opening shall not be permitted except in the presence of those of the notaries, and such of the witnesses who signed the act of superscription, as shall be found on the spot, or those summoned.

1008.

In the case in article 1006, if the will is olographic or mystic, the general legatee shall be bound to procure himself to be put in possession by an ordinance of the president, placed at the bottom of a request, to which shall be joined the act of deposit.

1009.

The general legatee who shall be in competition with an heir to whom the law reserves a portion of the property, shall be bound by debts and charges on the succession of the testator, personally for his own share and portion, and conditionally for the whole; he shall also be bound to discharge all legacies, saving the case of reduction, as it is explained in articles 926 and 927.

SECTION V.

Of Legacy by general Title.

1010.

The legacy by general title is that by which the testator bequeaths an aliquot part of the property of which the law allows him to dispose, such as a half, a third, or all his immoveables, or all his personalty.

or a fixed proportion of all his immoveables, or of all his personalty.

Every other legacy forms only a disposition by particular title.

1011.

Legatees by general title shall be bound to demand a transfer to the heirs to whom a proportion of the property is reserved by the law; failing such, to general legatees, and failing the latter, to the heirs called in the order established under the title "*Of Successions.*"

1012.

The legatee by general title shall be bound like the general legatee, by the debts and charges of the succession of the testator, personally for his own share and portion, and conditionally for the whole.

1013.

When the testator shall only have disposed of one part of the disposable portion, and shall have done so by general title, such legatee shall be bound to discharge the particular legacies by contribution with the natural heirs.

SECTION VI.

Of particular Legacies.

1014.

Every legacy absolute and unconditional shall, from the day of the testator's decease, confer upon the legatee a right to the thing bequeathed, a right transmissible to his heirs or assigns.

Nevertheless the particular legatee shall not be permitted to put himself in possession of the thing bequeathed, nor to claim the fruits or interests thereof, except as computing from the day of his demand of transfer, formed according to the order established by article 1011, or from the day on which such transfer shall have been voluntarily granted.

1015.

The interests or fruits of the thing bequeathed shall accrue for the benefit of the legatee, from the day of the death, and without his having made a petition according to law.

1st. When the testator shall have expressly declared his intention, in this respect, in the will;

2d. When an annuity or a pension shall have been bequeathed under title of alimony.

1016.

The expenses of the petition for transfer shall be at the charge of the succession, provided nevertheless that no reduction of the legal reserve shall be permitted to result therefrom.

The fees on registration shall be demandable from the legatee.

The whole if it have not been otherwise directed by the will.

Every legacy may be registered separately, although such registration may profit no one but the legatee or his assigns.

1017.

The heirs of the testator, or other debtors in a legacy, shall be personally bound to discharge it, each in proportion to the share and portion in which he shall have been benefitted by the succession.

They shall be conditionally bound for the whole thereof, up to the amount of the value of the immoveables of the succession of which they shall be holders.

1018.

The thing bequeathed shall be transferred with all necessary appurtenances, and in the state in which it shall be found on the day of the donor's death.

1019.

When he who has bequeathed the property of an immoveable, has afterwards augmented it by acquisitions, such acquisitions, though they be contiguous, shall not be deemed to form part of the legacy without a new disposition.

It shall be otherwise with embellishments, or new buildings formed on the estate bequeathed, or an enclosure with which the testator shall have enlarged the circumference.

1020.

If before or after the will, the thing bequeathed has been mortgaged for a debt of the succession, or even for the debt of a third person, or it it is encumbered with an usufruct, he who ought to acquit such legacy is not bound to redeem it, unless he have been charged to do so by an express disposition of the testator.

1021.

Where a testator shall have bequeathed an object belonging to another, the legacy shall be annulled, whether the testator were aware or not that it did not belong to him.

1022.

When the legacy shall be of a thing undetermined, the heir shall not be compelled to give it of the best quality, nor shall he be permitted to offer the worst.

1023.

A legacy made to a creditor shall not be deemed a compensation for his debt, nor the legacy made to a domestic a compensation for his wages.

1024.

The legatee by particular title shall not be bound by the debts of the succession; saving the reduction of the legacy as is said above, and saving the mortgage deed of creditors.

SECTION VII.

Of testamentary Executors.

1025.

The testator shall be at liberty to nominate one or more testamentary executors.

1026.

He may give them seisin of the whole or only of one part of his personalty; but it shall not be allowed to continue beyond a year and a day computing from his death.

If he has not given it them, they shall not be permitted to demand.

1027.

The heir may put an end to such possession, by offering to place in the hands of the testamentary executors a sum sufficient for the payment of the personal legacies, or by guaranteeing such payment.

1028.

He who is incapable of making a bond, cannot be a testamentary executor.

1029.

A married woman shall not be allowed to accept testamentary executorship except with her husband's consent.

If she enjoy separate property, either by the marriage-contract or by judgment, she may accept it with her husband's consent, or upon his refusal, with legal authority, conformably to what is prescribed by articles 217 and 219, under the title "*Of Marriage.*"

1030.

A minor shall not be allowed to become testamentary executor even with the authority of his guardian or curator.

1031.

Testamentary executors shall cause seals to be affixed if there are among the heirs, minors, interdicted persons, or absentees.

They shall cause an inventory of the property of the succession to be made in the presence of the heir presumptive ; or having duly summoned him,

They shall proceed to a sale of the personalty, on failure of sufficient money to pay the legacies.

They shall use vigilance that the will be executed; and they shall be authorized, in case of dispute respecting its execution, to interfere in order to sustain its validity.

They must render an account of their management at the expiration of a year from the death of the testator.

1032.

The powers of the testamentary executor shall not pass to his heirs.

1033.

If there are several testamentary executors who have accepted, one only may act in default of the others ; and they shall be responsible for the whole of the account of the personalty, which was confided to them, unless the testator have divided their functions, and unless each of them is circumscribed in that which has been allotted him.

1034.

The expenses incurred by the testamentary executor for the affixing of the seals, for the inventory, the account and other expenses relative to their functions, shall be at the charge of the succession.

SECTION VIII.

Of the Revocation and of the Lapse of Wills.

1035.

Wills shall be incapable of being revoked, in whole or in part, except by a later will, or by an act before notaries, containing a declaration of the change of intention.

1036.

Later wills, not revoking in an express manner the preceding ones, shall annul in the latter such dispositions only therein contained as shall be found inconsistent with the new ones, or which shall be contrary thereto.

1037.

The revocation made in a latter will shall produce its complete effect, although the new act remain unexecuted by reason of the incapacity of the heir appointed or of the legatee, or by reason of their refusal to accept the succession.

1038.

Every alienation, even that by sale with power of

repurchase or by exchange, which the testator shall make of the whole or of part of the thing bequeathed, shall import revocation of the legacy as respects all which has been alienated, although the posterior alienation be null, and the object be returned into the hands of the testator.

1039.

Every testamentary disposition shall lapse if he in whose favor it has been made does not survive the testator.

1040.

Every testamentary disposition made under a condition dependent on an uncertain event, and such that within the testator's intention, it must not be executed except so far as such event shall happen or not happen, shall be lapsed, if the heir appointed or the legatee dies before the accomplishment of the condition.

1041.

The condition which, within the testator's intention, merely suspends the execution of the disposition, shall not prevent the heir appointed, or the legatee, from having a vested right and transmissible to his heirs.

1042.

The legacy shall lapse, if the thing bequeathed have totally perished during the life of the testator.

The same rule holds, if it have psrished subsequently to his death, without the act and fault of the heir, although the latter have been guilty of delay in transferring it, provided it would have perished equally in the hands of the legatee.

1043.

The testamentary disposition shall lapse, when the heir appointed or the legatce shall reject it, or shall be found incapable of receiving it.

1044.

There shall be ground for increase for the benefit of legatees, in the case where the legacy shall be made to several conjointly.

The legacy shall be taken to be made conjointly when it shall be so by one single and the same disposition, and when the testator shall not have assigned the proportion of any of the colegatees in the thing bequeathed.

1045.

It shall moreover be taken to be made conjointly, when a thing which is not capable of being divided without deterioration, shall have been given by the same act to several persons, although separately.

1046.

The same causes which, according to article 954 and the first two regulations of article 955, shall authorize the petition for revocation of the donation during life, shall be admitted as a petition for revocation of testamentary dispositions.

1047.

If such petition be founded on a serious injury done to the memory of the testator, it must be instituted within the year, to be computed from the date of the crime.

CHAPTER VI.

Of Dispositions permitted in favor of the Grand-Children of the Donor or Testator, or of the Children of their Brothers and Sisters.

1048.

The property which fathers and mothers have the power to dispose of, may be by them conferred in whole or in part, on one or more of their children, by acts during life or by will, with the condition of surrendering such property to the children born or to be born, in the first degree only, of the said donees.

1049.

In case of death without children, the disposition which the deceased shall have made by act during life or testamentary, for the benefit of one or more of his brothers or sisters, of the whole or part of his property not reserved by the law in the succession, shall be valid on condition of restoring such property to children born and to be born, in the first degree only, to the said brothers and sisters donees.

1050.

The dispositions allowed by the two preceding articles, shall only be valid as far as the condition of restitution shall be for the benefit of all the children born and to be born of the party subjected thereto, without exception or preference of age or sex.

1051.

If in the cases mentioned above, the party subjected to restitution for the benefit of his children, dies, leaving children in the first degree and descendants of a child previously deceased, such last shall receive, by representation, the portion of the child previously deceased.

1052.

If the child, the brother or the sister to whom property shall have been given by act during life, without charge of restitution, accept a new gift made by act during life or testamentary, on condition that the property previously conferred shall be encumbered with such charge, it is no longer permitted them to divide the two dispositions made for their benefit, or to renounce the second in order to get possession of the first, even though they should offer to restore the property comprised in the second disposition.

1053.

The claims of parties summoned shall be opened at the period when, for any cause whatsoever, the enjoyment of the child of the brother or sister charged with restitution, shall cease: the previous renunciation of the enjoyment for the benefit of the parties summoned, shall not be permitted to prejudice the creditors of the party charged anterior to the abandonment.

1054.

The wives of tenants for life shall not be allowed to have, over the property to be restored, subsidiary redress, in case of insufficiency of unencumbered property, except for the capital of dowry-money, and in the case only where the testator has expressly ordered it.

1055.

He who shall make the dispositions authorized by the preceding articles, shall be allowed to nominate, in authentic form, by the same act or by a later one, a guardian charged with the execution of such dispositions; such guardian shall not be dispensed therefrom except for one of the causes expressed in section 6 of chap. 2, of the title "*Of Minority, Guardianship, and Emancipation.*"

1056.

In default of such guardian, one shall be named at the instance of the party charged, or of his guardian if he be a minor, within the interval of a month, to be computed from the day of the decease of the donor or testator, or from the day subsequent to such death, on which the act containing the disposition shall have been known.

1057.

The party charged, who shall not have satisfied the preceding article, shall be deprived of the benefit of the disposition; and in such case the right may be declared open for the benefit of the parties summoned, at the instance either of the summoned if they are of age, or of their guardian or curator if they are minors or interdicted persons, or of any relation of the summoned of age, minors or interdicted persons, or even officially at the instance of the commissary of government in the court of first instance in the place where the succession is opened.

1058.

After the decease of one who shall have made disposition with charge of restitution, it shall be proceeded in the ordinary forms, to the inventory of all the property and effects which shall compose his succession, excepting nevertheless the case where one particular legacy only is to be dealt with. This inventory shall contain a valuation at a fair price of the moveables and personal effects.

1059.

It shall be done at the request of the party charged with restitution, and within the delay fixed under the title "*Of Succession*," in presence of the guardian nominated for execution. The expenses shall be deducted from the property comprehended in the disposition.

1060.

If the inventory have not been made by the request of the tenant for life, within the interval abovementioned, it shall be proceeded in in the month following, at the instance of the guardian nominated for the execution, in presence of the tenant for life, or of his guardian.

1061.

If the two preceding articles have not been satisfied, the same inventory shall be proceeded in at the instance of the persons designated in article 1057, by calling thereto the tenant for life or his guardian, and the guardian nominated for the execution.

1062.

The tenant for life shall be bound to take proceedings for a sale, by notices, and to the highest bidder, of all the moveables and effects comprised in the disposition, with the exception nevertheless of those of which mention is made in the two following articles.

1063.

Household goods and other moveable effects which shall have been comprised in the disposition, with the express condition of preserving them in kind, shall be restored in the state in which they shall be found at the period of restitution.

1064.

Cattle and implements serving for the cultivation

of lands, shall be taken to be comprised in donations of such lands during life or testamentary; and the tenant for life shall only be bound to get them appraised and estimated, in order to render an equal value at the period of restitution.

1065.

The tenant for life shall, within the interval of six months, computing from the day of closing the inventory, employ the ready money, of such as arises from the price of the moveables and effects which shall have been sold, and of that which shall have been received from debts owing.

Such interval may be prolonged, if there be ground for it.

1066.

The tenant for life shall be in like manner bound to employ money proceeding from debts owing which shall be recovered and from payments of rents, and this within three months at the latest, after he shall have received such money.

1067.

This employment shall be made in conformity to what shall have been directed by the author of the disposition, if he have pointed out the nature of the effects in which the employment is to be made; if not, it can only be in immoveables, or with privilege over immoveables.

1068.

The employment directed by the preceding articles shall be made in presence and at the instance of the guardian nominated for the execution.

1069.

Dispositions by acts during life or testamentary, on condition of restitution, shall be made public, either by the party charged or by the guardian nominated for the execution ; that is to say, as regards immoveables, by the transcription of the acts into the registers of the office of mortgages of the place where they are situated ; and as regards sums placed out with priority of claim over immoveables, by inscription on the property subject to such priority.

1070.

The default of transcription of the act containing the disposition, may be objected by creditors and third persons purchasers, even to minors or interdicted persons; saving the remedy against the tenant for life and against the guardian for the execution, and without minors and interdicted persons being capable of being reinstated in spite of such failure of transcription, even though the tenant for life and the guardian be found insolvent.

1071.

The failure of transcription cannot be supplied nor regarded as cured by the knowledge which creditors or third persons creditors might have had of the disposition by other means than that of transcription.

1072.

Neither donees, legatees, nor even the legitimate heirs of him who shall have made the disposition, nor in like manner their donees, legatees or heirs, shall be allowed, in any case, to object to parties summoned the want of transcription or inscription.

1073.

The guardian nominated for the execution shall be personally responsible, unless he has, in every point, conformed to the rules above established for verifying the property, for the sale of the personalty, for the employment of the money, for transcription and inscription, and in general if he have not used all necessary diligence in order to the good and faithful acquittal of the condition of restitution.

1074.

If the tenant for life is a minor, he cannot, even in case of the insolvency of his guardian, be reinstated against failure in complying with the rules prescribed to him by the articles of the present chapter.

CHAPTER VII.

Of Distributions made by the Father, Mother, or other Ancestors, among their Descendants.

1075.

The father and mother and other ancestors may

make division and distribution of their property among their children and descendants.

1076.

These distributions are allowed to be made by acts during life or testamentary, with the formalities, conditions, and rules prescribed for donations during life and wills.

Distributions made by acts during life can only have present property for their object.

1077.

If all the property which the ancestor shall leave on the day of his death has not been comprised in the distribution, that portion of property which has not been comprehended therein shall be distributed conformably to law.

1078.

If the distribution has not been made among all the children who shall exist at the time of the death and the descendants of those who have previously died, the distribution shall be entirely null. A new one may therefore be claimed in legal form, either by the children or descendants who shall not have received any portion thereof, or even by those among whom the distribution shall have been made.

1079.

The distribution made by the ancestor may be impeached for cause of waste of more than a fourth;

it may also be so in case it should result from the distribution and from the dispositions made in preciput, that one of the coparceners shall have an advantage greater than the law permits him.

1080.

The child who, for one of the causes expressed in the preceding article, shall impeach the distribution made by the ancestor, must advance the expenses of the estimate; and he shall bear them eventually, as well as the charges of the contest, if the objection is not founded.

CHAPTER VIII.

Of Donations made by the Marriage-contract to the Parties, and to Children to be born of the Marriage.

1081.

Every donation during life of present property, though made by contract of marriage to the married parties, or to one of them, shall be subject to the general rules prescribed for donations made under this title.

It shall not take place for the benefit of children to be born, except in the cases enumerated in cap. 6 of the present title.

1082.

The fathers and mothers, the other ancestors, the collateral relations of the married parties, and even strangers, may, by the contract of marriage, dispose of the whole or of part of the property which they shall leave at the day of their death, as well for the benefit of the married parties, as for the benefit of children to be born of their marriage, in the case in which the donor shall survive the married party donee.

A similar donation, although made for the benefit only of the married parties or of one of them, shall be always, in the said case of survivorship by the donor, presumed to have been made for the benefit of the children and descendants to be born of the marriage.

1083.

The donation, in the form contained in the preceding article, shall be irrevocable, in this sense only that the donor shall be no longer capable of disposing by gratuitous title of the objects comprised in the donation, unless it be for moderate sums under the title of recompense or otherwise.

1084.

The donation by marriage-contract may be made cumulatively of present and future property, in whole or in part, on condition that there shall be annexed to the act a statement of the debts and charges of the donor existing at the day of the donation; in which case it shall be competent to the donee, at the death of the donor, to make election of the present property, renouncing the residue of the property of the testator.

38

1085.

If the statement of which mention is made in the preceding article has not been annexed to the act containing the donation of the present and future property, the donee shall be compelled to accept or reject such donation for the whole. In case of acceptance, he can only claim the property which shall be found in existence at the day of the donor's decease, and he shall be subject to the payment of all the debts and encumbrances of the succession.

1086.

The donation by marriage-contract in favor of married persons and of children to be born of their marriage, may furthermore be made, on condition of paying without distinction all the debts and encumbrances on the succession of the donor, or under other conditions, the execution of which might depend on his will, by whomsoever the donation shall have been made ; the donee shall be bound to fulfil such conditions, unless he prefer renouncing the donation ; and in case the donor, by the marriage-contract, shall reserve to himself the liberty of disposing of an article comprised in the donation of his present property, or of a fixed sum to be taken out of the same property, the article or the sum, if he die without having disposed thereof, shall be taken to be comprised in the donation, and shall belong to the donee or to his heirs.

1087.

Donations made by contract of marriage shall not

be impeached, or declared null, under pretence of want of acceptance.

1088.

Every donation made in favor of marriage shall be void, if the marriage do not follow.

1089.

Donations made to one of the married parties, in the terms of articles 1082, 1084, and 1086, above-mentioned, shall become void, if the donor survive the married party donee and his posterity.

1090.

All donations made to married persons by their marriage-contract shall, at the time of opening the succession of the donor, be reducible to the portion of which the law shall permit him to dispose.

CHAPTER IX.

Of Dispositions between Married Persons, either by Contract of Marriage, or during Marriage.

1091.

Wedded persons shall be allowed, by the marriage-contract, to make to each other, or one of the two to the other, such donation as shall be deemed convenient, subject to the modifications hereafter expressed.

1092.

Every donation during life of present property,

made between wedded persons by the marriage-contract, shall be taken not to have been made with condition of survivorship by the donee, unless such condition has been formally expressed ; and it shall be subject to all the rules and forms above prescribed touching donations of this description.

1093.

The donation of future property, or of present and future property, made between wedded persons by marriage-contract, whether single or mutual, shall be subject to the rules established by the preceding chapter, with regard to similar donations which shall be made to them by a third person ; saving that it shall not be transmissible to the issue of such marriage, in case of the death of the wedded person donee before the other.

1094.

The husband shall be allowed, either by marriage-contract, or during the marriage, in the case where he shall leave neither children nor descendants, to dispose in favor of his wife, absolutely, of every thing which he might dispose of in favor of a stranger, and in addition of the usufruct of the entirety of the portion of which the law prohibits the disposition to the prejudice of heirs.

And in the case where the husband donor shall leave children or descendants, he may give to his wife either a fourth absolutely, and another fourth in usufruct, or the moiety of his property in usufruct only.

1095.

A minor shall not be allowed by marriage-contract to give to his wife, either by single or mutual donation, except with the consent and assistance of those whose consent is requisite for the validity of his marriage; but with such consent he is permitted to give all that the law allows a husband of full age to give to his wife.

1096.

All donations made between wedded persons during marriage, shall be always revocable, although entitled as during life.

The revocation may be made by the wife, without being thereto authorized by the husband or by the law.

Such donations shall not be revoked by the circumstance of children.

1097.

Wedded persons shall not be permitted during marriage to make to each other, either by act during life or by will, any mutual and reciprocal donation by one and the same act.

1098.

The husband or wife who, having had children by another bed, shall contract a second or subsequent marriage, shall not be permitted to give to such new spouse more than one portion of a legitimate child, and provided that in no case such donations exceed a fourth of the property.

1099.

Wedded persons shall not be permitted to give each other indirectly beyond what is allowed them by the above regulations.

Every donation, either disguised, or made to intermediate persons, shall be null.

1100.

Donations by one of the wedded persons to the children or to one of the children of the other, the issue of a former marriage, shall be deemed to have been made to intermediate persons as well as those made by the donor to relations to whom the other wedded party shall be heir presumptive on the day of the donation, although the latter may not have survived his relation donee.

TITLE III.

OF CONTRACTS OR CONVENTIONAL OBLIGATIONS IN GENERAL.

Decreed the 7th of February, 1804. *Promulgated the* 17*th of the same Month.*

CHAPTER I.

Preliminary Regulations.

1101.

A contract is an agreement which binds one or

more persons, towards another or several others, to give, to do, or not to do something.

1102.

A contract is *synallagmatical* or *bilateral* when the contractors bind themselves mutually some of them towards the remainder.

1103.

It is *unilateral* when it binds one person or several towards one other or several others, without any engagement being made on the part of such latter.

1104.

It is *commutative* when each of the parties binds himself to give or to do a thing which is regarded as the equivalent for that which is given him, or for that which is done for him.

When the equivalent consists in the chance of gain or loss for each of the parties, in consequence of an uncertain event, the contract is *aleatory*.

1105.

The contract of *beneficence* is that in which one of the parties procures for the other an advantage purely gratuitous.

1106.

The contract by *onerous title* is that which subjects each of the parties to give or to do something.

1107.

Contracts, whether they have a particular denomination, or whether they have not, are subject to general rules, which are the objects of the present title.

Rules applicable to certain contracts are established under the titles relating to each of them; and the rules applicable to commercial transactions are established by the laws relating to commerce.

CHAPTER II.

Of Conditions essential to the Validity of Agreements.

1108.

Four conditions are essential to the validity of an agreement:

The consent of the party who binds himself;

His capacity to contract;

A certain object forming the matter of the contract;

A lawful cause in the bond.

SECTION I.

Of Consent.

1109.

There can be no valid consent if such consent have been given through mistake, or have been extorted through violence or surreptitiously obtained by fraud.

1110.

Mistake is not a cause for annulling the agreement except when it occurs in the very substance of the thing which is the object thereof.

It is not a cause for nullity when it occurs only in the person with whom it is intended to contract, unless the consideration of such person were the principal cause of the agreement.

1111.

Violence exercised toward him who has contracted the obligation, is a cause of nullity, although it have been exercised by a third person different from him for whose benefit the agreement has been made.

1112.

That is violence which is of a nature to make an impression on a reasonable person, and which may inspire him with fear of exposing his person or his fortune to a considerable and present injury.

Regard must be had, on this subject, to the age, to the sex, and condition of persons.

1113.

Violence is a cause of nullity of contract, not only when it has been exercised over the contracting party, but further when it has been so over his or her husband or wife, over their descendants or ancestors.

1114.

Reverential fear only towards a father, mother, or

other ancestor, without any violence having been exercised, does not suffice to annul a contract.

1115.

A contract can no longer be impeached for cause of violence, if, subsequently to the cessation of the violence, such contract have been approved, either expressly, or tacitly, or by suffering the time fixed by the law for remedy thereof to pass by.

1116.

Fraud is a cause of nullity of the agreement when the stratagems practised by one of the parties are such, that it is evident that without such stratagems the other party would not have contracted.

It is not to be presumed, but must be proved.

1117.

The agreement contracted by mistake, violence, or fraud, is not void absolutely; it only affords ground for an action for nullity or rescision, in the cases and in the manner explained in section 7 of cap. 5 of the present title.

1118.

Inquiry does not vitiate agreements except in certain cases or with regard to certain persons, as shall be explained in the same section.

1119.

A man cannot, in general, bind himself or stipulate in his own name except for himself.

1120.

Nevertheless a man may vouch for a third person, by guaranteeing the deed of the latter; saving the indemnity against him who has vouched or who has promised to get it ratified, if the third party refuse to keep his engagement.

1121.

A man may in like manner stipulate for the benefit of a third person, when such is the condition of a stipulation that a man makes for himself or of a donation which he makes to another. He who has made such stipulation can no longer revoke it, if the third party has declared his readiness to profit by it.

1122.

A man is deemed to have stipulated for himself and for his heirs and assigns, unless the contrary be expressed, or result from the nature of the agreement.

SECTION II.

Of the Capacity of the Contracting Parties.

1123.

Every person may contract who has not been declared by the law incapable of doing so.

1124.

Incapable of contracting are,

Minors,

Interdicted persons,

Married women in the cases expressed by the law,

And all those generally to whom the law has forbidden certain contracts.

1125.

The minor, the interdicted person, and the married woman, cannot, under pretext of incapacity, impeach their own engagements, except in the cases provided for by the law.

Persons capable of binding themselves cannot object the incapacity of the minor, of the interdicted person, or of the married woman, with whom they have contracted.

SECTION III.

Of the Object and Matter of Contracts.

1126

Every contract has for its object a thing which one party binds himself to give, or which one party binds himself to do or not to do.

1127.

The simple use or the simple possession of a thing may be, like the thing itself, the object of contract.

1128.

It is only things which are objects of commerce that can be the object of agreements.

1129.

It is necessary that the obligation have for its object a thing at least determinate as regards its kind.

The quantity of the thing is allowed to be uncertain, provided it is capable of being determined.

1130.

Things future may be the objects of an obligation.

A man cannot however renounce a succession not opened, or make any stipulation regarding such a succession, even with his consent whose succession was in agitation.

SECTION IV.

Of the Cause.

1131.

An obligation without a cause, or upon a false cause, or upon an unlawful cause, can have no effect.

1132.

The agreement is not less valid, although the cause be not expressed therein.

1133.

The cause is unlawful when it is prohibited by the law, when it is contrary to good morals or to public order.

CHAPTER III.

Of the Effect of Obligations.

SECTION I.

General Regulations.

1134.

Agreements legally formed have the force of law over those who are the makers of them.

They cannot be revoked except with their mutual consent, or for causes which the law authorizes.

They must be executed with good faith.

1135.

Agreements bind not only as to what is expressed therein, but further as regards all the consequences which equity, usage, or law attribute to an obligation by its nature.

SECTION II.

Of the Obligation of Giving.

1136.

The obligation of giving imports that of delivering the thing and of preserving it up to delivery, under pain of damages and interest towards the creditor.

1137.

The obligation of vigilance in the preservation of the thing, whether the agreement have for its object the advantage of one of the parties, or whether its object be their mutual profit, subjects him who is charged therewith to apply all his care like a good father of a family.

This obligation is more or less extended in relation to certain contracts, the effects of which, in this respect, are explained under the titles which apply to them.

1138.

The obligation to deliver the thing is perfect by the consent merely of the contracting parties.

It renders the creditor proprietor, and puts the thing upon his risk from the instant at which it ought to have been delivered, although the delivery have not been actually made unless the debtor should have delayed delivering it; in which case the thing remains at the risk of the latter.

1139.

The debtor is deemed guilty of delay, either by a summons or other equivalent act, or by the effect of the agreement, when it imports that, without need of an act and by the sole lapse of the term, the debtor shall be in delay.

1140.

The effects of the obligation to give or to deliver

an immoveable are regulated under the title "*Of Sales,*" and under the title "*Of Privileges and Mortgages.*"

1141.

If the thing which a party is bound to give or to deliver to two persons successively is purely moveable, that one of the two who has been put in actual possession thereof is preferred and remains proprietor thereof, although his title should be posterior in date, provided however that the possession be in good faith.

SECTION III.

Of the Obligation to do or not to do.

1142.

Every obligation to do or not to do resolves itself into damages, in case of non-performance on the part of the debtor.

1143.

Nevertheless the creditor has a right to demand that whatever shall have been done in contravention of the engagement, shall be destroyed; and he may procure himself to be authorized to destroy it at the expense of the debtor, without prejudice to his damages, if there be ground.

1144.

The creditor may also, in case of non-performance,

be authorized to procure the bond to be executed himself at the expense of the debtor.

1145.

If the obligation is not to do, he who contravenes it therein is indebted in damages and interest by the single act of contravention.

SECTION IV.

Of Damages and Interest resulting from the non-performance of the Obligation.

1146.

Damages and interest are only due when the debtor is in arrear in fulfilling his obligation ; except nevertheless when the thing which the debtor has bound himself to give or to do cannot be given or done but within a certain time which he has suffered to pass by.

1147.

The debtor is condemned, if there be ground, to the payment of damages and interest, either by reason of the non-performance of the obligation or by reason of delay in its execution, as often as he cannot prove that such non-performance proceeds from a foreign cause which cannot be imputed to him, although there be no bad faith on his part.

1148.

There is no ground for damages and interest, when

by consequence of a superior force or of a fortuitous occurrence, the debtor has been prevented from giving or doing that to which he has bound himself, or has done that from which he was interdicted.

1149.

The damages and interest due to the creditor are, in general, to the amount of the loss which he has sustained or of the gain of which he has been deprived; saving the exceptions and modifications following.

1150.

The debtor is only bound for the damages and interest which were foreseen, or which might have been foreseen at the time of the contract, when it is not in consequence of his fraud that the obligation has not been executed.

1151.

Even in the case where the non-performance of the contract results from the fraud of the debtor, the damages and interest must not comprehend, as regards the loss sustained by the creditor and the gain of which he has been deprived, any thing which is not the immediate and direct consequence of the non-performance of the contract.

1152.

When the agreement imports that he who shall fail in executing it shall pay a certain sum under the title of damages, there can be allowed to the other party neither a greater nor a less sum.

1153.

In the obligations which are limited to the payment of a certain sum, the damages and interest resulting from the delay in the performance consist only of a condemnation to the interest fixed by the law; saving the rules peculiar to commerce and security.

Such damages and interest are demandable without binding the creditor to prove any loss.

They are only due from the day of the demand, except in cases wherein the law makes them run absolutely.

1154.

Interest accruing from capital sums may produce interest either by a judicial demand or by a special agreement, provided that whether in the demand or in the agreement, the interest in question has been due for one entire year at least.

1155.

Nevertheless revenues falling due, such as rents of farms, houses, arrears of perpetual annuities, or those for life, produce interest from the day of demand or by the agreement.

The same rule applies to restrictions of fruits, and to interest paid by a third person to the creditor in discharge of the debtor.

SECTION V.

Of the Interpretation of Agreements.

1156.

In agreements it is necessary to search into the mutual intention of the contracting parties, rather than to stop at the literal sense of terms.

1157.

When a clause is susceptible of two meanings, it must rather be understood in that according to which it may have some effect, than in that whereby it cannot produce any.

1158.

Expressions susceptible of two meanings must be taken in that which agrees best with the matter of the contract.

1159.

Whatever is ambiguous must be interpreted according to the usage of the country where the contract is made.

1160.

Clauses usual in the contract must be supplied therein, although they are not expressed.

1161.

All the clauses of agreements are interpreted by each other, giving to each the sense derived from the entire act.

1162.

In case of doubt, the agreement is interpreted against him who has stipulated, and in favour of him who has contracted the obligation.

1163.

However general the terms may be in which an agreement is couched, it only comprehends things respecting which it appears that the parties intended to contract.

1164.

When a case has been put in a contract for the purpose of explaining the obligation, it is not to be inferred to have been designed to restrict the extent to which the engagement goes of right as regards cases not expressed.

SECTION VI.

Of the Effect of Agreements as respects third Persons.

1165.

Agreements have no effect but between the contracting parties; they do not work injury to a third person, nor can they profit him except in the case provided for by article 1121.

1166.

Nevertheless creditors may put in force all claims and suits belonging to their debtor, with the exception of those which are exclusively attached to the person.

1167.

They may also, in their own name, impeach acts made by their debtor in fraud of their rights.

They must nevertheless, as regards their rights, set forth under the title "*Of Succession,*" and under the title "*Of the Marriage Contract, and of the respective Rights of Married Persons,*" conform themselves to the rules which are therein prescribed.

CHAPTER IV.

Of the different Species of Obligations.

SECTION I.

Of conditional Obligations.

§ I. Of Conditions generally, and of their different Kinds.

1168.

The obligation is conditional when it is made to depend on an event future and uncertain, either by suspending it until the event happens, or by receding therefrom accordingly as the event shall happen or not.

1169.

A *casual* condition is that which depends on chance, and which is in no respect in the power of the creditor or of the debtor.

1170.

A *potestative* condition is that which causes the performance of the agreement to depend on an event which it is in the power of one or other of the contracting parties to cause to happen or to prevent from doing so.

1171.

A *mixed* condition is that which depends at once on the will of one of the contracting parties, and on the will of a third person.

1172.

Every condition of a thing impossible, or contrary to good morals, or prohibited by the law, is null, and renders null the agreement which depends thereon.

1173.

The condition of not doing an impossible thing does not render null the obligation contracted subject to such condition.

1174.

Every obligation is null when it has been contracted under a potestative condition on the part of him who binds himself.

1175.

Every condition must be accomplished in the manner in which the parties have probably wished and intended that it should be.

1176.

When an obligation is contracted under the condition that an event shall happen within a fixed time, such condition is deemed to have failed when the time is expired without the event having taken place. If there be no time fixed, the condition may always be accomplished; and it is not taken to have failed until it has become certain that the event will not happen.

1177.

When an obligation is contracted under the condition that an event shall not happen within a fixed time, such condition is accomplished when the time is expired without the event having occurred; it is equally so, if before the limit, it is certain that the event will not occur; and if there have been no determinate period, it is not accomplished until it is certain that the event will not happen.

1178.

The condition is taken to be accomplished, when the debtor, bound under such condition, has prevented the accomplishment thereof.

1179.

A condition accomplished has an effect retroactive to the day on which the engagement was contracted. If the creditor be dead before the accomplishment of the condition, his rights pass to his heirs.

1180.

A creditor may, before the condition is accomplished, put in force all acts preservative of his rights.

§ II. Of the suspensive Condition.

1181.

The obligation contracted under a condition suspensive, is that which depends either on an event future and uncertain, or on an event actually happened, but still unknown to the parties.

In the first case, the obligation cannot be performed until after the event.

In the second case, the obligation takes effect from the day on which it was contracted.

1182.

When the obligation has been contracted under a condition suspensive, the thing which forms the matter of the agreement remains at the risk of the debtor, who is not bound to deliver it except in case of the event of the condition.

If the thing have perished entirely without the fault of the debtor, the obligation is extinguished.

If the thing be deteriorated without the fault of the debtor, the creditor has the choice either to dissolve the obligation, or to demand the thing in the state in which it shall be found, without diminution of price.

If the thing be deteriorated by the fault of the debtor, the creditor has a right either to dissolve the obligation, or to demand the thing in the state in which it shall be found, with damages.

§ III. Of the Condition dissolutory.

1183.

A condition dissolutory is that which, when it is accomplished, operates the revocation of the obligation, and which again puts affairs in the same state as though the obligation had never existed.

It does not suspend the performance of the obligation; it merely obliges the creditor to restore what he may have received, in the case in which the event provided for by the condition happens.

1184.

A condition dissolutory is always intended in synallagmatical contracts, for the case in which one of the two parties shall not satisfy his engagement.

In this case the contract is not dissolved absolutely. The party towards whom the engagement has not been performed, has his election either to compel the other to performance of the agreement where it is possible, or to demand the dissolution thereof with damages and interest.

The dissolution may be demanded at law, and a delay may be granted to the defendant according to circumstances.

SECTION II.

Of Obligations for a Term.

1185.

A term differs from a condition, in that it does not suspend the engagement, of which it retards the execution only.

1186.

That which is not due until after a term, cannot be demanded until the expiration of the term ; but that which has been paid in advance, cannot be recovered.

1187.

A term is always presumed to be stipulated in favor of the debtor, unless it result from the stipulation, or from circumstances, that it has been also agreed in favor of the creditor.

1188.

A debtor can no longer claim the benefit of the term when he has become bankrupt, or when by his own act he has diminished the security which he had given by the contract to his creditor.

SECTION III.

Of alternative Obligations.

1189.

A debtor in respect of an alternative obligation is discharged by the delivery of one of two things which were comprehended in the obligation.

1190.

The election belongs to the debtor, if it have not been expressly accorded to the creditor.

1191.

A debtor may discharge himself by delivering one of two things promised; but he cannot compel the creditor to receive one part of one, and one part of the other.

1192.

An obligation is pure and simple, although contracted in an alternative manner, if the one of two things promised could not be the subject of obligation.

1193.

The obligation alternative becomes pure and simple, if one of the things promised perishes and is no longer capable of being delivered, even with the fault of the debtor. The price of such thing cannot be offered in its place.

If both have perished and the debtor is in fault with respect to one of them, he must pay the price of that which perished last.

1194.

When in the cases contemplated in the preceding article, the election has been deferred by agreement with the creditor:—

Either one of the things only has perished; and then if it is without the fault of the debtor, the creditor must have that which remains; if the debtor is in fault the creditor may demand the thing which remains or the price of that which has perished;

Or both the things have perished; and then if the debtor is in fault with regard to both, or even with regard to one of them only, the creditor may demand the price of either at his election.

1195.

If both the things have perished without the fault of the debtor, and before he is in delay, the obligation is extinguished, conformably to article 1302.

1196.

The same principles apply to cases in which there are more than two things comprehended in the alternative obligation.

SECTION IV.

Of Obligations, joint and several.

§ I. Of Creditors jointly and severally interested.

1197.

The obligation is joint and several among several creditors when the title gives expressly to each of them the right to demand payment of the whole of the debt, and when payment made to one of them discharges the debtor, although the benefit of the obligation be distributable and divisible between the different creditors.

1198.

It is within the election of the debtor to pay to one or other of the joint and several creditors, so long as he is not anticipated by the prosecution of one of them.

Nevertheless postponement, which is only made by one of the joint and several creditors, does not discharge the debtor, except on the part of such creditor.

1199.

Every act which interrupts prescription with regard to one of the joint and several creditors, benefits the other creditors.

§ II. Of Debtors jointly and severally interested.

1200.

Debtors are jointly and severally interested when they are bound to one and the same thing, in such manner that each one may be arrested for the entirety, and when payment made by one discharges the other towards the creditor.

1201.

The obligation may be joint and several, though one of the debtors be bound differently from the other to the payment of the same thing: for example, if one be bound only conditionally, while the engagement of the other is absolute, or if one has taken a term which is not granted to the other.

1202.

Joint and several obligation is not to be presumed; it is necessary that it should be expressly stipulated.

This rule is only suspended where the joint and several obligation takes place absolutely, by virtue of a regulation of the law.

1203.

The creditor of an obligation contracted jointly and severally may address himself to such one of the debtors as he may choose, without the latter being able to object the benefit of division.

1204.

Prosecutions directed against one of the debtors do not prevent the creditor from instituting the like against the others.

1205.

If the thing due have perished by the fault or during the delay of one or of several of the joint and several debtors, the other joint-debtors are not discharged from the obligation of paying the price of such thing; but the latter are not subject to damages.

A creditor can only recover damages against the debtors by whose fault the thing has perished and against those who are in delay.

1206.

Prosecutions made against one of joint and several debtors interrupt prescripiton with respect to all.

1207.

A demand for interest made against one of the joint and several debtors causes interest to run with respect to all.

1208.

A joint and several debtor prosecuted by the creditor must oppose all the objections which flow from the nature of the obligation, and all those which are personal to himself, as well as those which are common to all the joint debtors.

He cannot oppose objections which are purely personal to some of the joint-debtors.

1209.

When one of the debtors becomes sole heir of the creditor, or when the creditor becomes sole heir of one of the debtors, the intermixture does not extinguish the joint and several credit, except for the part and portion of such debtor or creditor.

1210.

A creditor who consents to a division of the debt with regard to one of the joint-debtors, preserves his joint and several action against the others, but subject to a deduction of the share of the debtor who was discharged from joint and several obligation.

1211.

A creditor who receives by division the share of one of the debtors, without reserving in the quittance his joint and several claims or his rights in general, only renounces joint and several obligation with regard to such debtor.

A creditor is not deemed to relinquish joint and several obligation to a debtor by receiving from him a sum equal to the portion in which he is bound.

if the acquittance do not import that it is for his share.

It is the same with regard to a simple demand made against one of the co-debtors for his share, if the latter have not acquiesced in the demand, or if a judgment of condemnation have not intervened.

1212.

The creditor who receives dividedly and without reserve the portion of one of the joint-debtors without arrears or interest of the debt, does not lose his joint and several obligation except as regards the arrears or interest fallen due, and not for those to fall due, nor as regards the capital, unless the divided payment have continued during ten consecutive years.

1213.

The obligation contracted jointly and severally towards the creditor divides itself absolutely among the debtors who are only bound therefore among themselves each for his own share and portion.

1214.

The joint debtor of a joint and several debt, who has paid it in entirety, cannot recover against the others beyond the part and portion of each of them.

If one of them is found to be insolvent, the loss which his insolvency occasions, is subdivided by contribution among all the other joint-debtors being solvent and him who has made the payment.

1215.

In the case in which a creditor has renounced his joint and several action against one of the debtors, if one or more of the remaining joint-debtors become insolvent, the portion of the insolvents shall be proportionably subdivided among all the debtors, even among those previously discharged from joint and several claims by the creditor.

1216.

If the matter for which the debt has been contracted jointly and severally relates only to one of the joint and several co-obligors, the latter shall be bound in the whole debt as respects the other joint-debtors, who shall only be considered with reference to him as his sureties.

SECTION V.

Of Obligations divisible and indivisible.

1217.

The obligation is divisible or indivisible accordingly as it has for its object either a thing which in its delivery, or an act which in its execution, is or is not susceptible of division, either material or intellectual.

1218.

The obligation is indivisible, although the thing or the act which is the object thereof is divisible in its nature, if the aspect under which it is considered in the obligation does not render it susceptible of partial execution.

1219.

Joint and several obligation stipulated does not confer the character of indivisibility.

§ I. Of the Effects of the divisible Obligation.

1220.

The obligation which is susceptible of division, must be executed between the creditor and the debtor as if it were indivisible. The divisibility has no application but with regard to their heirs, who cannot demand the debt or who are not bound to pay it, except in the portions of which they are seised, or in which they are bound as representing the creditor or the debtor.

1221.

The principle laid down in the preceding article admits of exceptions with regard to the heirs of the debtor,

1st. In the case where the debt is on mortgage;

2d. When it is of a certain property;

3d. When a debt alternative is in question regarding things in the election of the creditor, one whereof is indivisible;

4th. When one of the heirs is charged alone, by the document, with the execution of the obligation;

5th. When it may be collected, either from the nature of the engagement, or from the thing which forms the object thereof, or from the end which is proposed by the contract, that the intention of the contracting parties was that the debt should not be partially discharged.

In the first three cases, the heir who possesses the thing due or the estate pledged for the debt, may be sued for the whole out of the thing due or out of the estate pledged, saving the remedy against his coheirs. In the fourth case the heir alone charged with the debt, and in the fifth case every heir, may also be sued for the whole; saving his remedy against his coheirs.

§ II. Of the Effects of an indivisible Obligation.

1222.

Each one of those who have contracted conjointly an indivisible debt, is bound for the total thereof, although the obligation have not been contracted jointly and severally.

1223.

The same rule applies to the heirs of him who has contracted a similar obligation.

1224.

Every heir of the creditor may demand in totality the execution of the indivisible obligation.

He cannot alone remit the entirety of the debt; he cannot alone receive the value in place of the thing. If one of the heirs have alone remitted the debt or received the price of the thing, his coheir cannot demand the indivisible thing without accounting for the portion of the coheir who has made remittance or received the price.

1225.

The heir of the debtor, charged with the entirety of the obligation, may demand a delay in order to sue his coheirs, unless the debt should be of a nature not capable of being acquitted except by the heir charged, who may then be condemned alone; saving his remedy for indemnification against his coheirs.

SECTION VI.

Of Obligations with Penal Clauses.

1226.

The penal clause is that by which a person, in order to assure the performance of an agreement, binds himself to something in case of non-performance.

1227.

The nullity of the principal obligation carries with it that of the penal clause.

The nullity of the latter does not draw after it that of the principal obligation.

1228.

The creditor is allowed to sue for performance of the principal obligation, in lieu of demanding the penalty stipulated against the debtor who is in delay.

1229.

The penal clause is the compensation for the damages which the creditor is subjected to from the non-performance of the principal obligation.

He cannot demand at the same time the principal and the penalty, unless the latter have been stipulated for delay only.

1230.

Whether the original obligation contain, or whether it do not contain a term within which it must be accomplished, the penalty is not incurred until he who is bound either to deliver, or to take, or to do, is in delay.

1231.

A penalty may be modified by the judge when the principal obligation has been executed in part.

1232.

When the original obligation contracted with a penal clause relates to a thing indivisible, the penalty is incurred by the contravention of one only of the heirs of the debtor, and it may be demanded, either in entirety against him who has so acted in contravention, or against each of the coheirs for their part and portion, and conditionally for the whole, saving their remedy against him who has actually incurred the penalty.

1233.

When the original obligation contracted under a penalty is divisible, the penalty is only incurred by that one of the heirs who contravenes such obligation, and in the proportion only in which he was bound in the principal obligation, without any action against those who have performed it.

This rule admits exception when the penal clause having been added with the intention that the payment should not be made partially, one coheir has prevented the performance of the obligation in totality. In such case the entire penalty may be demanded against him and against the other coheirs for their portion only, saving their remedy.

CHAPTER V.

Of the Extinction of Obligations.

1234.

Obligations are extinguished,

By payment,

By novation,

By voluntary remission,

By compensation,

By intermixture,

By the loss of the thing,

By nullity or rescission,

By the effect of the condition dissolutory, which has been explained in the preceding chapter,

And by prescription, which shall form the subject of a particular title.

SECTION I.

Of Payment.

§ I. Of Payment in general.

1235.

Every payment supposes a debt; that which has been paid without being due is subject to recovery.

The recovery is not permitted with respect to natural obligations which have been voluntarily discharged.

1236.

An obligation may be discharged by every person who is interested therein, such as a co-obligor or a surety.

The obligation may even be discharged by a third person who is not interested therein, provided such third person act in the name and in discharge of the debtor, or that if he act in his own proper name, he is not substituted into the rights of the creditor.

1237.

The obligation to do an act cannot be discharged by a third person against the consent of the creditor, when the latter has an interest in its being performed by the debtor himself.

1238.

In order to pay validly, it is necessary to be proprietor of the thing given in payment, and capable of alienating it.

Nevertheless the payment of a sum in money or other thing which is consumed by using, cannot be recovered against the creditor who has consumed it bona fide, although payment thereof have been made by him who is not the proprietor thereof or who was not capable of alienating it.

1239.

The payment must be made to the creditor or to some one having authority from him, or who shall be authorized by the court or by the law to receive for him.

Payment made to one who shall not have authority to receive for the creditor, is valid, if the latter ratify it or if he have profited thereby.

1240.

Payment made bona fide to him who is in possession of the credit, is valid, although he be so by eviction.

1241.

Payment made to the creditor is not valid if he were incapable of receiving it, unless the debtor can prove that the thing paid has turned to the benefit of the creditor.

1242.

Payment made by the debtor to his creditor, to the prejudice of a seizure or opposition, is not valid with regard to the creditors seizing or opposing; the latter may, according to their claim, compel him to pay afresh, saving in such case only, his remedy against the creditor.

1243.

The creditor cannot be compelled to accept a thing different from that which is due to him, although the value of the thing tendered should be equal or even superior.

1244.

The debtor cannot oblige the creditor to receive partial payment of a debt, although divisible.

The judge may nevertheless, in consideration of the debtors situation, and using this power with great caution, award moderate delays for the payment, and suspend the course of the suit, putting all things in the same state.

1245.

A debtor in a certain and determinate property is discharged by the remittance of such object in the state in which it may be at the time of delivery, provided that the deteriorations which have occurred therein do not proceed from his act or fault, nor from that of persons for whom he is responsible; provided also that previously to such deteriorations he were not in delay.

1246.

If the debt consists of a thing which cannot be determined except by its species, the debtor shall not be bound, in order to his discharge, to give it of the best kind ; but he must not offer the worst.

1247.

The payment must be performed in the place appointed by the agreement. If the place be not designated therein, when a certain and determinate property is in question, it must be made in the place where the thing which is the object of the obligation was at the date thereof.

With the exception of these two cases, the payment must be made at the domicil of the debtor.

1248.

The expenses of the payment are at the charge of the debtor.

§ II. Of Payment with Substitution.

1249.

Substitution into the rights of the creditor for the benefit of a third person who pays him, is either conventional or legal.

1250.

Such substitution is conventional,

1st. When the creditor receiving his payment from a third person substitutes him into his rights, actions, privileges, or mortgages against the debtor, such substitution must be express, and made at the same time as the payment;

2d. When the debtor borrows a sum for the purpose of paying his debt, and of substituting the lender into the rights of the creditor, it is necessary to the validity of such substitution, that the act of borrowing and the acquittance should be made before notaries; that in the act of borrowing it should be declared that the sum has been borrowed in order to make payment, and that in the quittance it should be declared that the payment has been made with money furnished for that purpose by the new creditor. Such substitution is operative without the concurrence of the creditor's assent.

1251.

Substitution takes place absolutely,

1st. For his benefit who being himself a creditor pays another creditor who has a preferable claim on account of his privileges or mortgages;

2d. For the benefit of the purchaser of an immoveable, who employs the value of his purchase in payment of creditors to whom such estate was mortgaged;

3d. For his benefit who being bound with others or for others for the payment of the debt, had interest in discharging it;

4th. For the benefit of the beneficiary heir who has paid out of his own funds the debts of the succession.

1252.

The substitution established by the preceding articles takes place as well against sureties as against debtors: it is not allowed to work injury to the creditor where he has only been paid in part; in such case he may exercise his rights, as respects what remains due to him, by preference against him from whom he has only received a partial payment.

§ III. Of the Application of Payments.

1253.

He who owes several debts has the right to declare, when he pays, which debt it is his purpose to discharge.

1254.

He who owes one debt bearing interest or producing arrears cannot, without the consent of the creditor, apply the payment which he makes to the capital in preference to the arrears or interest: the payment made on the capital and interest, but which is not entire, is applied at first to the interest.

1255.

When he who owes divers debts has received an acquittance by which the creditor has deducted what he has received from one of the debts specifically, the debtor can no longer demand deduction from a different debt, unless there have been fraud or surprise on the part of the creditor.

1256.

When the quittance does not contain any application, the payment must be deducted from the debt which the debtor had at that time the most interest in acquitting among those which are equally due; otherwise, from the debt due, though less burdensome than those which are not so.

If the debts are of equal nature, the deduction is made from that of longest standing: all things being equal, it is made proportionably.

§ IV. Of Tenders of Payment, and of Deposit.

1257.

When the creditor refuses to receive his payment, the debtor may make him real offers, and on the refusal of the creditor to accept them, may deposit the sum or the thing offered.

Real offers followed by a deposit discharge the debtor; they have with respect to him the effect of payment, when validly made, and the thing thus deposited remains at the risk of the creditor.

1258.

In order that real offers should be valid, it is necessary,

1st. That they should be made to the creditor capable of receiving, or to a person who has authority to receive for him;

2d. That they should be made by a person capable of paying;

3d. That they should consist of the entire sum demandable, of arrears or interest due, of liquidated damages, and of a sum for unliquidated damages, saving to perfect it;

4th. That the term be expired, if it have been stipulated in favor of the creditor;

5th. That the condition under which the debt has been contracted has occurred;

6th that the offers were made at the place agreed on for the payment, and that, if there be no special agreement on the place of payment, they should be made personally to the creditor, or at his domicil, or at the domicil chosen for the performance of the agreement;

7th. That the offers be made by a ministerial officer having authority for these descriptions of acts.

1259.

It is not necessary to the validity of the deposit that it should have been authorized by the judge; it suffices,

1st. That it have been preceded by a summons signified to the creditor, and containing an indication of the day, the hour, and the place, where and when the thing offered will be deposited;

2d. That the debtor divest himself of the thing offered, by sending it to the depot marked out by the law for the reception of deposits, with the interest up to the day of the deposit;

3d. That a statement have been drawn up by the ministerial officer, of the nature of the commodities offered, of the refusal which the creditor has made to receive them, or of his non-appearance, and finally of the deposit;

4th. That in case of non-appearance on the part

of the creditor, the statement respecting the deposit have been signified to him with a summons to take away the thing deposited.

1260.

The expenses of real offers and of deposit are, if valid, charged upon the creditor.

1261.

So long as the deposit is not accepted by the creditor, the debtor may withdraw it; and if he do withdraw it, the parties jointly indebted with him and his sureties are not discharged.

1262.

When the debtor has himself obtained a judgment passed with force of a matter decided, which has declared his offers and his deposit good and valid, he is no longer at liberty, even with the consent of the creditor, to withdraw his deposit, to the prejudice of those jointly indebted with him, or of his sureties.

1263.

A creditor who has consented that the debtor should withdraw his deposit after it has been declared valid, by a judgment which has acquired the force of a matter decided, can no longer, with a view to the payment of his demand, exercise the privileges or mortgages attached thereto; the mortgage ceases to exist except from the day on which the act by which he consented that the deposit should be withdrawn shall be reinvested with the forms requisite to re-establish the mortgage.

1264.

If the thing due is a certain property which must be delivered in the place where it is found, the debtor must give the creditor notice to remove it, by act notified personally to him or at his domicil, or at the domicil elected for the execution of the agreement. Such notice having been given, if the creditor do not remove the thing, and the debtor wants the place in which it stood, the latter may obtain from the court permission to put it in deposit in some other place.

§ V. Of the Cession of Property.

1265.

The cession of property is the abandonment made by a debtor to his creditors of all his property, when he finds himself no longer in condition to pay his debts.

1266.

The cession of property is voluntary or judicial.

1267.

The voluntary cession of property is that which the creditors accept voluntarily, and which has no effect beyond that which results from the contract passed between them and the debtor.

1268.

Judicial cession is a benefit which the law accords to the unfortunate and *bona fide* debtor, to whom it is allowed, in order to secure the liberty of his person, to make judicially an abandonment of all his property to his creditors, notwithstanding any stipulation to the contrary.

1269.

Judicial cession confers no property on the creditors; it gives them the right only of making sale of the property for their own benefit, and of enjoying the revenues thereof until the sale.

1270.

Creditors cannot refuse a judicial cession unless it be within the cases excepted by the law.

It operates a discharge from corporeal restraint.

Further, it does not liberate the debtor beyond the amount of the value of the property abandoned: and in the cases where that shall prove insufficient, and other property shall come to his hands, he is compelled to abandon it until complete payment.

SECTION II.

Of Novation.

1271.

Novation is effected in three ways;

1st. When the debtor contracts towards his creditor a new debt which is substituted for the ancient one, which latter is extinguished ;

2d. When a new debtor is substituted for the ancient one who is discharged by the creditor ;

3d, When, by the effect of a new engagement, a new creditor is substituted for the ancient one, towards whom the debtor becomes discharged.

1272.

Novation can only be effected between persons capable of contracting.

1273.

Novation is not to be presumed ; it is necessary that the intention to effect it should clearly result from the act.

1274.

Novation by the substitution of a new debtor, may be effected without the concurrence of the first.

1275.

The delegation by which a debtor gives to a creditor another debtor who binds himself towards the creditor, does not operate novation, if the creditor has not expressly declared that he intended to discharge his debtor who has made the delegation.

1276.

The creditor who has discharged the debtor by whom delegation has been made, has no remedy against such debtor, if the delegated person become insolvent, unless the acts contain an express reservation thereof, or that the delegated party has been already openly a bankrupt, or has fallen into embarrassment at the moment of the delegation.

1277.

The simple indication made by the debtor, of a person who is to pay in his place, does not operate novation.

The same rule applies to the simple indication made by the creditor, of a person who is to receive for him.

1278.

The privileges and mortgages of an ancient debt do not pass to that which is substituted for it, unless the creditor have expressly reserved them.

1279.

When the novation is effected by the substitution of a new debtor, the original privileges and mortgages of the debt cannot pass to the property of the new debtor.

1280.

When the novation is effected between the creditor and one of the joint and several debtors, the privileges and mortgages of the ancient debt cannot be reserved except upon his property who contracts the new debt.

1281.

Joint debtors are discharged by novation made between the creditor and one of the joint debtors.

Novation operated with respect to the principal debtor discharges his securities.

Nevertheless, if the creditor have required in the first case the addition of the joint debtors, or in the second that of the securities, the ancient debt subsists, if the joint debtors or the securities refuse to accede to the new arrangement.

SECTION III.

Of the Remission of a Debt.

1282.

Voluntary remittance of the original document under private signature, by the creditor to the debtor, forms proof of discharge.

1283.

Voluntary surrender of an obligatory deed forms presumption of the remission of the debt or payment, without prejudice to contrary proof.

1284.

The surrender of the original document under private signature, or of an engrossed copy of the document to one of the joint and several debtors, has the same effect for the benefit of his joint debtors.

1285.

Conventional remittance or discharge for the benefit of one of the joint and several debtors, liberates all the rest, unless the creditor have expressly reserved his rights against them.

In which latter case, he can no longer recover the debt without deduction made of his share to whom he has made remittance.

1286.

Delivery of a thing given by way of security does not suffice to raise presumption of the remission of the debt.

1287.

Conventional remission or discharge accorded to the principal debtor discharges the sureties ;

The same accorded to the surety does not liberate the principal debtor ;

The same accorded to one of the sureties does not discharge the others.

1288.

What a creditor has received from a surety in discharge of his suretyship, must be deducted from the debt, and applied to the discharge of the principal debtor and of the other sureties.

SECTION IV.

Of Compensation.

1289.

When two persons find themselves in each other's debt, a compensation is effected between them extinguishing both debts in the manner and in the cases hereafter expressed.

1290.

Compensation is effected absolutely by force of law only, even without the knowledge of the debtors; the two debts are reciprocally extinguished the instant at which they are found to exist at the same time up to the amount of their respective proportions.

1291.

Compensation only takes place between two debts which have equally for their object a sum of money, or a certain quantity of articles of consumption of the same species, and which are equally liquidated and demandable.

Loans of grain or commodities not contested, and of which the value is regulated by the prices current, may be balanced against sums liquidated and demandable.

1292.

The term of grace is not an obstacle to compensation.

1293.

Compensation takes place whatever may be the causes of one or other of the debts, except in the case,

1st. Of a demand for restitution of a thing of which the proprietor has been unjustly deprived;

2d. Of the demand of restitution of a deposit and of a loan on usance;

3d. Of a debt founded on alimony declared not seisable.

1294.

The surety may oppose the compensation of that which the creditor owes to the principal debtor;

But the principal debtor cannot oppose the compensation of that which the creditor owes to the surety.

The joint and several debtor may in like manner oppose the compensation of that which the creditor owes to his co-debtor.

1295.

The debtor who has accepted absolutely and unconditionally the cession which a creditor has made of his rights to a third person, can no longer oppose to the assignee the compensation, which he might before acceptance have opposed to the ceder.

With respect to cession which has not been accepted by the debtor, but which has been notified to him, it only prevents the compensation of debts posterior to such notification.

1296.

When the two debts are not payable in the same place, compensation thereof can only be opposed by accounting for the expenses of the remission.

1297.

When there are several debts subject to compensation due from the same person, the rules must be followed for their compensation, which are established touching deduction by article 1256.

1298.

Compensation does not take place to the prejudice of rights acquired by a third person. Thus he who, being a debtor, is become creditor subsequently to seisure and arrest made by a third person into his hands, cannot oppose compensation to the prejudice of such seiser.

1299.

He who has paid a debt which was of right extinguished by compensation, can no longer, by pursuing the demand, the compensation of which he has neglected to oppose, avail himself, to the prejudice of third persons, of the privileges and mortgages which were attached thereto, unless he had a sufficient excuse for not being aware of the claim which was to compensate his debt.

SECTION V.

Of Confusion.

1300.

When the characters of debtor and creditor are united in the same person, a confusion arises by law which extinguishes the two claims.

1301.

The confusion which is effected in the person of the principal debtor, benefits his sureties.

The same effected in the person of the surety does not draw after it the extinction of the principal obligation; that which is effected in the person of the creditor, does not benefit those jointly and severally indebted with him, except for the portion in which he was debtor.

SECTION VI.

Of the Loss of the Thing due.

1302.

When the certain and determinate property which was the object of the obligation happens to perish, is put out of traffic, or is lost in such manner that its existence is absolutely unknown, the obligation is extinguished if the thing have perished, or have been lost without the fault of the debtor, and before he have been in delay.

Even when the debtor is in delay, and if he have not been charged with fortuitous occurrences, the obligation is extinguished in the case where the thing would equally have perished at the house of the creditor if it had been delivered to him.

The debtor is bound to prove the fortuitous occurrence which he alleges.

In whatsoever manner a thing stolen have perished, or have been lost, its loss does not exonerate him who has removed it from restitution of the price.

1303.

When the thing has perished, been put out of traffic, or lost, without fault on the part of the debtor, he is bound, if there are any claims or actions for indemnity in reference to such thing, to yield them to his creditor.

SECTION VII.

Of the Action for Nullity, or for Rescission of Agreements.

1304.

In all cases in which the action for nullity or for rescission of an agreement is not limited to a less time by the law, such action enures for ten years.

Such time does not run, in the case of duress, except from the day on which it ceases; in the case of mistake or fraud from the day on which they have been discovered; and as respects acts passed by married women unauthorized, from the day of the dissolution of the marriage.

The time does not run with respect to acts made by interdicted persons, except from the day on which the interdiction is removed; and with respect to those made by minors, only from the day of majority.

1305.

Simple injury gives ground for rescission in favor of the minor not emancipated, against all kinds of agreements; and in favor of the minor emancipated against all agreements which exceed the bounds of his capacity, as was determined under the title "*Of Minority, Guardianship, and Emancipation.*"

1306.

The minor is not relievable for cause of injury, when it was merely the result of a casual and unforeseen event.

1307.

The simple declaration of majority, made by the minor, forms no obstacle to his relief.

1308.

The minor being a tradesman, banker, or artisan, is not relievable against engagements to which he is liable in respect of his trade or craft.

1309.

The minor is not relievable against agreements contained in his contract of marriage, when they have been made with the consent and assistance of those whose consent is requisite for the validity of his marriage.

1310.

He is not relievable against obligations resulting from his own wrong or quasi wrong.

1311.

He is no longer permitted to disclaim an engagement which he subscribed in minority, when he has ratified it in majority, whether such engagement were null in its form, or whether it were only liable to be relieved against.

1312.

When minors, interdicted persons, or married women, are admitted in such capacities to obtain relief against their engagements, the reimbursment of what, in consequence of such engagements, shall have been paid during minority, interdiction, or marriage, cannot be exacted from them, unless it be proved that what has been paid has turned to their advantage.

1313.

Persons of full age are not relieved for cause of injury except in the cases and under the conditions especially mentioned in the present code.

1314.

When the formalities required with respect to minors or interdicted persons, either for alienation of immoveables, or in a distribution of succession, have been complied with, they are in reference to such acts considered as having done them during majority or before interdiction.

CHAPTER VI.

Of the Proof of Obligations and of that of Payment.

1315.

The party who claims performance of an obligation, must prove it.

On the other hand, he who claims to be exonerated, must establish payment, or verify the act which led to the extinction of his obligation.

1316.

The rules which relate to literal proof, testimonial proof, presumptions, acknowledgment, and oath of parties, are explained in the following sections.

SECTION I.

Of Literal Proof.

§ I. Of an authentic Document.

1317.

An authentic act is that which has been taken by public officers whose duty it is to draw up instruments in the place where the act was reduced to writing, and with the requisite solemnities.

1318.

The act which is not authentic through the incompetence or incapacity of the officer, or through a defect of form, is equivalent to a private writing, if it were signed by the parties.

1319.

The authentic act supplies full credit to the agreement which it contains between the contracting parties and their heirs or assigns.

Nevertheless, in case of complaint of capital forgery, the execution of the act charged to be forged shall be suspended by the institution of the charge; and in case of inscription of forgery incidentally made, the courts may, according to circumstances, suspend provisionally the execution of the act.

1320.

The act, whether authentic or under private signature, affords proof between the parties even of that which is expressed therein only in declaratory terms, provided the declaration have a direct reference to the disposition. Declarations foreign to the disposition can only serve as commencement of proof.

1321.

Defeasances can only produce their effect between the contracting parties; they have no operation against third persons.

§ II. Of an Act under private Signature.

1322.

The act under private signature, acknowledged by the party against whom it is produced, or held by law to have been acknowledged, obtains between those who have subscribed it, their heirs and assigns, the same credit as an authentic act.

1323.

The party against whom an act under private signature is produced, is obliged formally to avow or disavow his writing or signature.

His heirs or assigns may content themselves with declaring that they do not know the writing or the signature of their principal.

1324.

In the case in which the party disavows his writing or his signature, and in the case in which his heirs or assigns declare they do not know it, the verification thereof is ordered by the court.

1325.

Acts under private signature which contain synallagmatical agreements are not valid except so far as there has been made a number of originals equal to that of the parties who have a distinct interest.

One original is sufficient for all the parties having the same interest.

Every original must include mention of the number of originals which have been made thereof.

Nevertheless, failure in mentioning that the originals have been made double, triple, &c. cannot be objected by him who has executed on his part the agreement contained in the act.

1326.

A note or promise under private signature, by which one single party binds himself towards another in the payment of a sum of money, or of a thing capable of being valued, must be written throughout by the hand of the subscriber; or at least it is necessary that besides his signature he should write "*bon*," or "*approuve*," bearing in all letters the sum or the quantity of the thing:

Excepting in the case where the act emanates from tradesmen, artisans, laborers, vine-dressers, day-laborers, and servants.

1327.

When the sum expressed in the body of the instrument is different from that which is expressed in the "*bon*," the obligation is presumed only to extend to the smaller sum, even when the act, as well as the "*bon*," are written throughout by the hand of the party bound, unless it can be proved on whose part the mistake lies.

1328.

Acts under private signature only take date against third persons from the day on which they have been registered, from the day of the death of the subscriber, or one of the subscribers, or from the day on which the substance of them is verified in acts drawn up by public officers, such as statements of sealing or of inventory.

1329.

The registers of tradesmen do not supply against those who are not so, proof of goods furnished as contained therein, saving what shall be said with respect to the oath.

1330.

The books of tradesmen afford proof against them;

but the party who desires to derive advantage therefrom, cannot separate them as to what they contain contrary to his claim.

1331.

Domestic registers and papers do not form vouchers for the party who has written them. They furnish proof against him, 1st, in all cases where they declare formally payment received; 2d, where they contain express mention that the memorandum has been made to supply the want of a document in favor of him for whose benefit they declare an obligation.

1332.

Writing inserted by the creditor at the end, in the margin, or on the back of a document which has always remained in his possession, is evidence, though not signed and dated by him, when it tends to establish the liberation of the debtor.

The same applies to writing inserted by the creditor on the back, or in the margin, or at the end of the duplicate of a document or quittance, provided such duplicate be in the hands of the debtor.

§ III. Of Tallies.

1333.

Tallies correlative to their patterns afford proof between parties who are in the habit of thus verifying commissions which they make and receive in retail.

§ IV. Of Copies of Documents.

1334.

Where the original document is in existence, copies only afford proof of what is contained in such document, the production of which may always be required.

1335.

When the original document no longer exists, copies furnish proof, agreeably to the following distinctions :

1st. Engrossments, or the first copies, supply the same proof as the original. It is the same with regard to copies which have been taken by authority of the magistrate, the parties having been present or duly summoned, or with regard to such as have been taken in presence of the parties, and with their mutual consent.

2d. Copies which, without the authority of the magistrate, or without the consent of the parties, and subsequently to the deliverance of the engrossments or first copies, shall have been taken from the minute of the act by the notary who received it, or by one of his successors, or by public officers, who in such capacity are the depositaries of the minutes, may in case of the loss of the original, be made evidence when they are ancient.

They are considered as ancient when they are more than thirty years old.

If they are less than thirty years old they can only be made use of as commencement of proof in writing.

3d. When copies taken from the minute of an act shall not have been so by the notary who received it, or by one of his successors, or by public officers who are in such capacity depositaries of the minutes, they can only be made use of, notwithstanding any degree of antiquity, as the commencement of proof in writing.

4th. Copies of copies may, according to circumstances, be considered as corroborative.

1336.

The transcription of an act upon the public registers shall only be made use of as commencement of proof in writing; and it is necessary even for that,

1st. That it be manifest that all the minutes of the notary, of the year in which the act appears to have been made, are lost, or that it be proved that the loss of the minute of this act have arisen from a particular accident;

2d. That there exist a regular docket of the notary, proving that the act was made at the precise date.

When, by reason of the concurrence of these two circumstances, proof by witnesses shall be admitted, it shall be necessary that those who were witnesses of the act, if they are still in existence, should be heard.

§ V. Of Acts of Recognition and Confirmation.

1337.

Acts of recognition do not dispense with the production of the original document, unless its tenor be therein specially set forth.

That which they contain in addition to the original document, or that which is found therein different from it, has no effect.

Nevertheless, where there are several corresponding acknowledgments confirmed by possession, and of which one is thirty years old, the creditor may be excused from producing the original document.

1338.

An act confirming or ratifying an obligation against which the law admits an action for nullity or rescission, is only valid when it contains within it the substance of such obligation, mention of the motive for the action for rescission, and an intention to remedy the defect on which such action was founded.

Failing such act of confirmation or ratification, it is sufficient that the obligation be executed voluntarily after the period at which the obligation may be validly confirmed or ratified.

Confirmation, ratification, or voluntary execution, in the forms and at the period determined by the law, imports renunciation of the arguments and exceptions which may be opposed to such act, without prejudice nevertheless to the right of third persons.

1339.

The donor cannot remedy by any confirmative act the defects of a donation during life; null in form, it is necessary that it should be re-executed in legal form.

1340.

Confirmation, ratification, or voluntary performance of a donation by the heirs or assigns of the donor, after his decease, imports their renunciation of opposition either to defects of form or any other objection.

SECTION II.

Of Testimonial Proof.

1341.

An act must be made before notaries or under private signature, respecting all things exceeding the sum or value of one hundred and fifty francs, even in the case of voluntary deposits; and no proof can be received by witnesses against or beyond what is contained in such acts, nor touching what shall be alleged to have been said before, at the time of or subsequently to such acts, although there may be question of a sum or value less than 150 francs;

The whole without prejudice to what is prescribed in the laws relative to commerce.

1342.

The above rule applies to the case in which the instrument contains, besides the demand of capital, a demand for interest, which, added to the capital, exceeds the sum of one hundred and fifty francs.

1343.

The party who has made a demand exceeding one hundred and fifty francs, can no longer be admitted to testimonial proof even on reducing his original demand.

1344.

Proof testimonial, on the demand of a sum even less than one hundred and fifty francs, cannot be admitted when such sum is declared to be the residue or to form part of a larger credit which is not proved by writing.

1345.

If in the same suit a party make several demands of which there is no evidence in writing, and where, if united together, they exceed the sum of one hundred and fifty francs, proof by witnesses cannot be admitted thereon, although the party allege that such credits arise from different causes, and that they accrued at different times, unless it be that such claims proceed from succession, donation, or otherwise from different persons.

1346.

All demands, of whatsoever description they may be, which shall not be entirely proved by writing, shall be formed by one single instrument; after which, other demands, of which there shall be no proof in writing, shall not be admitted.

1347.

The rules above-mentioned admit of exception when there is a commencement of proof in writing.

This denomination is applied to every act in writing which emanates from the party against whom the demand is made, or from him whom such party represents, and who renders probable the fact alleged.

1348.

They admit moreover of exception in all cases where it is impossible for the creditor to obtain a literal proof of the obligation which has been contracted with him.

This second exception applies,

1st. To obligations which spring from quasi-contracts and from crimes or quasi-crimes;

2d. To necessary deposits made in case of fire, fall of buildings, tumult or shipwreck, and to those made by travellers lodging at an inn, the whole according to the condition of the persons and the circumstances of the act;

3d. To obligations contracted on the occurrence of unforeseen accidents, in which it would have been impossible to have had acts in writing;

4th. In the case where the creditor has lost the document which served him for literal proof, in consequence of a fortuitous circumstance, unforeseen, and resulting from superior force.

SECTION III.

Of Presumptions.

1349.

Presumptions are the conclusions which the law or the magistrate draws from a fact known or a fact unknown.

§ I. Of Presumptions established by Law.

1350.

Legal presumption is that which is attached by an express law to certain acts or to certain facts; such are,

1st. Acts which the law declares null, as presumed to have been made in fraud of its regulations, regarding their quality only;

2d. Cases in which the law declares property or liberation to result from certain determinate circumstances;

3d. The authority which the law attributes to a matter decided;

4th. The force which the law attaches to the confession of the party or to his oath.

1351.

The authority of a matter decided has no place except with regard to that which formed the object of the judgment. It is necessary that the thing de-

47

manded should be the same; that the demand should be founded on the same cause; that the demand should be between the same parties, and made by and against them in the same capacity.

1352.

Legal presumption dispenses with all proof on his part for whose benefit it exists.

No proof is admitted against presumption of law, when, on the basis of such presumption, it annuls certain acts or restrains an action, unless it have reserved contrary proof, and saving what shall be said touching the oath and judicial confession.

§ II. Of Presumptions which are not established by Law.

1353.

Those presumptions which are not established by law are committed to the sagacity and prudence of the magistrate, who must only admit presumptions grave, precise, and concordant, and in those cases only in which the law admits testimonial proofs, unless the act should be impeached for cause of fraud or deceit.

SECTION IV.

Of the Acknowledgment of the Party.

1354.

The acknowledgment which is objected to a party, is either judicial or extrajudicial.

1355.

The allegation of an extrajudicial acknowledgment purely is useless in all cases where a demand is in question in which testimonial proof would not be admissible.

1356.

Judicial acknowledgment is a declaration made in court by the party or his attorney specially appointed.

It furnishes complete proof against the party who made it.

It cannot be divided against him.

It cannot be revoked, unless it can be proved that it proceeded from a mistake of fact.

It cannot be revoked under pretext of a mistake in law.

SECTION V.

Of Oath.

1357.

The judicial oath is of two species;

1st. That which one party tenders to another in order to make the judgment of the cause depend thereon: it is called "*decisory*;"

2d. That which is administered officially by the judge to either of the parties.

§ I. Of the Oath decisory.

1358.

The oath decisory may be tendered in any description of dispute whatsoever.

1359.

It can only be tendered touching a fact personal to the party to whom it is put.

1360.

It may be tendered in every stage of a cause, and although there exist no commencement of proof of the demand or of the objection on which it is claimed.

1361.

The party to whom the oath is tendered, who refuses it or who does not consent to tender it in return to his adversary, or the adversary to whom it has been tendered in return and who refuses it, must yield in his claim or in his objection.

1362.

The oath cannot be tendered in return when the fact which is the object thereof does not lie between the two parties, but is purely personal to him to whom the oath was originally tendered.

1363.

When the oath tendered or offered in return has been taken, the adversary is not admissible to prove the falsity thereof.

1364.

The party who has tendered the oath or offered it in return, is not allowed to retract after the adversary has declared that he is ready to take such oath.

1365.

The oath when taken only affords proof in favor of the party taking it, or against him and in favor of his heirs and assigns, or against them.

Nevertheless the oath tendered by one of the joint and several creditors to the debtor, only discharges the latter as regards the share of such creditor;

The oath tendered to the principal debtor discharges equally his sureties;

The same tendered to one of the joint and several debtors benefits those jointly indebted with him;

And the same tendered to a surety benefits the principal debtor.

In the two latter cases, the oath of the joint and several debtor or of the surety, does not benefit the other joint debtors or the principal debtor except when it has been tendered touching the debt, and not in respect of the fact of the joint and several claims or security.

§ II. Of the Oath officially administered.

1366.

The judge may tender the oath to one of the parties, either to make the decision of the cause depend thereon, or simply in order to determine the amount of the sentence.

1367.

The judge cannot administer the oath officially, either upon the demand, or on the objection which is opposed thereto, except under the two following conditions: it is necessary,

1st. That the demand or the objection should not be fully proved;

2d. That it be not totally destitute of proofs.

Except in these two cases, the judge must either admit or reject the demand absolutely and unconditionally.

1368.

The oath administered officially by the judge to one of the parties, cannot be offered in return by such party to the other.

1369.

The oath touching the value of the thing demanded cannot be administered by the judge to the demandant, except where it is impossible by other means to verify such value.

The judge must, even in this case, determine the sum up to the amount of which the demandant shall be thereon worthy of credit upon his oath.

TITLE IV.

OF ENGAGEMENTS WHICH ARE FORMED WITHOUT CONTRACT.

Decreed the 9th of February, 1804. Promulgated the 19th of the same Month.

1370.

Certain engagements are formed without the intervention of any agreement, either on the part of him who is bound thereby, or on his towards whom he has become bound.

Some result from the simple authority of law. others spring from a fact personal to the party who finds himself bound.

The first are engagements formed involuntarily, such as those between neighboring proprietors, and those of guardians and other administrators who are not at liberty to refuse the functions cast upon them.

The engagements which spring from a fact personal to him who finds himself bound, result either from quasi-contracts, or from quasi-crimes. They form the subject of the present title.

CHAPTER I.

Of Quasi-Contracts.

1371.

Quasi-contracts are the purely voluntary acts of the party from which results any engagement whatsoever towards a third person, and sometimes a reciprocal engagement of two parties.

1372.

When a person voluntarily manages the affairs of others, whether the proprietor is aware of such management or whether he is ignorant of it, he who so manages contracts a tacit engagement to continue the management which he has begun and to complete it until the proprietor shall be in condition to provide for it himself; he must himself take the charge in like manner of all the dependencies of the same affairs.

He subjects himself to all the obligations which would result from an express commission given him by the proprietor.

1373.

He is compelled to continue his management, notwithstanding the master may happen to die before the affair is completed, until the period at which the heir is competent to take the direction thereof.

1374.

He is bound to apply in the management of the affair all the cares of a good father of a family.

Nevertheless the circumstances which led him to charge himself with the affair, may authorize the judge to moderate the damages which would result from the faults or negligence of the manager.

1375.

The principal whose business has been well administered, must fulfil the engagements which the party who managed it has contracted in his name, must indemnify him against all personal engagements which he has undertaken, and reimburse him in all the useful or necessary expenses which he has been put to.

1376.

He who receives through mistake or knowingly that which is not due to him, is bound to restore it to the party from whom he has unduly received it.

1377.

When a person through mistake, believing himself a debtor, discharges a demand, he has a claim for recovery against the creditor.

Nevertheless such claim ceases in the case where the creditor has destroyed his title in consequence of payments, saving the remedy of the party paying against the real debtor.

1378.

If there have been bad faith on the part of him who has received, he is bound to restore, as well the capitol as the interest or the fruits, from the day of payment.

1379.

If the thing unduly received is an immoveable or a corporeal moveable, he who has received it is bound to restore it in kind, if in existence, or its value if it have perished or become deteriorated by his fault; he is even responsible for its loss by accident, if he have obtained it through bad faith.

1380.

If he who has received bona fide has sold the thing, he is only bound to refund the produce of such sale.

1381.

He to whom the thing is restored must allow even to the possessor through bad faith, all the necessary and useful expenses which have been incurred for its preservation.

CHAPTER II.

Of Crimes and Quasi-crimes.

1382.

Every action of man whatsoever which occasions injury to another, binds him through whose fault it happened to reparation thereof.

1383.

Every one is responsible for the damage of which he is the cause, not only by his own act, but also by his negligence or by his imprudence.

1384.

A person is responsible not only for the injury which is caused by his own act, but also for that which is caused by the act of persons for whom he is bound to answer, or by things which he has had under his care.

The father, and the mother after the decease of her husband, are responsible for the injury caused by their children being minors and residing with them; masters and trustees, for the injury caused by their servants and managers in the functions in which they have employed them;

Tutors and artisans for the injury caused by their pupils and apprentices during the period in which they are under their superintendence.

The responsibility above mentioned is incurred unless the father and mother, tutors and artisans, can prove that they were not able to prevent the act which gives rise to such responsibility.

1385.

The owner of an animal, or he who makes use of it while it is in his employment, is responsible for the injury which the animal has occasioned, whether the animal were in his custody, or whether it had strayed or escaped.

1386.

The proprietor of a building is responsible for the injury caused by its fall, when it has happened in consequence of the want of necessary repairs or from defect in its construction.

TITLE V.

OF THE CONTRACT OF MARRIAGE AND OF THE RESPECTIVE RIGHTS OF MARRIED PERSONS.

Decreed the 10*th of February,* 1804. *Promulgated the* 20*th of the same Month.*

CHAPTER I.

General Regulations.

1387.

The law does not regulate the conjugal association, as respects property, except in default of special agreements, which the married parties may make as they shall judge convenient, provided they are not contrary to good morals, and, moreover, subject to the modifications which follow.

1388.

Married persons cannot derogate from the rights resulting from the power of the husband over the persons of his wife and of his children, or which belong to the husband as head, nor from the rights conferred on the survivor of the married parties by the title "*Of the Paternal Power*," and by the title "*Of Minority, Guardianship, and Emancipation*," nor from the prohibitory regulations of the present code.

1389.

They are not allowed to make any agreement or renunciation, the object of which shall be to change the legal order of successions, whether with reference to themselves in the succession of their children or descendants, or with reference to their children between themselves; without prejudice to donations during life or by will, which may take place according to the forms and in the cases determined by the present code.

1390.

The married parties can no longer stipulate in a general manner that their union shall be regulated by one of the customs, laws, or local ordinances which heretofore governed the different parts of the French territory, and which are repealed by the present code.

1391.

They may nevertheless declare in a general manner that they intend to be married either under the law of community, or under the law of dowry. In the first case, and under the law of community, the rights of the married parties, and of their heirs, shall be governed by the regulations of chapter 2 of the present title.

In the second case, and under the law of dowry, their rights shall be governed by the regulations of chapter 3.

1392.

The simple stipulation that the wife settles upon herself, or that there is settled upon her property in dowry, does not suffice to subject such property to law of dowry, if there be not in the marriage contract an express declaration in this respect.

Neither does liability to law of dowry result from the simple declaration of the married parties, that they are married without community, or that they shall be separated as to property.

1393.

In default of special stipulations which derogate from the law of community or modify it, the rules established in the first part of chapter 2, shall form the common law of France.

1394.

All matrimonial agreements shall be reduced to writing before the marriage, by act before a notary.

1395.

They cannot receive any alteration after the celebration of marriage.

1396.

The changes which shall be made therein before

such celebration must be verified by act passed in the same form as the contract of marriage.

No change or defeasance moreover is valid without the presence and simultaneous consent of all the persons who have been parties in the contract of marriage.

1397

All changes and defeasances, even invested with the forms prescribed by the preceding article, shall be without effect as regards third persons, unless they have been reduced to writing at the end of the minute of the contract of marriage: and the notary is forbidden, on pain of damages to the parties, and under the greatest penalty if there be ground for it, to deliver either engrossments or copies of the contract of marriage without transcribing at the end the change or the defeasance.

1398.

The minor competent to contract marriage is competent to consent to all the agreements of which such contract is susceptible; and the agreements and donations which he has made therein are valid, provided he have been assisted in the contract by the persons whose consent is necessary to render such marriage valid.

CHAPTER II.

Of the law respecting Community.

1399.

The community, whether legal or conventional, commences from the day of the marriage contracted before the officer of the civil power: they cannot stipulate that it shall commence at another date.

PART I. OF LEGAL COMMUNITY.

1400.

The community which is established by the simple declaration that the parties marry under the law of community, or in default of contract, is subjected to the rules explained in the six following sections.

SECTION I.

Of that which composes Community actively and passively.

§ I. Of the active Part of the Community.

1401.

Community is composed actively,

1st. Of all the moveable property which the married parties possessed at the day of the celebration of the marriage, together with all moveable property which falls to them during the marriage by title of succession, or even of donation, if the donor have not expressed himself to the contrary;

2d. Of all the fruits, revenues, interests, and arrears, of what nature soever they may be, fallen due or received during the marriage, and arising from property which belonged to the married persons at the time of the celebration, or from such as has fallen to them during the marriage, by any title whatsoever;

3d. Of all the immoveables which are acquired during marriage.

1402.

Every immoveable is reputed to have been acquired in community, unless it be proved that one of the married parties had the property or legal possession thereof at a period anterior to the marriage, or that it has fallen to such party since by title of succession or donation.

1403.

Cuttings of wood and the productions of quarries and mines fall under community as regards all which can be considered as usufruct, according to the rules explained under the title "*Of Usufruct, Right of Common and Habitation.*

If the cuttings of wood which, according to those rules, might have been made during community, have not been so, recompense shall therefore be payable to the married party not being proprietor of the estate, or to his heirs.

If the quarries and mines have been opened during the marriage, the produce thereof only falls under community saving a compensation or indemnity to the married party who has claim thereto.

1404.

The immoveables which married persons possess on the day of the celebration of marriage, or which fall to them during its continuance by title of succession, do not enter into community.

Nevertheless, if one of the married persons have acquired an immoveable subsequently to the contract of marriage containing condition of community, but before the celebration of the marriage, the immoveable acquired in such interval shall enter into community, unless the acquisition have been made in the execution of some article of marriage; in which case it shall be regulated according to the agreement.

1405.

Donations of immoveables which are made during marriage to one only of the married parties, do not fall into community, but belong to the donee only, unless the donation expressly declare that the thing given shall belong to both in community.

1406.

An immoveable abandoned or ceded by the father, mother, or other ancestor, to one of the two married parties, either to satisfy what shall be owing to such party, or on condition of paying debts due from the donor to strangers, does not enter into community, saving compensation or indemnity.

1407.

An immoveable acquired during marriage, by title of exchange for an immoveable belonging to one of the two married parties, does not enter into community; but is substituted instead and in place of that which was alienated, saving recompense, if there be any difference of value.

1408.

The acquisition made during the marriage, by title of auction or otherwise, of the portion of an immoveable, of which one of the married parties was proprietor in coparcenary, does not constitute a purchase; saving indemnity to the community for the sum which it has supplied for such acquisition.

In the case where the husband shall become, alone and in his own proper name, purchaser or highest bidder for a portion or the entirety of an immoveable belonging in coparcenary to his wife, the latter, at the dissolution of the community, has the election either to abandon the object to the community, which thereupon becomes debtor to the wife in the price of the portion which belonged to her, or to withdraw the immoveable, reimbursing to the community the price of its acquisition.

§ II. Of the passive Part of Community, and of Actions which result therefrom against the Community.

1409.

Community is composed passively,

1st. Of all personal debts with which the married parties were encumbered on the day of the celebration of their marriage, or with which those successions were charged which fell to them during the marriage, saving compensation for those relating to immoveables proper to one or other of the married parties;

2d. Of debts, as well in capital sums as in arrears or interest, contracted by the husband during the community, or by the wife with her husband's consent, saving compensation in cases where there is ground for it;

3d. Of those arrears and interest only of rents or debts due to others which are personal to the two married parties;

4th. Of usufructuary repairs of immoveables which do not enter into community;

5th. Of alimony of married persons, of the education and maintenance of children, and of every other charge of marriage.

1410.

Community is not maintained with respect to personal debts contracted by the wife before marriage, except so far as they result from an authentic act anterior to marriage, or as they have received before that event a certain date, either by enrolment, or by the decease of one or more of those who signed the said act.

The creditor of the wife cannot, by virtue of an act which has not received a certain date before the marriage, sue for the payment of his debt against her, except on the bare property of her personal immoveables.

The husband, who has undertaken to pay for his wife a debt of this nature, cannot demand compensation therefor, either of his wife or of her heirs.

1411.

The debts of successions purely moveable, which

have fallen to married persons during the marriage, are entirely at the charge of the community.

1412.

The debts of a succession purely immoveable which falls to one of the married parties during the marriage, are not at the charge of the community; saving the right which the creditors have to sue for their payment out of the immoveables of the said succession.

Nevertheless, if the succession have fallen to the husband, the creditors of the succession may sue for their payment, either out of all the property peculiar to the husband, or even out of that of the community; saving in the second case, the compensation due to the wife, or to her heirs.

1413.

If a succession purely immoveable have fallen to the wife, and the latter have accepted it with the consent of her husband, the creditors of the succession may sue for their payment out of all the wife's personal property; but if the succession have only been accepted by the wife with the authority of the law on her husband's refusal, the creditors, in case of deficiency in the immoveables of the succession, can only obtain relief out of the wife's bare property in other personal goods.

1414.

When a succession fallen to one of the married

persons is partly moveable and partly immoveable, the debts with which it is encumbered are not at the charge of the community, except to the amount of the rateable proportion of personalty in such debts, regard being had to the value of such moveables compared with that of the immoveables.

Such reateable portion is regulated by the inventory to which the husband must cause them to proceed, either in his own right, if the succession concern him personally, or as directing and authorizing the actions of his wife, if the question relate to a succession fallen to her.

1415.

In default of the inventory, and in all cases where such default prejudices the wife, she or her heirs may, at the dissolution of the community, sue for compensation of right, and even make proof as well by private documents and papers as by witnesses, and in case of necessity by common rumor, of the existence and value of the personalty not inventoried.

The husband is never admissible to make such proof.

1416.

The regulations of article 1414 do not form any obstacles to the creditors of a succession partly moveable and partly immoveable suing for payment out of the property of the community, whether the succession have fallen to the husband, or whether it have fallen to the wife, when the latter has accepted it with the consent of her husband ; the whole saving the respective compensations.

The same rule applies where the succession has only been accepted by the wife as authorized by the law, and though the moveables thereof have nevertheless been confounded with those of the community without a previous inventory.

1417.

If the succession have only been accepted by the wife as authorized by the law on the refusal of her husband, and if there have been an inventory, the creditors can only sue for payment out of the property as well moveable as immoveable of the said succession, and in case of insufficiency, on the bare property of the wife in the other personal goods.

1418.

The rules established by article 1411 and those following govern debts dependent upon a donation, as well as those resulting from a succession.

1419.

Creditors may sue for the payment of debts contracted by the wife with her husband's consent, as well out of the whole property of the community as out of that of the husband or wife ; saving compensation due to the community, or indemnity due to the husband.

1420.

Every debt which is contracted by the wife in

virtue only of the general or special procuration of her husband, is at the charge of the community; and the creditor cannot sue for the payment thereof either against the wife or against her personal property.

SECTION II.

Of the Administration of the Community, and of the Effect of the Acts of either of the married Parties relating to the conjugal Union.

1421

The husband alone administers the property of the community.

He may sell it, alienate and pledge it without the concurrence of his wife.

1422.

He cannot make disposition during life by gratuitous title of the immoveables of the community, nor of the entirety or a proportion of the moveables, except for the establishment of their common children.

He may nevertheless dispose of moveable effects by gratuitous and particular title, for the benefit of any persons, provided he do not reserve to himself the usufruct thereof.

1423.

A testamentary donation made by the husband must not exceed his portion in the community.

If he have given in this form any article of the community, the donee cannot claim it in kind, except so far as such article by the event of distribution fall to the lot of the heirs of the hnsband ; if the article do not fall to the lot of such heirs, the legatee has his recompense for the total value of the article given, out of the portion of the heirs of the husband in the community and out of the personal property of the latter.

1424.

Fines incurred by the husband for a crime not importing civil death, may be sued for out of the property of the community, saving the compensation due to the wife ; such as are incurred by the wife cannot be put in execution except out of her bare property in her personal goods, so long as the community continues.

1425.

Sentences pronounced against one of the married parties for crime importing civil death, affect only such party's portion in the community, and his or her personal property.

1426.

Acts done by the wife without her husband's consent and even with the authority of the law, do not bind the property of the community, except when she contracts as a public trader and for the purposes of her traffic.

1427.

The wife cannot bind herself nor engage the property of the community, even to free her husband from prison, or for the establishment of their children in case of her husband's absence, until she shall have been thereto authorized by the law.

1428.

The husband has the management of all the personal property of the wife.

He may prosecute alone all possessory actions and those relating to moveables, which belong to his wife.

He cannot alienate the personal immoveables of his wife without her consent.

He is responsible for all waste in the personal goods of his wife, occasioned by the neglect of conservatory acts.

1429.

Leases which the husband has made alone of the property of his wife for a time which exceeds nine years, are not, in case of the dissolution of the community, obligatory against the wife or her heirs, except for the time which has still to run either of the first period of nine years, if the parties are still within it, or of the second, and so in succession, in such manner that the former shall only have a right to complete his enjoyment for that period of nine years which may be in progress.

1430.

Leases of his wife's property, which the husband has made or renewed alone for nine years or under, more than three years before the expiration of the current lease, if it relate to rural property, and more than two years before the same period if houses be in question, are void, unless their execution have commenced before the dissolution of the community.

1431.

The wife who becomes bound jointly and severally with her husband in respect of affairs in the community, or of her husband, is not deemed bound with regard to the latter, except as security; she may be indemnified against the obligation which she has contracted.

1432.

The husband who guarantees jointly and severally, or otherwise, the sale which his wife has made of a personal immoveable, has in like manner a remedy against her, either out of her portion in the community, or out of her personal goods, if he be troubled thereon.

1433.

If an immoveable belonging to one of the married parties be sold, as also if redemption be made in money of manorial services claimable from estates peculiar to one of them, and the price thereof be paid into the community, and all without compensation, there is ground for deduction of the price from the community, for the benefit of the married party who was proprietor, either of the immoveable sold, or of the services redeemed.

1434.

Compensation is deemed to have been made with respect to the husband whenever at the period of a purchase he has declared that it was made with money arising from the alienation of an immoveable which was personal to himself, and to be in lieu of compensation.

1435.

The declaration of the husband that the acquisition is made with money arising from an immoveable sold by the wife, and as regards her to serve instead of compensation, is not sufficient, if such compensation have not been formally accepted by the wife; if she have not accepted it, she has simply the right, at the dissolution of the community, to reimbursement of the price of her immoveable sold.

1436.

Recompense for the price of an immoveable belonging to the husband can only be claimed out of the mass of the community: that for the price of the immoveable belonging to the wife is claimable out of the personal goods of the husband, in case of insufficiency in the goods of the community. In all cases, the compensation only takes place on the footing of the sale, whatever allegation may be made touching the value of the immoveable alienated.

1437.

As often as a sum is withdrawn from the community, whether to discharge debts or incumbrances personal to one of the married parties, such as the price or part of the price of an immoveable peculiar to such party, or the redemption of manorial services, or for the recovery, preservation, or improvement of their personal property, and generally whenever one of the married parties has derived a personal profit from the goods of the community, a compensation is therefore due.

1438.

If the father and mother have conjointly endowed their common child without expressing the proportion in which they intended to contribute thereto, they are deemed to have endowed it each in a moiety, whether the dowry have been paid or promised in the effects of the community, or whether it have been so in goods personal to one of the two married parties.

In the second case, the married party whose immoveable or personal effects have been settled as dowry, has an action for indemnity in a moiety of the said dowry, against the goods of the other; regard being had to the value of the article given at the time of the donation.

1439.

A dowry settled by the husband alone on a common child, in the effects of the community, is at the charge of the community; and in the case in which community is accepted by the wife, the latter may contribute a moiety of the dowry, unless the husband have expressly declared that he charged himself with the whole thereof, or with a portion greater than a moiety.

1440.

Warranty of dower is due from every person who has settled it; and interest thereon runs from the day of marriage, even though there be a fixed time for payment, unless there be a stipulation to the contrary.

SECTION III.

Of the Dissolution of Community and of some of its Consequences.

1441.

Community is dissolved, 1st, by natural death; 2d, by civil death; 3d, by divorce; 4th, by separation of body; 5th, by separation of goods.

1442.

The want of an inventory after the natural or civil death of one of the married parties, does not give rise to a continuation of community: saving the prosecutions of parties interested, relatively to the condition of goods and effects in community of which the proof may be made as well by document as by common rumor.

If there be children under age, the want of inventory causes in addition a loss to the surviving married party of the enjoyment of their revenues; and the supplementary guardian who shall not have compelled such party to make inventory, is bound jointly and severally with the party by all sentences which may be pronounced for the benefit of minors.

1443.

Separation of goods can only be sued for in court by the wife whose dowry is put in peril, and when the disorder of the husband's affairs gives room to fear that the goods of the latter will not be sufficient to satisfy the prior claims and demands of the wife.

Every voluntary separation is null.

1444.

The separation of property, though pronounced in court, is null, unless it have been executed by the actual payment of the claims and demands of the wife, effectuated by authentic act, up to the amount of the husband's goods, or at least by prosecutions commenced within the fortnight following the judgment, and not interrupted since.

1445.

Every separation of goods must, before its exceution, be made public by a notice upon a list destined to this purpose, in the principal hall of the court of first instance, and further, if the husband be a merchant, banker, or tradesman, in that of the court of commerce at the place of his domicil; and this on pain of nullity of the execution.

The judgment pronouncing separation of goods,

has relation backward, as to its effects, to the day of the petition.

1446.

The personal creditors of the wife cannot, without her consent, demand separation of goods.

Nevertheless, in case of bankruptcy or embarrassment of the husband, they may avail themselves of the claims of their debtor up to the amount of their debts.

1447.

The creditors of the husband may obtain redress against the separation of property pronounced and even executed in fraud of their rights; they may even interpose in the suit on the petition for separation in order to contest it.

1448.

The wife who has obtained separation of goods, must contribute, in proportion to her means and those of her husband, as well to the charges of the household as to those of the education of their common children.

She must entirely sustain those charges, if nothing remain to the husband.

1449.

The wife separated either in body and goods, or in goods only, regains the uncontrolled government thereof.

She may dispose of her moveables, and alienate them. She cannot alienate her immoveables without the consent of her husband, or without being thereto authorized by the court on his refusal.

1450.

The husband is not responsible for any failure in the employment or re-employment of the price of an immoveable which the wife after separation has alienated under the authority of the court, unless he have concurred in the contract, or unless it be proved that the money has been received by him, or has been turned to his advantage.

He is responsible for failure in its employment or re-employment if the sale have been made in his presence and with his consent; he is not so with regard to the utility of such employment.

1451.

Community dissolved either by separation of body and goods, or of goods only, may be re-established with the consent of both parties.

This can only be done by an act before notaries and with a minute, of which a copy must be hung up in the form of article 1445.

In this case community re-established resumes its operation from the day of marriage; affairs return to the same state as though there had been no separation, without prejudice nevertheless to the execution of acts which, during such interval, may have been made by the wife in conformity with article 1449.

Every agreement by which the married parties

would re-establish their community under conditions different from those which regulated it previously, is null.

1452.

The dissolution of community operated by divorce or by separation either of body and goods, or of goods only, does not give origin to claims of survivorship by the wife ; but the latter retains the power of exercising them at the civil or natural death of her husband.

SECTION IV.

Of the Acceptance of Community, and of the Renunciation which may be made thereof, with the Conditions relating thereto.

1453.

After the dissolution of community, the wife or her heirs and assigns have the power of accepting or renouncing it. Every agreement to the contrary is null.

1454.

The wife who has intermeddled in the goods of the community, cannot afterwards renounce.

Acts purely administrative or conservatory do not imply intermeddling.

1455.

A wife of age who has admitted in an act the existence of community, is no longer at liberty to renounce, or relievable against the character she has assumed, although she have made such admission before the forming an inventory, provided there be no fraud on the part of her husband's heirs.

1456.

The surviving wife who is desirous of retaining the power of renouncing community, must, within three months from the day of her husband's decease, cause an exact and faithful inventory to be made of all the goods of the community, in the presence of the heirs of the husband, or after having duly summoned them.

Such inventory must be by her affirmed to be just and veritable, at the time of its closure, before the public officer who took it.

1457.

Within three months and forty days after the decease of the husband, she must make her renunciation at the registry of the court of first instance in the circle in which the husband had his domicil; this act must be enrolled on the register established for the reception of renunciations of succession.

1458.

The widow may, according to circumstances, demand of the civil court an extension of the interval prescribed by the preceding article for her renunciation; such extension is, if there be ground, pronounced in presence of the heirs of the husband, or after they have been duly summoned.

1459.

The widow who has not made her renunciation within the interval above prescribed, is not deprived of the power of renouncing if she have not intermeddled and if she have formed an inventory; she can only be sued as in community until she have renounced, and she is liable to charges incurred against her up to her renunciation.

She may equally be sued after the expiration of the forty days from the closing of the inventory, if it have been closed within the three months.

1460.

The widow who has converted or concealed any of the effects of the community, is declared subject thereto, notwithstanding her renunciation: it is the same with regard to her heirs.

1461

If the widow die before the expiration of the three months without having made or completed the inventory, the heirs shall, for the purpose of making or completing the inventory, have a new interval of three months, to be computed from the decease of the widow, and of forty days for deliberation after the closing of the inventory.

If the widow die after the termination of the inventory, her heirs shall have a fresh interval of forty days for deliberation, to be computed from her decease.

They may moreover renounce community in the

forms established above; and articles 1458 and 1459 are applicable to them.

1462.

The regulations of articles 1456 and those following are applicable to the wives of individuals civilly dead, commencing from the moment at which civil death took place.

1463.

The wife divorced or separated in body, who has not within three months and forty days after the divorce or separation definitively pronounced, accepted community, is deemed to have renounced it, unless, while yet within the interval, she has obtained an extension from the court, in her husband's presence, or after having daily summoned him.

1464.

The creditors of the wife may impeach renunciation which shall have been made by her or by her heirs in fraud of their demands, and accept community in their own right.

1465.

The widow, whether she accept or whether she renounce, has a right during the three months and forty days which are allowed her to form the inventory and to deliberate, to take for her own sustenance and that of her domestics from the provisions which remain, and in default thereof to borrow on account of the common stock, on condition of making moderate use thereof.

She is not liable to any rent by reason of her residence, during such intervals, in a house dependent on the community or belonging to the heirs of her husband; and if the house which the married parties occupied at the period of the dissolution of the community, was held by them subject to rent, the wife shall not contribute, during the same intervals, to the payment of the said rent, but it shall be deducted from the mass.

1466.

In the case of dissolution of community by the death of the wife, her heirs may renounce the community within the intervals and in the forms which the law prescribes to the surviving wife.

SECTION V.

Of the Distribution of the Community after Acceptance.

1467.

After the acceptance of community by the wife or her heirs, the active is distributed and the passive is sustained in the manner hereinafter determined.

§ I. Of the Partition of the Active.

1468.

The married persons or their heirs bring into the mass of existing goods every thing in which they are debtors to the community by title of compensation or indemnity, according to the rules above prescribed, in section 2 of the first part of the present chapter.

1469.

Every married person or the heir brings in in like manner the sums which have been drawn from the community, or the value of the property which the married party may have taken therefrom to endow a child by another bed, or to endow personally a common child.

1470.

From the mass of property, each married person or the heir deducts,

1st. Personal goods which have not entered into community if they exist in kind, or those which have been acquired in compensation ;

2d. The price of immoveables which have been alienated during the community, and for which compensation has not been made ;

3d. Indemnities due to such party from the community.

1471.

The shares of the wife take precedence of those of her husband.

This right is exercised in respect of goods which no longer exist in kind, first out of ready money, next out of moveable property, and subsidiarily out of the immoveables of the community ; in the last case, the election of the immoveables is yielded to the wife and to her heirs.

1472.

The husband cannot exercise his claims, except out of the goods of the community.

The wife and her heirs are entitled, in case of insufficiency in the community, to exercise their claims out of the personal goods of the husband.

1473.

The repayments and compensations due from the community to the married parties, and the compensations and indemnities due from them to the community, carry interest absolutely from the day of the dissolution of the community.

1474.

After all the deductions of the two married parties from the mass have been completed, the residue is distributed in moieties between the parties or their representatives.

1475.

If the heirs of the wife are divided, so that one has accepted the community which the other has renounced, he who has accepted can only take his personal and hereditary share in the property which fell to the lot of the wife.

The residue remains with the husband, who is charged towards the heir renouncing, with the claims which the wife would have been permitted to exercise in case of renunciation, but up to the amount only of the personal hereditary share of the party renouncing.

1476.

Further, the partition of the community, as to all which concerns its forms, the auction of the immoveables when there is ground for it, the effects of the partition, the warranty which results therefrom, and the balance, are submitted to the rules which are established under the title "*Of Successions,*" for distributions among heirs.

1477.

Such of the married parties as shall have converted or concealed any effects of the community, is deprived of a portion in the said effects.

1478.

After partition consummated, if one of the married parties is the creditor of the other, as when the price of the property of one has been employed in paying the personal debt of the other, or through any other means, such party exercises his claim over the property in the community which has fallen to the latter, or over the personal property of the latter.

1479.

Personal credits which married persons have to put in force against each other, do not carry interest except from the day of demand in court.

1480.

Donations which one of the married parties may have made to the other, are executed only out of the portion of the donor in the community, or out of his personal property.

1481.

The mourning of the wife is at the charge of the heirs of her husband previously deceased.

The value of such mourning is regulated by the fortune of the husband.

It is claimable even by a wife who renounces community.

§ II. Of the Passive in the Community, and of Contribution to Debts.

1482.

The debts of the community are to the amount of a moiety at the charge of each of the married parties or of their heirs : the expenses of sealing, inventory, sale of moveables, liquidation, auction and partition form part of such debts.

1483.

The wife is not bound for the debts of the community either with respect to her husband or with respect to creditors, except to the amount of her emolument, provided that there have been a good and faithful inventory, and provided she render account as well of the contents of such inventory as of that which has fallen to her in the partition.

1484.

The husband is bound for the whole of the debts of the community contracted by him, saving his remedy against his wife or her heirs for a moiety of such debts.

1485.

He is not bound beyond a moiety, for those personal to his wife and which fell to the charge of the community.

1486.

The wife may be sued for the whole of the debts which accrued in he own right and which entered into the community, saving her remedy against her husband or his heir, for a moiety of the said debts.

1487.

The wife even personally bound for a debt of the community, cannot be sued for more than a moiety of such debt, unless the obligation be joint and several.

1488.

The wife who has paid a debt of the community beyond her moiety has no right to recover against the creditor the excess, unless the acquittance express that what she has paid was for her moiety.

1489.

The one of two married persons who, by the effect of a mortgage executed upon an immoveable which has fallen to him by partition, finds himself sued for the whole of a debt of the community, has of right his remedy for a moiety of such debt against the other married party or her heirs.

1490.

The preceding regulations form no impediment to this; that by the partition, either of the coparceners should be charged with the payment of a proportion of the debts other than the moiety, even with discharging them entirely.

As often as one of the coparceners has paid the debts of the community beyond the portion in which he was bound, there is ground for a remedy for him who has paid too much against the other.

1491.

All which has been said above with regard to the husband or the wife, applies with regard to the heirs of either; and such heirs exercise the same rights and are subject to the same actions as the married party whom they represent.

SECTION VI.

Of the Renunciation of Community and of its Effects.

1492

The wife who renounces forfeits every description of claim upon the goods of the community, and even upon the moveables which have become part thereof in her right.

She retains only linen and clothes for her own use.

1493.

The wife who renounces has a right to resume,

1st. The immoveables belonging to her when they exist in kind, or the immoveable which has been acquired by compensation ;

2d. The price of her immoveables alienated for which compensation has not been made and accepted, as is mentioned above ;

3d. All indemnities which may be due to her from the community.

1494.

The wife renouncing is discharged from all contribution to the debts of the community as well with regard to the husband as with regard to creditors. She nevertheless remains bound towards the latter, when she is under obligation conjointly with her husband, or when the debt, become a debt of the community, accrued originally in her right ; the whole saving a remedy against the husband or his heirs.

1495.

She may exercise all actions and previous demands above detailed, as well against the goods of the community as against the personal goods of her husband.

Her heirs may do the same, saving in what relates to deduction of linen and clothes, as well as lodging and sustenance during the interval given for making the invéntory and for deliberating ; which rights are purely personal to the wife surviving.

Regulation relative to legal Community, when one of the married Parties or both of them have Children of previous Marriages.

1496.

All which has been said above shall be observed even when one of the married parties or both of them shall have children by precedent marriages.

If however the intermixture of the personalty and of the debts operate, for the benefit of one of the married parties, an advantage superior to that which is authorized by article 1098, under the title "*Of Donations during Life, and of Wills,*" the children of the first bed of the other married party shall have an action for compensation.

PART II. OF CONVENTIONAL COMMUNITY, AND OF AGREEMENTS WHICH MAY MODIFY AND EVEN EXCLUDE LEGAL COMMUNITY.

1497.

Married persons may modify legal community by every description of agreements not contrary to articles 1387, 1388, 1389, and 1390.

The principal modifications are those which take place in stipulating in one or other of the modes following; that is to say,

1st. That the community shall only embrace purchases;

2d. That the present or future moveables shall not form part of the community, or shall only form part of it for one party;

3d. That the whole or part of the present or future immoveables shall be comprehended therein, by making them moveable;

4th. That the married parties shall pay separately their debts anterior to marriage;

5th. That in cases of renunciation, the wife may resume her contributions free and unencumbered;

6th. That the survivor shall have a reversion;

7th. That the married parties shall have unequal shares;

8th. That there shall be between them community by general title.

SECTION I.

Of Community confined to Property acquired.

1498.

When married persons stipulate that there shall be a community between them of acquisitions only, they are deemed to exclude from community both the debts of each of them existing and future, and their respective moveables present and future.

In this case, and after that each of the married persons has deducted the contributions, duly proved, the partition is limited to acquisitions made by the married persons together or separately during the marriage, and arising as well from their common industry as from the savings out of the fruits and revenues of the property of both the married persons.

1499.

If the moveable property existing at the time of the marriage, or fallen since, have not been proved by inventory or statement in correct form, it is reputed acquired.

SECTION II.

Of the Clause which excludes from the Community the moveable Property in Whole or in Part.

1500.

The married parties may exclude from their community all their moveable property present and future.

When they stipulate that they will thereout mutually contribute to the amount of a sum or value determinate, they are by that alone deemed to have reserved the surplus.

1501.

This article renders the married party debtor to the community in the sum promised to be brought in, and obliges such party to prove such contributions.

1502.

The contribution is sufficiently proved as regards the husband, by the declaration contained in the marriage contract, that his moveable property is of such value.

It is sufficiently proved with regard to the wife, by the acquittance which the husband gives her, or those who have endowed her.

1503.

Every married person has the right to resume and take up, at the time of dissolving the community, the value of that in which the moveable property brought in by him at the time of the marriage, or which has fallen to him since, exceeded his contribution to the community.

1504.

The moveable property which falls to each of the married parties during the marriage, must be verified by an inventory.

In default of such inventory of moveable property fallen to the husband, or of a title proper to justify its existence and value, deduction being made of debts, the husband cannot exercise his previous claim thereon.

If the default of inventory reach to moveables fallen to the wife, the latter or her heirs are admitted to make proof, either by documents or by witnesses, or even by common rumor, of the value of such moveables.

SECTION III.

Of the Clause making moveable.

1505.

When the married parties or one of them cause the whole or a portion of their immoveables present or future to form part of the community, such clause is called "*making moveable.*"

1506.

The act of making moveable may be determinate or indeterminate.

It is determinate when the married party has declared that such an immoveable is rendered moveable and added to the community, wholly or up to the amount of a given sum.

It is indeterminate when the married party has simply declared that the immoveables are brought into community up to the amount of a certain sum.

1507.

The effects of determinately making moveable is to render the immoveable or the immoveables which are affected thereby, goods of the community even as moveables.

When the immoveable or immoveables of the wife are wholly rendered moveable, the husband may dispose thereof as of the other goods of the community and alienate them entirely.

If the immoveable is only rendered moveable for a certain sum, the husband cannot alienate it but with the consent of his wife; but he may pledge it without her consent, to the amount only of the portion rendered moveable.

1508.

The act of making moveable indeterminately does not render the community proprietor of immoveables which are affected thereby; its effect is limited to obliging the married party, who has consented to it, to include within the mass, at the time of dissolving the community, some of the immoveables of such party up to the amount promised.

The husband cannot, as in the preceding article, alienate in whole or in part, without the consent of his wife, the immoveables which have been rendered moveable indeterminately; but he may pledge them up to the amount to which they have been made moveable.

1509.

The married party who has rendered an estate moveable, has, at the time of partition, the power of retaining it, on making a deduction from his portion of its then value; and his heirs have the same right.

SECTION IV.

Of the Article of Separation of Debts.

1510.

The article by which married persons stipulate that they will separately pay their personal debts, compels them, at the dissolution of the community, to render to each other mutual accounts of the debts which are proved to have been paid by the community in discharge of such of the married parties as was debtor therein.

This obligation remains the same, whether, there have been an inventory or not; but if the moveable property contributed by the married parties have not been verified by an inventory or authentic statement anterior to marriage, the creditors of both the married parties may, without having regard to any of the distinctions which shall be claimed, sue for payment out of the moveable property not contained in the inventory, as well as out of all the other goods of the community.

The creditors have the same right over the moveable property which shall have fallen to the married parties during community, unless it have been likewise verified by an inventory or authentic statement.

1511.

When married persons bring into the community a sum certain, or a certain property, such a contribution carries with it a tacit agreement that it is not burdened with debts anterior to marriage ; and an account must be rendered by the married party who has debts to the other, of all those which will diminish the contribution promised.

1512.

The article of separation of debts does not prevent the community from being charged with interest and arrears which have accrued subsequently to marriage.

1513.

When the community is sued for debts of one of the married parties, declared by the contract free and unburthened with any debts anterior to the marriage, the other party has a right to an indemnity operating either upon that portion in the community which would revert to the married party debtor, or upon the personal goods of the said party;

and in case of insufficiency, such indemnity may be prosecuted by way of warranty against the father, mother, ancestor or guardian who shall have declared such party free and unburthened.

This warranty may even be exercised by the husband during the community, if the debt accrue on the part of the wife; saving in such case compensation due from the wife or her heirs to the warrantors, after the dissolution of the community.

SECTION V.

Of the Power granted to the Wife of resuming her Contribution free and unencumbered.

1514.

The wife may stipulate that in case of renunciation of the community, she shall resume the whole or part of what she shall have contributed thereto, either at the time of the marriage, or since; but this stipulation cannot be extended beyond things formally expressed, nor for the benefit of persons other than those designated.

Thus the power of resuming the moveables which the wife contributed at the time of the marriage does not extend to those which fell during the marriage.

So also this power allowed to the wife does not extend to children; the same allowed to the wife and children does not extend to heirs ascending or collateral.

In no case can the contributions be resumed

without deduction made of debts personal to the wife, and which the community shall have discharged.

SECTION VI.

Of conventional Reversion (Préciput).

1515.

The article by which the married party surviving is authorized to deduct and retain, before any partition, a certain sum or a certain quantity of moveable effects in kind, does not confer a right to the benefit of such deduction on the surviving wife, only when she accepted community, unless the contract of marriage have reserved to her such right even on renunciation thereof.

Except in case of such reservation, reservation is only exercised over the distributable mass, and not over the personal property of the married party previously deceased.

1516.

Reversion is not regarded as an advantage subject to the formalities of donations, but as a covenant of marriage.

1517.

Natural or civil death gives opening to reversion.

1518.

When the dissolution of the community is effected by divorce or by separation of body, there is no ground for the actual delivery of the reversionary property; but the married party who has obtained either divorce or separation of body retains reversionary rights in case of survivorship. If it be the wife, the sum or the thing which constitutes her jointure remains always with the husband provisionally, on condition of giving security.

1519.

The creditors of the community have always the right to effect a sale of the property comprised in the reversion, saving the remedy of the married party, conformably to article 1515.

SECTION VII.

Of the Articles by which unequal Portions in the Community are assigned to either of the Married Parties.

1520.

Married persons may depart from the equal partition established by the law, either by only giving the survivor or the heirs of such survivor a portion in the community less than a moiety, or by giving the survivor a fixed sum in lieu of every claim upon the community, or by stipulating that the entire community shall, in certain cases, belong to the survivor or to one of the parties only.

1521.

Where it has been stipulated that a married person or his heirs shall have only a certain portion in the community, as a third or a fourth, the party thus limited or his heirs shall not be liable to the debts of the community, except proportionably to the share they take in the active.

The agreement is null if it binds the party thus limited or his heirs to sustain a larger share, or if it exonerate them from sustaining a share in the debts equal to that which they take in the active.

1522.

Where it is stipulated that one of the married parties or the heirs of such party shall not claim beyond a certain sum in lieu of every right in the community, the article is a penal obligation which binds the other party or the heirs of such latter party to pay the sum agreed on, whether the community be good or bad, sufficient or not to discharge such sum.

1523.

If the article only establish the penal undertaking with regard to the heirs of the married party, the latter, in case of survivorship, has a right to legal partition by moieties.

1524.

The husband or his heirs who retain, by virtue of the stipulation set forth in article 1520, the entirety of the community, is obliged to discharge all the debts thereof.

The creditors have not in such case any action against the wife or against her heirs.

If the wife be the survivor who has, for a sum

agreed upon, the right of retaining all the community against the heirs of the husband, she has her election either to pay them such sum, becoming bound for all the debts, or to renounce the community, and abandon the goods and charges thereof to the heirs of her husband.

1525.

It is permitted to the married parties to stipulate that the entirety of the community shall belong to the survivor or to one of them only, saving to the heirs of the other the previous resumption of contributions and capital sums fallen into the community in right of their principal.

This stipulation is not deemed an advantage subject to the rules relative to donations, whether as to substance, or as to form, but simply a covenant of marriage and between partners.

SECTION VIII.

Of Community by general Title.

1526.

Married persons may establish by their contract a general community of their property as well moveable as immoveable, present and future, or of all their present property only, or of all their future property only.

Regulations common to the eight preceding Sections.

1527.

That which has been said in the eight previous sections, does not confine to their precise regulations the stipulations of which conventional community is susceptible.

Married persons may make any other agreements, as has been said in article 1387, and saving the modifications contained in articles 1388, 1389 and 1390.

Nevertheless, in the case where there shall have been children by a preceding marriage, every agreement which shall tend to give to one of the married parties more than the portion regulated by article 1098, under the title "*Of Donations during Life and by Will,*" shall be void as to all which exceeds such portion; but the simple benefit resulting from the common labor and savings of the two married persons out of their respective revenues, though unequal, shall not be considered as an advantage made to the prejudice of the children of the former bed.

1528.

Conventional community continues subject to the rules of legal community in all cases in which they have not been superseded explicitly or impliedly by the contract.

SECTION IX.

Of Agreements excluding Community.

1529.

If, without submitting to condition of dower, the parties declare that they marry without community.

or that they will be separate in property, the effects of such stipulation are regulated as follows.

§ I. Of the Clause implying that the Parties marry without Community.

1530.

The article importing that the parties marry without community does not confer upon the wife a right to administer her property, nor to enjoy the fruits thereof: such fruits are deemed to have been given to the husband to sustain the expenses of marriage.

1531.

The husband retains the administration of the property of his wife moveable and immoveable, and by consequence, the right to the enjoyment of all the moveable property which she brings as dowry, or which falls to her during the marriage; saving the restitution thereof which he is bound to make after the dissolution of the marriage, or after the separation of property which shall be pronounced by the court.

1532.

If among the moveables brought as dowry by the wife, or which have fallen to her during the marriage, there are things which cannot be enjoyed without consuming them, an estimatory statement thereof must be annexed to the contract of marriage, or an inventory thereof must be made at the time they so fall to the wife, and the husband must restore their value according to the estimate.

1533.

The husband is bound for all charges of the usufruct.

1534.

The article set forth in the present section forms no objection to an agreement that the wife shall receive annually, on her single acquittance, a certain portion of her revenues for her support and personal wants.

1534.

The immoveables settled as dower, in the case of the present section, are not inalienable.

Nevertheless they cannot be alienated without the consent of the husband, and upon his refusal, without the authority of the court.

§ II. Of the Clause of Separation of Property.

1536.

Where the parties have stipulated by their marriage contract that they will be separate in goods, the wife retains the entire management of her property moveable and immoveable, and the free enjoyment of her revenues.

1537.

Each of the parties contributes to the expenses of marriage, according to the covenants contained in their contract; and if there be none on this head, the wife contributes to such expenses up to the amount of one third of her income.

1538.

In no case, nor by virtue of any stipulation, can the wife alienate her immoveables without the special consent of her husband, or upon his refusal, without being authorized by the court.

Every general authority granted to the wife of alienating immoveables, either by the marriage contracts or subsequently, is null.

1539.

Where the wife under separation has given up to her husband the enjoyment of her property, the latter is only bound, either upon demand made by his wife, or upon the dissolution of the marriage, to a production of the existing fruits, and he is not accountable for those which have been consumed up to that period.

CHAPTER III.

Of Regulation of Dowry,

1540.

The dowry, under this regulation as under that of cap. 2, is the property which the wife brings to her husband in support of the charges of marriage.

1541

All that which the wife settles or which is conferred upon her by contract of marriage, appertains to her dowry, if there be no stipulation to the contrary.

SECTION I.

Of Settlement of Dowry.

1542.

The settlement of dowry may reach to all the present and future property of the wife, or all her present property only, or a part of her present and future property, or even an individual article.

The settlement in general terms, of all the wife's property, does not comprehend future property.

1543.

Dowry cannot be settled or even augmented during the marriage.

1544.

If the father and mother settle a dowry conjointly, without distinguishing the share of each, it shall be taken to be settled by equal portions.

If the dowry be settled by the father only in respect both of paternal and maternal rights, the mother, though present at the contract, shall not be bound, and the dowry remains entirely at the charge of the father.

1545.

If the father or mother surviving settle a dowry in respect of paternal and maternal property, without specifying the portions, the dowry shall be taken first from the rights of the intended husband in the property of the party previously deceased, and the residue out of the property of the party making settlement.

1546.

Although the daughter endowed by her father and mother have property in her own right of which they have the enjoyment, the dowry shall be taken from the property of the settlers, if there be no stipulation to the contrary.

1547.

Those who settle a dowry are bound to warranty of the objects settled.

1548.

Interest upon a dowry runs absolutely, from the day of marriage, against those who have promised it, although a term be fixed for its payment, unless there be a stipulation to the contrary.

SECTION II.

Of the Rights of the Husband over the Property in Dowry, and of the inalienable Nature of the Funds of the Dower.

1549.

The husband alone has the management of the property in dowry, during the marriage.

He has alone the right to sue the debtors and detainers thereof, to enjoy the fruits and interest thereof, and to receive reimbursements of capital.

Nevertheless it may be agreed, by the marriage contract, that the wife shall receive annually, on her single acquittance, a part of her revenues for her maintenance and personal wants.

1550.

The husband is not bound to find security for the receipt of the dowry, unless he have been subjected thereto by the contract of marriage.

1551.

If the dowry or part of the dowry consist of moveable articles fixed at a price by the contract, without declaration that such estimate does not amount to a sale, the husband becomes proprietor thereof, and is only debtor in the price given to the moveables.

1552.

An estimate put upon an immoveable settled in dowry does not transfer property therein to the husband without an express declaration thereof.

1553.

An immoveable acquired by money in dowry does not appertain to the dowry unless the condition of expending it have been stipulated by the marriage contract.

It is the same with respect to an immoveable given in payment of dowry settled in money.

1554.

Immoveables settled in dowry cannot be alienated or pledged during the marriage, either by the husband, or by the wife, or by the two conjointly; saving the exceptions which follow.

1555.

The wife may, with the authority of her husband, or upon his refusal, with the permission of the court, bestow the goods of her dowry in the establishment of children which she may have by a former marriage; but if she is only authorized by the court, she must reserve the enjoyment to her husband.

1556.

She may also with the authority of her husband, bestow the goods of her dowry for the establishment of their common children.

1557.

The immoveable in dowry may be alienated whenever the alienation thereof has been permitted by the marriage contract.

1558.

The immoveable in dowry may also be alienated with the permission of the court, and by auction, after three public notices,

In order to relieve the husband or wife from prison;

To furnish sustenance for the family in the cases provided for by articles 203, 205, and 206, under the title "*Of Marriage;*"

To pay the debts of the wife or of those who have

settled the dowry, when such debts have a certain date anterior to the contract of marriage;

To make substantial reparations indispensable to the preservation of the immoveable in dowry;

In short, when such immoveable is found in coparcenary with third persons, and when it is acknowledged to be indistributable.

In all these cases, the excess of the price of the sale above the acknowledged exigencies shall continue to form part of the dowry, and shall as such be expended for the benefit of the wife.

1559.

The immoveable in dowry may be exchanged, but with the consent of the wife, for another immoveable of equal value, of four-fifths at least, on proving the utility of the exchange, or obtaining the authority of the court, and after an estimate by competent persons officially named by the court.

In this case, the immoveable received in exchange shall appertain to the dowry; so also shall the excess of price, if there be any, and it shall be expended as such for the benefit of the wife.

1560.

If out of the excepted case, which is hereafter to be explained, the wife or the husband, or both conjointly alienate the funds of the dower, the wife or her heirs may cause the alienation to be revoked after the dissolution of the marriage, without power of objecting any prescription during its continuance; the wife shall have the same right after separation of property.

The husband himself may cause the alienation to be revoked during the marriage, becoming nevertheless liable in damages to the purchaser, unless he have declared in the contract that the property sold was in dower.

1561.

Immoveables in dower not declared alienable by the contract of marriage are imprescriptible during the marriage, unless the prescription have commenced before.

They become nevertheless liable to prescription after separation of property, at whatever period the prescription may have begun.

1562.

The husband is bound, as respects all property in dower, by all the obligations of the usufructuary.

He is responsible for all prescriptions gained and deteriorations occurring by his negligence.

1563.

If the dowry be put in peril, the wife may sue for separation of property, as has been mentioned in article 1443 and those following.

SECTION III.

Of the Restitution of Dower.

1564.

If the dowry consist of immoveables,

Or of moveables not estimated by the marriage contract, or fixed at a just price, with a declaration that the estimate does not take away the wife's property therein,

The husband or his heirs may be compelled to restore it without delay, after the dissolution of the marriage.

1565.

If it consist of a sum in money,

Or in moveables, to which a price has been affixed by the contract, without declaration that the estimate does not render the husband proprietor thereof,

The restitution cannot be exacted within a year after the dissolution.

1566.

If the moveables of which the wife retains the property have perished by using and without the fault of the husband, he shall be only bound to restore those which remain, and in the state in which they shall happen to be.

Nevertheless the wife may, in all cases, select linen and clothes for her actual use, saving a deduction of their value when such linen and clothes shall have been originally settled with estimate.

1567.

If the dowry comprehend obligations and annuities which have perished, or suffered retrenchments which cannot be imputed to negligence in the husband, he shall not be responsible for them, but shall be entirely discharged on restoring the contracts.

1568.

If an usufruct have been settled in dowry, the husband or his heirs are only bound, at the dissolution of the marriage, to restore the right of usufruct, and not the fruits fallen in during the marriage.

1569.

If the marriage have continued ten years subsequently to the expiration of the term assigned for the payment of the dowry, the wife or her heirs may demand it again from the husband after the dissolution of marriage, without being held to prove that he has received it, unless he is able to show diligence employed in vain in order to procure the payment thereof to himself.

1570.

If the marriage be dissolved by the death of the wife, the interest and fruits of the dowry to be restored run in full right for the benefit of her heirs subsequently to the day of the dissolution.

If it be so by the death of the husband, the wife has the choice of demanding the interest of the dowry during the year of mourning, or of causing alimony to be supplied to her during the said period at the expense of her husband's succession; but, in both cases, her lodging during such year, and her mourning weeds, must be supplied to her from the succession, and without deduction from the interest due to her.

1571.

On the dissolution of the marriage, the fruits of the immoveables in dowry are distributed between the husband and the wife, or their heirs, in proportion to the time it has continued, during the last year.

The year begins to run from the day on which the marriage was celebrated.

1572.

The wife and her heirs have no privilege for the recovery of the dowry from mortgage creditors prior to herself.

1573.

If the husband were already insolvent, and had no trade or profession when the father settled a dowry on his daughter, the latter shall only be bound to bring into the succession of her father the action which she has against that of her husband, in order to procure reimbursement thereof.

But if the husband have not become insolvent until after the marriage,

Or if he have a calling or profession which serves him in place of fortune,

The loss of the dowry falls singly on the wife.

SECTION IV.

Of Paraphernalia.

1574.

All the property of the wife which has not been settled in dowry, constitutes paraphernalia.

1575.

If all the goods of the wife are paraphernalia, and if there be no covenant in the contract that she shall sustain a portion of the expenses of marriage, the wife contributes thereto to the amount of one third of her revenues.

1576.

The wife has the management and enjoyment of her paraphernalia.

But she cannot alienate such property, nor become party to a suit in respect of the said property, without the authority of her husband, or upon his refusal, without the permission of the court.

1577.

If the wife give her procuration to her husband to administer her paraphernalia, on condition, of rendering account to her of the fruits, he shall be bound towards her as every other agent.

1578.

If the husband have enjoyed the paraphernalia of his wife not as her agent, and nevertheless without opposition on her part, he is only bound, on the dissolution of the marriage, or at the first demand of his wife, to the production of the existing fruits, and he is not accountable for those which have been consumed up to that period.

1579.

If the husband have enjoyed the paraphernalia, in spite of opposition manifested by his wife, he is accountable to her for all the fruits as well existing as consumed.

1580.

The husband enjoying the paraphernalia, is bound by all the obligations of the usufructuary.

PARTICULAR REGULATION.

1581.

On submitting to condition of dowry, married parties may nevertheless stipulate for an union of acquisitions, and the effects of such union are regulated as is mentioned in articles 1498 and 1499.

TITLE VI.

OF SALES.

Decreed the 6th of March, 1804. Promulgated the 16th of the same Month.

CHAPTER I.

Of the Nature and Form of Sales.

1582.

A sale is an agreement by which one person is bound to deliver a thing, and another to pay for it.

It may be made by authentic act, or under private signature.

1583.

It is complete between the parties, and the property is acquired in law by the purchaser with regard to the seller, as soon as the thing and the price are agreed on, though the thing have not been delivered nor the price paid.

1584.

The sale may be made absolutely and unconditionally, or subject to a condition which may either suspend or annul it.

It may also have for its object the alternative of two things or more.

In all these cases its effect is regulated by the general principles of agreements.

1585.

When merchandise is sold not in bulk, but by weight, tale, or measure, the sale is not complete, in this sense, that the articles sold remain at the risk of the vendor until they shall be weighed, counted, or measured ; but the purchaser may demand either delivery thereof or damages, if there be ground, in case of non-performance of the engagement.

1586.

If, on the contrary, the merchandise have been sold in bulk, the sale is perfect, although the merchandise have not been weighed, counted, or measured.

1587.

With respect to wine, oil, and other things which persons are in the habit of tasting before making purchase thereof, there is no sale so long as the purchaser have not tasted or approved of them.

1588.

A sale made on trial is always presumed to have been made under a suspensive condition.

1589

The promise of sale is equivalent to a sale, where there is a mutual agreement of the two parties upon the article and the price.

1590.

If the promise to sell have been made with earnest,

each of the contracting parties is at liberty to depart therefrom ;

He who has given it, on losing it ;

He who has received it, by restoring double.

1591.

The price of the sale must be determined and designated by the parties.

1592.

It may nevertheless be left to the arbitration of a third person : if such third party will not or cannot make an estimate, there is no sale.

1593.

The expenses of acts and other appendages of the sale, are at the charge of the purchaser.

CHAPTER II.

Who may buy or sell.

1594.

All persons not interdicted by the law are capable of buying or selling.

1595.

The contract of sale cannot take place between married persons, except in the three following cases:

1st. That in which one of the married parties cedes property to the other judicially separated, in payment of the claims of such separated party ;

2d. That in which the cession which the husband makes to the wife, even when not separated, has a lawful cause, such as reimbursment of her immoveables alienated, or of money belonging to her, if such immoveables or money do not fall into community;

3d. That in which the wife cedes property to her husband in satisfaction of a sum which she has promised him in dowry, and where community has been excluded;

Saving, in these three cases, the rights of the heirs of the contracting parties, if there be indirect advantage.

1596.

The following persons are forbidden to become purchasers, either by themselves or by the intervention of others, on pain of nullity:

Guardians of the property of those of whom they have the guardianship;

Factors of goods which they are charged to sell;

Administrators of the property of communes and public establishments confided to their care;

Public officers of national property, of which sale is made by their means.

1597.

Judges, their deputies, the commissaries of government, their substitutes, registrars, tipstaves, pastors of churches, official conductors of defences and notaries, cannot become assignees of suits, claims, and actions at law which are within the jurisdiction of the court within whose cognizance they exercise their functions, on pain of nullity, and expenses and damages.

CHAPTER III.

Of Things which may be sold.

1598.

Every thing which is the object of commerce may be sold, where particular laws have not prohibited the alienation thereof.

1599.

A sale of another's property is null: it may afford ground for damages where the purchaser was ignorant that the thing belonged to another.

1600.

The succession to a living person cannot be sold, even with his consent.

1601.

If at the moment of sale the thing sold had entirely perished, the sale shall be null.

If a part only of the thing have perished, it is in the election of the purchaser to relinquish the sale, or to demand the part preserved, causing the price thereof to be determined by valuation.

CHAPTER IV.

Of the Obligations of the Seller.

SECTION I.

General Regulations.

1602.

The seller is bound to explain clearly what it is he binds himself to.

Every obscure or ambiguous bargain is construed against the seller.

1603.

He has two principal obligations, that of delivering and that of warranting the thing which he sells.

SECTION II.

Of Delivery.

1604.

Delivery is the transferring the thing sold into the power and possession of the purchaser.

1605.

The obligation to deliver immoveables is fulfilled on the part of the vendor, when he has handed over the keys, if the question be of a building, or when he has handed over the titles to the property.

1606.

Delivery of moveable effects is completed,

Either by actual transfer,

Or by handing over the keys of the buildings which contain them,

Or even by the single consent of the parties, if the transfer thereof cannot be made at the moment of the sale, or if the purchaser have them already in his custody by another title.

1607.

The delivery of incorporeal rights is made, either by surrender of the titles, or by the use which the purchaser makes thereof with the consent of the seller.

1608.

The expenses of the delivery are at the charge of the seller, and those of removal at the charge of the purchaser, if there be no stipulation to the contrary.

1609.

The delivery must be made at the place where, at the time of sale, the thing which formed the object thereof, was, unless it be otherwise agreed upon.

1610.

If the seller fail to make delivery within the time agreed between the parties, the purchaser may at his election demand the rescinding of the sale, or to be put into possession, if the delay have occurred entirely through the act of the seller.

1611.

The seller must, in all cases, be condemned in damages, if an injury result to the purchaser through failure in delivery at the term agreed on.

1612.

The seller is not bound to deliver the article if the purchaser do not pay the price thereof, provided the seller have not allowed him an interval for the payment.

1613.

Further he shall not be obliged to delivery, although he may have allowed an interval of payment, if subsequently to the sale, the purchaser has become bankrupt, or be in a state of embarrassment, in such sort that the seller finds himself in imminent peril of losing the price; unless the purchaser give him security to pay at the end of the term.

1614.

The article must be delivered in the state in which it is at the moment of sale.

After that day all the fruits belong to the purchaser.

1615.

The obligation to deliver the article comprises its appurtenances, and every thing which has been designed for its perpetual use.

1616.

The seller is bound to deliver the full extent as

contained in the contract, subject to the modifications hereafter expressed.

1617.

If the sale of an immoveable have been made with indication of extent, at the rate of so much measure, the seller is bound to deliver to the purchaser, if he require it, the quantity indicated in the contract;

And if the thing is impossible to him, or if the purchaser do not require it, the seller is compelled to suffer a proportional diminution of the price.

1618.

If on the contrary, in the case of the preceding article, there be found an extent greater than that expressed in the contract, the purchaser has the election to supply the remainder of the price, or to relinquish the contract, if the excess be a twentieth beyond the extent declared.

1619.

In all other cases,

Whether sale be made of a certain and limited property,

Whether it have for its object funds distinct and separate,

Whether it commence by the measure, or by designation of the object sold followed by measure,

The expression of such measure does not give place to any additional price in favor of the seller, to any diminution of the price for less measure, except when the difference between the real measure and that expressed in the contract is a twentieth more or less, regard being had to the total value of the objects sold, if there be no contrary stipulation.

1620.

In the case in which, according to the preceding article, there is ground for augmenting the price on account of excess of measure, the purchaser has the election either to recede from the contract, or to furnish the additional price, and this with interest if he have kept the immoveable.

1621.

In all cases in which the purchaser has a right to recede from the contract, the seller is bound to restore to him, beyond the price, if he have received it, the expenses of the contract.

1622.

The action for addition to the price on the part of the seller and that for diminution of price or that for disengagement from the contract on the part of the purchaser, must be brought within a year, computing from the day of the contract, on pain of nonsuit.

1623.

If two estates be sold by the same contract, and for one and the same price, with designation of the measure of each, and there be found too little extent in the one and too much in the other, compensation takes place until both be rendered accurate; and the action, either for addition, or for diminution of price, only holds according to the rules established above.

1624.

The inquiry for ascertaining upon whom the loss or deterioration of the thing sold must fall before delivery, whether on the seller or on the purchaser, is determined according to the rules prescribed under the title "*Of Contracts or Conventional Obligations in general.*"

SECTION III.

Of Warranty.

1625.

The warranty due from the vendor to the purchaser embraces two points: the first is the peaceable possession of the thing sold; the second, the secret defects of the article, or such as would annul the sale.

§ I. Of Warranty in case of Eviction

1626.

Although at the time of sale no stipulation have been made respecting warranty, the seller is obliged by the law to warrant the purchaser against eviction which he may sustain in the whole or part of the thing sold, or against encumbrances on such object, and not declared at the time of sale.

1627.

The parties may, by private agreements, add to such obligation of law, or diminish the effect thereof; they may even covenant that the seller shall not be subject to any warranty.

1628.

Although it be said that the seller shall not be subject to any warranty, he continues nevertheless bound by that which results from an act personal to himself: every agreement to the contrary is void.

1629.

In the same case of stipulation of non-warranty, the seller in case of eviction is bound to restitution of the price;

Unless the purchaser knew at the time of the sale the danger of evication, or unless he purchased at his own peril and risk.

1630.

When warranty has been promised, or nothing has been stipulated on the subject, if the purchaser is evicted, he has a right to demand from the seller,

1st. Restitution of the price;

2d. That of the fruits, when he is compelled to give them up to the proprietor who has evicted him;

3d. The expenses incurred by the demand of warranty from the purchaser, and those incurred by the original demandant;

4th. In short, damages as well as the expenses and lawful costs of the contract.

1631.

Where at the period of eviction the thing sold is found to be diminished in value, or considerably deteriorated, either by the negligence of the purchaser, or by the intervention of superior force, the seller is not bound to restore the entirety of the price thereof.

1632.

But if the purchaser have derived profit from the spoliations committed by him, the seller has a right to keep back from the price a sum equal to such profit.

1633.

If the thing sold be found augmented in price at the period of eviction, although independently of the act of the purchaser, the seller is bound to pay him what it is worth beyond the price of sale.

1634.

The seller is bound to reimburse, or to cause to be reimbursed, to the purchaseer, by the party evicting, all the useful reparations and improvements which he shall have made in the estate.

1635.

If the seller have in bad faith disposed of the estate of another, he shall be compelled to reimburse to the purchaser all the expenses, even though mere matters of taste, which the latter shall have made on the estate.

1636.

If the purchaser be evicted only from one part of the thing, but which is of such consequence, as respects the whole, that the purchaser would not have bought it without the part from which he has been evicted, he may be permitted to recede from the purchase.

1637.

If, in the case of eviction from one part of the estate sold, the sale have not been rescinded, the value of the part from which the purchaser is found to be evicted is reimbursed to him according to its value at the period of eviction, and not in proportion to the total price of the sale, whether the thing sold have augmented or diminished in value.

1638.

If the estate sold be found to be burthened, a declaration thereof having been made, with non-apparent servitudes, which shall be of such importance that there is ground for presuming that the purchaser would not have bought if he had been informed thereof, he may demand to have the contract rescinded, unless he shall rather prefer an indemnity.

1639.

The other questions which may arise respecting damages accruing to the purchaser from the non-performance of the sale, must be decided according to the general rules established under the title "*Of Contracts or Conventional Obligations in general.*"

1640.

The warranty for cause of eviction ceases when the purchaser has suffered himself to be condemned in a judgment in the last resort, or from which an appeal is not allowed, without summoning his vendor, if the latter prove that sufficient grounds existed for rejecting the suit.

§ II. Of the Warranty against Defects in the Thing sold.

1641.

The seller is bound to warranty in respect of secret defects in the thing sold which render it improper for the use to which it is destined, or which so far diminish such use, that the buyer would not have purchased it, or would not have given so large a price, if he had known them.

1642.

The seller is not bound against apparent faults and such as the purchaser might have taken cognizance of himself.

1643.

He is bound against concealed faults, even though he was not aware of them, unless in such case it have been stipulated that he should not be bound to any warranty.

1644.

In the cases of articles 1641 and 1643, the purchaser has the election to return the thing and to obtain restitution of the price, or to keep the thing and to cause such a portion of the price to be restored to him as shall be settled by competent persons.

1645.

If the seller was acquainted with the faults of the thing, he is bound, beyond the restitution of the price which he has received for it, in all damages towards the purchaser.

1646.

If the seller was ignorant of the faults of the thing, he shall only be bound to a restitution of the price, and to reimburse to the purchaser the expenses occasioned by the sale.

1647.

If the faulty thing have perished in consequence of such bad qualities, the loss falls upon the seller, who shall be bound towards the purchaser to a restitution of the price and to other compensations explaned in the two preceding articles.

But a loss happening by accident is placed to the account of the purchaser.

1648.

The action resulting from faults annulling the sale must be brought by the purchaser, within a short interval, according to the nature of such faults, and the usage of the place where the sale was made.

1649.

It does not take place with respect to sales made by authority of law.

CHAPTER V.

Of the Obligations of the Purchaser.

1650.

The principal obligation of the purchaser is to pay the price at the day and in the place appointed by the sale.

1651.

If nothing be settled on this head at the time of sale, the purchaser must pay at the time and in the place where delivery is to be made.

1652.

The purchaser is indebted in interest on the price of sale up to the payment of the capital, in the three following cases:

If it have been already agreed on at the time of sale;

If the thing sold and delivered produces fruits or other revenues;

If the purchaser have been summoned to pay.

In the last case, interest runs only from the day of the summons.

1653.

If the purchaser be harassed or has a just ground for fearing he shall be troubled by an action either of mortgage, or of counter-claim, he may suspend the payment of the price until the seller have put an end to such harassment, unless the latter prefer giving security, or unless it have been stipulated, that notwithstanding such annoyance, the purchaser shall pay.

1654.

If the purchaser does not pay the price, the seller may demand annulment of the contract.

1655.

Annulling of the sale of immoveables is pronounced immediately if the seller is in danger of losing the thing and the price.

If such danger do not exist, the judge may accord to the purchaser a delay more or less extended according to circumstances.

Such interval being passed without the purchaser having paid, rescission of the sale shall be pronounced.

1656.

If it have been stipulated at the time of the sale of immoveables, that on failure of payment of the price within the term agreed on, the sale shall be annulled absolutely, the purchaser may nevertheless pay after the expiration of the interval, so long as he shall not have been sued for payment; but after such suit, the judge cannot grant him any delay.

1657.

In the matter of sale of provisions and moveable effects, the disannulling of the sale shall take place absolutely and without summons, for the benefit of the purchaser, after the expiration of the term agreed on for taking them away.

CHAPTER VI.

Of the Nullity and Rescinding of Sales.

1658.

Independently of the causes of nullity or of rescinding already explained in this title, and of those which are common to all agreements, the contract of sale may be rescinded by the exercise of the power of repurchase and by the inconsiderableness of the price.

SECTION I.

Of the Power of Repurchase.

1659.

The power of repurchase or of redemption is a compact by which the seller reserves to himself the resumption of the thing sold, on restitution of the principal price, and the reimbursement of which mention is made in article 1673.

1660.

The power of repurchase cannot be stipulated for, for a term exceeding five years.

If it have been stipulated for, for a longer term, it is reduced to such term.

1661.

The term fixed is imperative, and must not be prolonged by the judge.

1662.

On failure by the seller to exercise his action of redemption within the term prescribed, the purchaser becomes irrevocable proprietor.

1663.

The interval runs against all persons, even against a minor, saving, if there be ground, legal remedy.

1664.

The seller with covenant of repurchase may put his action in force against a second purchaser, even though the power of redemption shall not have been declared in the second contract.

1665.

The purchaser with covenant of repurchase exercises all the rights of his vendor; he may prescribe as well against the true owner as against those who set up claims or mortgages against the thing sold.

1666.

He may oppose the benefit of seizure and sale to the creditors of his vendor.

1667.

If the purchaser with covenant of redemption of an undivided portion of an estate have become highest bidder for the entirety at an auction claimed against him, he may oblige the vendor to redeem the whole when the latter is desirous to make use of his covenant.

1668.

If several persons have sold conjointly, and by a single contract, an estate common to them all, each one can only exercise his action for redemption as to the portion which he had therein.

1669.

It is the same if the party who has sold an estate alone leaves several heirs.

Each of such coheirs can only use the power of repurchase as regards the portion which he takes in the succession.

1670.

But, in the case of the two preceding articles, the purchaser may demand that all the co-vendors or all their coheirs should be made parties to the suit, in order to obtain their agreement to the resumption of the entire estate; and if they cannot agree, the petition shall be remanded.

1671.

If the sale of an estate belonging to several persons have not been made conjointly and of the whole estate together, and if each have sold only the portion which he had therein, they may put in force separately the action for redemption in respect to the portion which belonged to them;

And the purchaser cannot compel the party who shall exercise it in such manner, to redeem tho whole.

1672.

If the purchaser have left several heirs, the action for redemption can be exercised against each of them only for his portion, in the case in which it is still undivided, and in that in which the thing sold has been distributed between them.

But if distribution of the inheritance have been made, and the thing sold have fallen to the lot of one of the heirs, the action for redemption may be brought against him for the whole.

1673.

The seller who makes use of the covenant of repurchase, must reimburse not only the principal price, but also the expenses and lawful costs of the sale, the necessary repairs, and those which have augmented the value of the estate, up to the amount of such augmentation. He cannot enter into possession until after having satisfied all these obligations.

Where the seller re-enters into his estate by virtue

of the covenant of redemption, he takes it exempt from all the charges and mortgages with which the purchaser has encumbered it: he is bound to execute leases made without fraud by the purchaser.

SECTION II.

Of annulling Sales for Cause of Injury.

1674.

If the vendor have been damnified in more than seven-twelfths of the price of an immoveable, he has a right to demand annulment of the sale, even though he should have expressly renounced in the contract the power of demanding such annulment, and though he shall have declared he has given up the excess.

1675.

In order to ascertain if there be injury to the amount of more than seven-twelfths, it is necessary to estimate the immoveable according to its state and value at the moment of sale.

1676.

The petition is not admissible after the expiration of two years, computing from the day of sale.

Such interval runs against married women, and against absentees, interdicted persons, and minors coming in right of a vendor of full age.

1677.

Proof of injury cannot be admitted except by a

judgment, and in the case only in which the facts alleged shall be sufficiently probable and sufficiently important to raise presumption of injury.

1678.

Such proof cannot be made except by a report from three competent persons, who shall be bound to draw up one single common statement, and to form only one single resolution by plurality of voices.

1679.

If there be different opinions, the statement shall contain the motives thereof, without its being permitted to appear of what opinion each competent person was.

1680.

The three competent persons shall be named officially, unless the parties shall agree in naming all three conjointly.

1681.

In the case in which the action for annulment is permitted, the purchaser has the election either to restore the thing, receiving back the price which he has paid therefor, or to keep the estate on paying the remainder of the just price, subject to a deduction of a tenth of the total price.

The third possessor has the same right, saving the warranty against his vendor.

1682.

If the purchaser prefer keeping the thing on furnishing the remainder regulated by the preceding article, he is indebted in interest on the remainder, from the day of the petition for rescission.

If he prefer restoring it and receiving the price, he must restore the fruits from the day of the petition.

The interest on the price which he has paid, is also calculated to him from the day of the same petition or from the day of payment, if he have not received any fruits.

1683.

Annulment for injury does not take place in favor of the purchaser.

1684.

It does not take place in any sales, which, according to law, can only be made with the authority of the court.

1685.

The rules explained in the preceding section for cases in which several persons have sold conjointly or separately, and for that in which the seller or purchaser has left several heirs, are equally observed for the exercise of the action for rescission.

CHAPTER VII.

Of Auctions.

1686.

If one thing common to several persons cannot be commodiously divided and without loss;

Or if in a partition made with mutual consent of common property, there be found some goods which none of the coparceners can or will take.

The sale thereof is made by auction, and the price thereof is distributed between the joint-proprietors.

1687.

Each of the joint-proprietors is at liberty to demand that strangers should be summoned to the auction: they are necessarily summoned when one of the joint-proprietors is a minor.

1688.

The mode and the formalities to be observed in the auction are explained under the title "*Of Successions,*" and in the judicial code.

CHAPTER VIII.

Of the Transfer of Credits and other Incorporeal Rights.

1689.

In the transfer of a credit, of a claim, or of an action against a third person, the delivery is effected between the party ceding and the party receiving by assignment of the title.

1690.

The assignee is not seized with regard to third persons, except by the notification of the transfer made to the debtor.

Nevertheless the assignee may be equally seized by the acceptance of the transfer made by the debtor in an authentic act.

1691.

If, before the assignor or the assignee have signified the transfer to the debtor, the latter have paid the assignor, he shall be validly discharged.

1692.

The sale or cession of a credit comprises the accessories of the credit, such as security, privilege, and mortgage.

1693.

He who sells a credit or other incorporeal right, must guarantee the existence thereof at the time of the transfer, although it be made without warranty.

1694.

He does not answer for the solvency of the debtor, except when he is bound thereto, and up to the amount only of the price which he has gained for the credit.

1695.

Where he has promised to guarantee the solvency of the debtor, such promise is only understood of actual solvency, and does not extend to a future time, if the assignor have not expressly stipulated for it.

1696.

He who sells an inheritance without specifying in

detail the objects thereof, is only bound to warrant his quality of heir.

1697.

If he have already profited by the fruits of any estate, or received the amount of any credit belonging to such inheritance, or sold any effects of the succession, he is bound to reimburse them to the purchaser, if he have not expressly reserved them at the time of the sale.

1698.

The purchaser must on his part reimburse to the vendor what the latter has paid for the debts and charges of the succession, and render him an account of all in which he was creditor, if there be no contrary stipulation.

1699.

He against whom has been ceded a disputed right may get himself relieved therefrom by the assignee, on reimbursing to him the real price of the cession with the charges and lawful costs, and with interest to be computed from the day on which the assignee paid the price of the cession made to him.

1700.

The thing is deemed disputed as soon as there is a suit and contest on the ground of right.

1701.

The regulation contained in article 1699 ceases,

1st. In the case in which the cession has been made to a co-heir or co-proprietor of the right ceded;

2d. When it has been made to a creditor in payment of what is due to him ;

3d. When it has been made to the possessor of the estate subject to disputed claim.

TITLE VII.

OF BARTER.

Decreed the 7th of March, 1804. *Promulgated the* 17*th of the same Month.*

1702.

Barter is a contract by which the parties mutually give one thing for another.

1703.

Barter is effected by consent only, in the same manner as a sale.

1704.

If one of the exchanging parties have already received the thing given him in barter, and if it afterwards prove that the other contractor is not the proprietor of such thing, he cannot be compelled to deliver that which he has promised to deliver, but only to restore that which he has received.

1705.

The exchanging party who is evicted from the thing which he has received in exchange, has the election to compromise for damages or to recover his property.

1706.

Annulment for cause of injury does not take place in the contract of barter.

1707.

All the other rules prescribed for the contract of sale apply also to barter.

TITLE VIII.

OF THE CONTRACT OF HIRING.

Decreed the 7th of March, 1804. *Promulgated the* 17*th of the same Month.*

CHAPTER I.

General Regulations.

1708.

There are two kinds of contracts of hiring:

That of things,

And that of work.

1709.

The hiring of things is a contract by which one of the parties binds himself to give up to another the enjoyment of a thing during a certain time, and for a certain price, which the latter binds himself to pay him.

1710.

The hiring of work is a contract by which one of

the parties engages to do something for another for a price agreed upon between them.

1711.

These two kinds of hiring are again subdivided into several particular species:

Lease is the name given to the hiring of houses, and that of moveables;

Farming-lease to that of rural heritages;

Hire, the hiring of labor or of service;

Hiring in cheptel, to that of animals of which the advantage is distributed between the proprietor and him to whom they are intrusted.

Proposal, estimate, and contract for the undertaking of a work at a determined price, are also a hiring, when the material is furnished by the party for whom the work is done.

The three last species have particular rules.

1712.

Leases of national property, of that of communes, and public establishments, are subject to particular rules.

CHAPTER II.

Of the Hiring of Things.

1713.

All descriptions of property moveable and immoveable may be hired.

SECTION I.

Of the Rules common to Leases of Houses and rural Property.

1714.

Hiring may take place either verbally or by writing.

1715.

If the lease made without writing have not yet received any execution, and if one of the parties deny it, proof cannot be received by witnesses, however moderate the price thereof may be, and though it be alleged that earnest has been given.

The oath can only be tendered to him who denies the lease.

1716.

Where there shall be a dispute touching the price of a verbal lease, of which the execution has begun, and no acquittance shall exist, the proprietor shall be believed therein upon his oath, unless the hirer shall rather prefer to demand an estimate by competent persons: in which case the charges of the view remain at his cost, if the estimate exceed the price which he has declared.

1717.

The lessee has the right to underlet, or even to assign his lease to another, if such power have not been restricted.

He may be restricted as respects the whole or part.

This article is always peremptory.

1718.

The articles of the title "*Of the Contract of Marriage and of the respective Rights of Married Persons,*" relative to leases of the property of married women, are applicable to leases of the property of minors.

1719.

The lessor is bound by the nature of the contract, and without the necessity of any particular stipulation,

1st. To deliver to the hirer the thing hired;

2d. To maintain such thing in a state to be employed for the use for which it was hired;

3d. To put the hirer in peaceable possession thereof during the continuance of his lease.

1720.

The lessor is bound to deliver the thing in a good state of complete repair.

He must make in it, during the continuance of the lease, all the reparations which may become necessary other than tenant's repairs.

1721.

Warranty is due to the lessee against all faults or defects of the thing hired, which may impede the use thereof, even though the lessor should not have known them at the time of the lease.

If from such faults or defects any loss result to the hirer, the lessor is bound to indemnify him.

1722.

If, during the continuance of the lease, the thing hired is destroyed in entirety by fortuitous events, the lease is rescinded absolutely; if it be only in part destroyed, the lessee may, according to circumstances, demand either a diminution of the price, or the rescinding of the lease itself. In neither case is there any ground for indemnification.

1723.

The lessor cannot, during the continuance of the lease, change the form of the thing hired.

1724.

If, during the lease, the thing hired have urgent need of reparations, such as cannot be deferred to the end thereof, the lessee must sustain them whatever inconvenience they may cause him, and though he should be deprived, while they are going on, of one part of the thing hired.

But if such reparations endure more than forty days, the price of the lease shall be diminished in proportion to the time and to the part of the thing hired of which he shall have been deprived.

If the reparations are of such a nature that they render that uninhabitable which is necessary for the lodging of the lessee and his family, the latter may cause the lease to be rescinded.

1725.

The lessor is not bound to warrant the lessee, against molestation which third persons may cause him by acts committed against his enjoyment, without moreover setting up any claim against the thing hired; saving to the lessee a prosecution under his own name.

1726.

If, on the contrary, the hirer or the farmer have been disturbed in their enjoyment in consequence of an action concerning the ownership of the estate, they are entitled to a proportionate diminution of the price of the lease or farming-lease, provided that such molestation and impediments have been announced to the proprietor.

1727.

If those who have committed such acts pretend to have any claim to the thing hired, or if the lessee is himself cited in court in order to see himself condemned to an abandonment of the whole or of part of such thing, or to submit to the exercise of any servitude, he must summon the lessor on his warranty, and must be put out of the suit, if he require it, on naming the lessor, in whose right he possesses.

1728.

The lessee is subject to two principal obligations:

1st. To use the thing hired in a careful manner, and according to the destination which was given to it by the lease, or according to that which may be presumed from circumstances, in default of agreement:

2d. To pay the price of the lease in the terms agreed upon.

1729.

If the lessee employ the thing hired for another purpose than that to which it has been destined, or from which may result a damage to the lessor, the latter may, according to circumstances, cause the lease to be rescinded.

1730.

If there have been a plan of the premises between the lessor and the hirer, the latter must restore the object such as he recevied it, excepting what has perished, or become deteriorated by antiquity or superior force.

1731.

If a statement of places have not been made, the lessee is presumed to have received them in a good condition as to tenant's repairs, and must restore them such, saving contrary proof.

1732.

He is responsible for deteriorations or losses which happen during his enjoyment, unless he can prove that they occurred without his fault.

1733.

He is answerable in case of fire, unless he can prove that the fire happened by accident or superior force, or by faulty construction;

Or that the fire was communicated from a neighbouring house.

1734.

If there be several hirers, all are jointly and severally responsible for fire, unless they can prove that the fire began in the house of one of them; in which case the latter alone is bound therein;

Or unless some of them can prove that the fire did not commence in their lodging, in which case the latter are not bound therein.

1735.

The lessor is bound for deteriorations and losses which happen by the act of the persons of his house or of his sub-tenants.

1736.

If the lease were made without writing, one of the parties cannot give discharge to the other without observing the intervals fixed by the usage of the places.

1737.

The lease ceases absolutely at the expiration of the term fixed, where it has been made in writing, without its being necessary to give discharge.

1738.

If at the expiration of written leases, the lessee remains and is left in possession, a new lease is effected, the operation of which is regulated by the article relative to hirings made without writing.

1739.

Where there has been a discharge signified, the lessee, though he has continued his enjoyment, cannot insist upon a tacit rehiring.

1740.

In the case of the two preceding articles, security given for the lease does not extend to obligations resulting from the prolongation.

1741.

The contract for hiring is dissolved by the loss of the thing hired, and by the respective default of the lessor and lessee, in fulfilling their engagements.

1742.

The contract for hiring is not dissolved by the death of the lessor, nor by that of the lessee.

1743.

If the lessor sell the thing hired, the purchaser cannot expel the farmer or the lessee who has an authentic lease or one of which the date is certain, unless such right be reserved by the contract of lease.

1744.

If it has been agreed, at the time of the lease, that in case of sale the purchaser may eject the farmer or hirer, and no stipulation have been made touching damages, the lessor is bound to indemnify the farmer or the lessee in the following manner.

1745.

If the question be touching a house, apartment, or shop, the lessor pays under the head of damages, to the hirer evicted, a sum equal to the price of the rent, during the time which, according to the usage of the place, is allowed between discharge and quitting.

1746.

If rural property be in question, the indemnity which the lessor must pay to the farmer, is of a third of the price of the lease for the whole time which has to run.

1747.

The indemnity shall be regulated by competent persons, if the question relate to manufactures, machinery, or other establishments which require great advances.

1748.

The purchaser who desires to make use of the power reserved by the lease, of ejecting the farmer or lessee in case of sale, is moreover bound to give the lessee the previous notice usual in the place for discharges.

He must also advertise the farmer of rural property, at least a year in advance.

1749.

Farmers or lessees cannot be ejected unless they be paid by the bailor, or on his default, by the new purchaser, the damages above explained.

1750.

If the lease have not been made by authentic act, or have not a certain date, the purchaser is not subject to any costs.

1751.

The purchaser with covenant of redemption cannot make use of his power of ejecting the tenant until, by the expiration of the delay fixed for repurchase, he become unchangeable proprietor.

SECTION II.

Of particular Rules and Leases.

1752.

The lessee who does not furnish the house with sufficient moveables, may be expelled, unless he give securities capable of answering for the rent.

1753.

The under-lessee is not bound towards the proprietor, except to the amount of the price of his under-lease in which he may be debtor at the moment of his occupation, and without his being able to object payments made in anticipation.

Payments made by the under lessee, whether by virtue of a stipulation contained in his lease, or in consequence of the usage of places, are not deemed to be made by anticipation.

1754.

Tenant's repairs or ordinary reparations in which the lessee is bound, if there be no article to the contrary, are those marked out as such by the usage of places, and among others the reparations to be made are,

To hearths, chimney-backs, jambs, and chimney-pieces;

To the plastering of the bottom of the walls of apartments and other places of habitation, to the height of a meter;

To the pavement and windows of chambers, when some of them only are broken;

To glass, unless it be broken by hail, or other extraordinary accidents, or arising from superior force, for which the tenant shall not be bound;

To doors, casements, bars or shutters of shops, hinges, window-bolts, and locks.

1755.

None of the reparations deemed to belong to tenants are chargeable on lessees, when they are only occasioned by antiquity or superior force.

1756.

The cleansing of wells and houses of office are at the charge of the lessor, if there be no clause to the contrary.

1757.

A lease of furniture supplied for the purpose of fitting up an entire house, an entire set of lodgings, a shop, or any other apartments, is deemed to be made for the ordinary duration of the leases of houses, sets of apartments, shops or other apartments, according to the usage of places.

1758.

The lease of a furnished apartment is taken to have been made for a year, when it has been made at so much a year;

By the month, when it has been made at so much a month;

By the day, if it have been made at so much a day.

If there be nothing to show that the lease was made at so much a year, a month, or day, the hiring is deemed to have been made according to the custom of the place.

1759.

If the party hiring a house or an apartment continue his enjoyment after an expiration of the lease in writing, without opposition on the part of the lessor, he shall be taken to occupy them on the same conditions, for the term fixed by the usage of the places, and shall not be at liberty to quit nor liable to be ejected therefrom, until after a discharge given according to the interval fixed by the usage of the places.

1760.

In case of rescinding by the fault of the hirer, the latter is bound to pay the price of the lease during the time necessary to reletting, without prejudice to the damages which may result from the wrong.

1761.

The lessor cannot dissolve the hiring, although he declare his desire to occupy by himself the house hired, if there have been no agreement to the contrary.

1762.

If it have been agreed, in the contract of hiring, that the lessor may come and occupy his house, he is bound to signify beforehand a discharge at the periods determined on by the usage of the places.

SECTION III.

Of the Rules peculiar to Farming Leases.

1763.

The party who cultivates, under condition of a partition of fruits with the lessor, can neither underlet nor assign, if such power have not been expressly granted to him by the lease.

1764.

In case of infringement, the proprietor has a right to re-enter into enjoyment, and the lessee is condemned in damages resulting from the non-performance of the lease.

1765.

If, in a farming lease, an extent is given to an estate exceeding more or less that which it really has, there is no ground for augmentation or diminution of the price for the farmer, except in the cases and according to the rules expressed under the title "*Of Sales.*"

1766.

If the lessee of a rural heritage do not stock it with cattle and implements necessary for its cultivation; if he abandon its culture; if he do not cultivate it in a husbandlike manner; if he employ the thing hired to another use than that for which it was destined; or if he do not generally execute the articles of the lease, and damage thereby result to the lessor, the latter may, according to circumstances, cause the lease to be rescinded.

In case of rescinding proceeding from the act of the lessee, the latter is bound for damages, as has been mentioned in article 1764.

1767.

Every hirer of rural property is bound to lay up his corn in the places destined for this purpose, according to the lease.

1768.

The lessor of rural property is bound, under pain of all expenses and damages, to advertise the proprietor of encroachments which may be committed on his estate.

Such notice must be given within the same interval as that which is regulated in case of summons, according to the distance of places.

1769.

If the lease is made for several years, and if, during the continuance of the lease, the whole or a moiety of one crop at least be carried away by fortuitous events, the farmer may demand a remission of the price of his hiring, unless he be indemnified by preceding harvests.

If he be not indemnified, the estimate of the remission can only take place at the end of the lease, at which period a balance shall be made of all the years of enjoyment;

But the judge may nevertheless, relieve the lessee provisionally from the payment of a part of the price, by reason of loss sustained.

1770.

If the lease be only for one year, and the loss be of the whole of the fruits, or at least of a moiety, the lessee shall be discharged from a proportional part of the price of the hiring.

He cannot claim any remission if the loss be less than a half.

1771.

The farmer cannot obtain remission, when the loss of the fruits occurs after they are severed from the soil, unless the lease give to the proprietor a proportional part of the fruits in kind; in which case the proprietor must sustain his part of the loss, provided the lessor have been guilty of no delay in delivering him his portion of the crop.

Neither is the farmer entitled to remission, when the cause of the damage was in existence, and known at the period at which the lease was made.

1772.

The hirer may be charged with accidents by express stipulation.

1773.

Such stipulation is only understood of ordinary accidents, such as hail, lightning, frost, or dropping of grapes.

It does not extend to extraordinary accidents, such as the ravages of war, or an inundation, to which the country is not ordinarily subject, unless the lessee has been charged with all accidents foreseen or not foreseen.

1774.

A lease, without writing, of a rural estate, is deemed to have been made for the time which is necessary, in order that the lessee may collect all the fruits of the heritage farmed.

Thus, the lease of a meadow, of a vineyard, and of any other estate of which the fruits are entirely collected in the course of a year, is deemed to have been made for a year.

A lease of arable lands, when they are divided by courses of husbandry or seasons, is deemed to have been made for so many years as there are crops.

1775.

The lease of rural heritages, although made without writing, ceases absolutely at the expiration of the time for which it is taken to have been made, according to the preceding article.

1776.

If, at the expiration of rural leases in writing, the lessee remain and is suffered to remain in possession, a new lease is operated, of which the effect is regulated by article 1774.

1777.

A farmer, on quitting, must leave to him who succeeds him in the cultivation, suitable buildings and other conveniences for the labors of the succeeding year; and on the other hand, the farmer entering must supply to him who quits, suitable buildings and other conveniences for the consumption of the fodder, and for the crops remaining to be gathered.

In both cases, the usage of the places must be conformed to.

1778.

The farmer, on quitting, must also leave straw and feed-corn for the year, if he received them at the time of his entry upon possession ; and even though he should not have received them, the proprietor may retain them according to estimate.

CHAPTER III.

Of the hiring of Labor and Industry.

1779.

There are three principal species of hiring of labor and industry :

1st. The hiring of workmen who engage themselves in the service of any one ;

2d. That of carriers, as well by land as by water, who are charged with the conveyance of persons or commodities ;

3d. That of persons who undertake works by estimate or by contract.

SECTION I.

Of the hiring of Domestics and Artificers.

1780.

Services can only be engaged for a term, or for a determinate undertaking.

1781.

The master is believed on his affirmation—
For the proportion of wages;
For the payment of the salary for the year elapsed;
And for sums paid on account for the current year.

SECTION II.

Of Carriers by Land and by Water.

1782.

Carriers by land and by water are subjected, for the protection and preservation of the articles which are confided to them, to the same obligations as innkeepers, of which mention is made under the title "*Of Deposit and Sequestration.*"

1783.

They are answerable not only for what they have already received within their vessel or carriage, but also for what has been delivered at the wharf or warehouse, in order to be placed in their vessel or carriage.

1784.

They are responsible for the loss and average of things intrusted to them, unless they can prove that they have been lost and damaged by fortuitous circumstances, or superior force.

1785.

Those who undertake public conveyances by land

and by water, and also public wagons, must keep a register of money, of goods and packages, of which they have the charge.

1786.

The managers and directors of carriages and public wagons, the masters of barges and boats, are moreover, subjected to particular regulations, which form the law between them and other citizens.

SECTION III.

Of Estimates and Works by Contract.

1787.

When a party is charged with the performance of a work, it may be agreed that he shall supply only his labor or skill, or further, that he shall also supply materials.

1788.

If, in the case in which the workman furnishes the material, the thing happens to perish, in whatsoever manner it may be, before being delivered, the loss thereof falls on the workman, unless the master be guilty of negligence in not receiving the thing.

1789.

In the case in which the workman supplies only his labor or his skill, if the thing happen to perish, the workman is only bound for his own misconduct.

1790.

If, in the case of the preceding article, the thing happens to perish, though without any fault on the part of the workman, before the work has been received, and without the master having been guilty of delay in showing it, the workman has no wages to claim, unless the thing have perished by the fault of the material.

1791.

If the question respect work in several parts, or by measure, the proof thereof may be made in parts ; it is deemed to have been made for all the parties paid, if the master pay the workman in proportion to the work done.

1792.

If the edifice, built at a set price, perish in whole or in part by defect in its construction, even by defect in the foundation, the architect and the contractor are responsible therefor for ten years.

1793.

When an architect or contractor has undertaken to erect a building upon a penalty, after a plan settled and agreed with the proprietor of the soil, he cannot demand any augmentation of price, neither under pretext of augmentation of the value of labor, or of materials, nor under that of alterations or enlargements of such plan, if such alterations or enlargements have not been authorized in writing, and the price agreed with the proprietor.

1794.

The master may rescind by his single will the bargain with penalty, although the work be already begun on indemnifying the contractor for all his expenses, for all his labor, and for all which he might have gained in such undertaking.

1795.

The contract for hiring of work is dissolved by the death of the workman, of the architect, or contractor.

1796.

But the proprietor is bound to pay according to the price contained in the agreement, to their succession, the value of work done and that of materials prepared, at the time only when such labors and such materials may be of service to him.

1797.

The contractor is responsible for the act of the persons he employs.

1798.

Masons, carpenters, and other workmen, who have been employed in the construction of a building, or of other works done by contract, have no action against the party for whom such work has been done, except to the amount in which he is found to be debtor towards the contractor, at the moment at which their action is brought.

1799.

Masons, carpenters, locksmiths, and other workmen, who directly make bargains at fixed prices, are bound by the rules prescribed in the present section: they are contractors in the calling in which they deal.

CHAPTER IV.

Of Lease in Cheptel.

SECTION I.

General Regulations.

1800.

A lease in *cheptel* is a contract by which one of the parties gives to the other a stock of cattle to keep, feed, and take care of, on the conditions agreed between them.

1801.

There are several sorts of cheptels:

Simple or ordinary cheptel.

Cheptel by moiety.

Cheptel allowed to a farmer or other cultivator.

There is, besides, a fourth species of contract improperly called *cheptel*.

1802.

Every species of animal may be given in cheptel which is susceptible of increase and profit in agriculture or commerce.

1803.

In default of particular agreements, such contracts are regulated by the principles which follow.

SECTION II.

Of simple Cheptel.

1804.

A lease in cheptel is a contract by which one party gives to another beasts to keep, to feed, and to take care of, on condition that the lessee shall enjoy the benefit of half the increase, and that he shall sustain also half the loss.

1805.

An estimated value given in the lease in cheptel does not transfer the property to the lessee; it has no other object than to ascertain the loss or gain which may be found at the expiration of the lease.

1806.

The lessee must employ all the care of a good manager in the preservation of the cheptel.

1807.

He is not bound as to a fortuitous occurrence, except when it has been preceded by some fault on his part, without which the loss would not have happened.

1808.

In case of dispute, the lessee is bound to prove the accident, and the lessor is bound to prove the fault which he imputes to the lessee.

1809.

The lessee who is discharged as to the accident, is always bound to render an account of the skins of the beasts.

1810.

If the cheptel perish entirely without the fault of the lessee, the loss thereof falls on the lessor.

If it only perish in part, the loss is sustained in common, according to the price of the original estimate, and that of the estimate at the expiration of the cheptel.

1811.

Parties cannot stipulate,

That the lessee shall sustain the total loss of the cheptel, although happening by accident and without his fault;

Or that he shall sustain, in the loss, a larger proportion than in the gain;

Or that the lessor shall take by preference, at the end of the lease, something more than the cheptel which he has supplied.

Every similar agreement is void.

The lessee alone has the benefit of the milk, of the dung, and of the labor of the animals given in cheptel. The wool and the increase are divided.

1812.

The lessee cannot dispose of any beast of the flock, whether of the stock or of the young, without the consent of the lessor, who cannot himself dispose thereof without the consent of the lessee.

1813.

When the cheptel is given to the farmer of another's estate, it must be notified to the proprietor of whom such farmer holds; without which he may seize it, and cause it to be sold for what such farmer owes him.

1814.

The lessee must not shear without previously informing the lessor thereof.

1815.

If there be no time fixed by the agreement for the duration of the cheptel, it is taken to have been made for three years.

1816.

The lessor may demand an earlier dissolution thereof, if the lessee do not fulfil his obligations,

1817.

At the end of the lease, or at the time of its dissolution, a new valuation of the cheptel is to be made.

The lessor may previously select beasts of each species, to the amount of the original valuation; the excess is divided.

If a sufficient number of beasts does not exist to complete the first valuation, the lessor takes what remains, and the parties adjust the loss between them.

SECTION III.

Of Cheptel *by Moiety.*

1818.

Cheptel by moiety is an association in which each of the contractors supplies a moiety of the cattle, which remain common for profit or for loss.

1819.

The lessee alone receives the benefit as in simple *cheptel* of the milk, of the manure, and of the labor of the beasts.

The lessor has a right only to a moiety of the young and of the wool.

Every contrary agreement is void, unless the lessor be proprietor of the farm of which the lessee is farmer, or partial cultivator.

1820.

All the other rules of simple *cheptel* apply to cheptel by moiety.

SECTION IV.

Of Cheptel given by the Proprietor to his Farmer or Joint-Cultivator.

§ I. Of *Cheptel* given to the Farmer.

1821.

This *cheptel* (called also *cheptel de fer*) is that by which the proprietor of a farm gives it to farm, on condition that at the expiration of the lease, the farmer shall leave cattle of a value equal to the price of the estimate of those which he shall have received.

1822.

The valuation of the *cheptel* given to the farmer does not transfer to him the property; but nevertheless places it at his risk.

1823.

All the profits belong to the farmer during the continuance of his lease, if there be no agreement to the contrary.

1824.

In cheptels given to the farmer, the dung is not among the personal profits of lessees, but belongs to the farm, in the cultivation of which it must be entirely employed.

1825.

The loss, even total and by accident, falls entirely on the farmer, if there be no contrary agreement.

1826.

At the end of the lease, the farmer cannot retain the cheptel by paying the original valuation thereof; he must leave one of value equal to that which he has received.

If there be a deficiency he must pay it; and it is the excess only which belongs to him.

§ II. Of Cheptel given to the Joint-Cultivator.

1827.

If the cheptel perish entirely without the fault of the husbandman, the loss falls on the lessor.

1828.

The party may stipulate that the husbandman shall give up to the lessor his share of the fleece at a price inferior to the ordinary value;

That the lessor shall have a larger part of the profit;

That he shall have a moiety of the milk:

But a stipulation cannot be made that the husbandman shall be bound by the whole loss.

1829.

This *cheptel* ceases with the lease of the farm.

1830.

It is besides subjected to all the rules of simple *cheptel.*

SECTION V.

Of the Contract improperly called Cheptel.

1831.

When one or more cows are given to be housed and fed, the lessor preserves the property therein; he has only the profit of the calves produced by them.

TITLE IX.

OF THE CONTRACT OF PARTNERSHIP.

Decreed the 8*th of March,* 1804. *Promulgated the* 18*th of the same Month.*

CHAPTER I.

General Ordinances.

1832.

Partnership is a contract by which two or more persons agree to put something in common, with a view to share the benefit which may result therefrom.

1833.

Every partnership must have a lawful object, and be contracted for the common interest of the parties.

Every partner must bring thereto either money or other property, or his skill.

1834.

Every partnership must be reduced to writing when the object is of a value exceeding one hundred and fifty francs.

Testimonial proof is not admitted against or beyond what is contained in the act of partnership, nor touching that which shall be alleged to have been said before, at the time, or subsequently to such act, although the question be of a sum or value less than one hundred and fifty francs.

CHAPTER II.

Of the different Species of Partnerships.

1835.

Partnerships are general or particular.

SECTION I.

Of general Partnerships.

1836.

Two sorts of general partnerships may be distinguished, a partnership of all present property, and a general partnership of profits.

1837.

A partnership of all present property is that by which the parties put in common all the property moveable or immoveable of which they are actually possessed, and the profits which they may draw therefrom.

They may also comprehend therein every other species of profits; but the property which may accrue to them by succession, donation, or legacy, does not enter into such partnership, except for enjoyment; every stipulation tending to make the ownership of such property form part thereof, is prohibited, saving between married persons, and conformably to what has been ordained respecting them.

1838.

A general partnership of profits includes all that the parties shall acquire by their industry, by whatsoever title it may be, during the course of the partnership; the moveables which each of the partners possesses at the time of the contract are also comprised therein; but their personal immoveables are included therein for enjoyment only.

1839.

The simple agreement of general partnership, made without any explanation, imports only a general partnership of profits.

1840.

No general partnership can take place but between persons respectively capable of mutually giving and receiving, and to whom it is not forbidden to derive advantage at the expense of other persons.

SECTION II.

Of particular Partnerships.

1841.

Particular partnership is that which applies only to certain determinate objects, or to their use, or to fruits to be reaped therefrom.

1842.

The contract by which several persons are associated, either for a proposed undertaking or for the exercise of some trade or profession, is also a particular partnership.

CHAPTER III.

Of the Engagements of Partners among themselves, and with regard to third Persons.

SECTION I.

Of the Engagements of Partners to each Other.

1843.

The partnership commences at the very instant of the contract, if it do not point out another period.

1844.

If there be no agreement concerning the duration of the partnership, it is taken to have been contracted for the whole life of the partners, subject to the modification contained in article 1869; or if an affair be in question of which the duration is limited, for the whole time which such affair continues.

1845.

Each partner is debtor to the partnership in all which he has promised to contribute thereto.

When such contribution consists of a certain property, and the partnership is evicted therefrom, the partner is surety therefore to the society, in the same manner as a vendor is to his purchaser.

1846.

The partner who was to contribute a sum to the partnership, and who has not done so, becomes, absolutely and without demand, debtor for the interest of such sum, computing from the day on which it ought to have been made.

It is the same with regard to sums which he has taken from the partnership chest, computing from the day on which he shall have drawn them for his private advantage;

The whole without prejudice to more ample damages if there be ground.

1847.

The partners who are bound to contribute their skill to the partnership, owe to it an account of all the profits which they have made by the species of industry which is the object of such partnership.

1848.

When one of the partners is, on his own private account, a creditor in a sum due towards a person who is found also to owe to the partnership a sum equally due, the deduction of what he receives from such debtor must be made from the credit of the partnership, and from his own in the proportion of the two credits, although he may in his acquittance have directed the entire deduction to be made from his private credit: but if he have expressed in his acquittance that the deduction shall be made entirely from the credit of the partnership, such stipulation shall be executed.

1849.

When one of the partners has received his entire share of a common debt, and the debtor has subsequently become insolvent, such partner is bound to contribute what he has received to the common stock, although he may have specially given acquittance *for his share.*

1850.

Each partner is bound towards the partnership for damages which he has caused it by his own fault, without being at liberty to balance against such damages the profits which his skill shall have procured to it in other affairs.

1851.

If things of which the enjoyment only has been given up to the partnership are certain and determinate objects, which do not consume by use, they are at the risk of the partner who is their proprietor.

If such things do consume, if they grow worse by keeping, if they have been destined to be sold, or if they have been given up to the partnership at a valuation contained in an inventory, they are at the risk of the partnership.

If the thing have been estimated, the partner can only recover the amount of his estimate.

1852.

A partner has an action against the partnership, not only on account of sums which he has disbursed for it, but also by reason of obligations which he has contracted bona fide in the affairs of the partnership, and for risks inseparable from the management of them.

1853.

When the act of partnership does not determine the share of each partner in the profits or losses, the share of each is in proportion to his contribution to the funds of the partnership.

With respect to him who contributes only his skill, his share in the benefit or in the losses is regulated as if his contribution had been equal to that of the partner who contributed the least.

1854.

If the partners have agreed to refer to one of themselves or to a third person for the regulation of the shares, such regulations cannot be impeached unless it be evidently contrary to equity.

No opposition is admitted on this subject, if more than three months have elapsed since the party who pretends to be injured has had knowledge of the regulation, or if such regulation have received on his part a commencement of execution.

1855.

An agreement which would give to one of the partners the whole of the profits is void.

The same rule holds with a stipulation which would set free from all contribution to losses, sums or effects added to the funds of the partnership by one or more of the partners.

1856.

The partner charged with the management by a special clause of the contract of partnership may, notwithstanding the opposition of the other partners, do all acts depending on his management, provided it be without fraud.

Such power cannot be revoked without lawful cause, so long as the partnership continues; but if it have been given only by an act subsequent to the contract of partnership, it is revocable like a simple authority.

1857.

Where several partners are charged with management without having determinate functions, or without its having been expressed that one cannot act without the other, they may each separately perform all acts of administration.

1858.

If it have been stipulated that one of the managers shall do nothing without the other, one cannot act alone, without a new agreement, in the absence of the other, even though the latter shall have been under an actual incapability of concurring in acts of management.

1859.

In default of special stipulations touching the mode of management, parties may observe the following rules.

1st. The partners are taken to have mutually given each other the power of managing one for another. What each does is alike valid for the share of his partners without his having obtained their consent; saving the right which the latter have, or one of them, to oppose the execution before it be concluded.

2d. Each partner may make use of things belonging to the partnership, provided he employ them for the use to which they were destined, and that he do not make use of them contrary to the interest of the partnership, or in such manner as to prevent his partners from making use of them according to their right.

3d. Each partner has a right to oblige his copartners to bear with him expenses necessary to the preservation of the property of the partnership.

4th. One of the partners cannot make alterations in immoveables depending on the partnership, even though he maintain them advantageous to such partnership, if the other partners do not consent thereto.

1860.

The partner who is not manager cannot alienate or encumber property, even moveable, which is dependent on the partnership.

1861.

Every partner may, without the consent of his copartners, connect himself with a third person in reference to his own share in the partnership: he cannot, without their consent, connect such person with the partnership, even though he have the management thereof.

SECTION II.

Of the Engagements of Partners with respect to third Persons.

1862.

In other partnerships than those for commercial purposes, the partners are not bound jointly and severally by partnership debts, and one of the partners cannot bind the others unless the latter have bestowed on him that power.

1863.

Partners are bound towards the creditor with whom they have contracted, each in an equal sum and share, although the share of one of them in the partnership should be less, if the act have not specially restricted the obligation of the latter to the footing of such last-mentioned share.

1864.

A covenant that the obligation is contracted on account of the society, binds only the partner contracting and not the others, unless the latter have given him authority, or unless the thing have turned to the benefit of the partnership.

CHAPTER IV.

Of the different Modes by which Partnership is put an end to.

1865.

Partnership is put an end to,

1st. By the expiration of the time for which it was contracted;

2d. By the destruction of the object, or the completion of the negotiation;

3d. By the natural death of one of the partners;

4th. By the civil death, interdiction, or embarrassment of one of them;

5th. By the desire expressed by one only or more of them no longer to continue in partnership.

1866.

The prolongation of a partnership for a limited time can only be proved by writing invested with the same formalities as the contract of partnership.

1867.

When one of the partners has promised to put in common the property in any thing, a loss occurring before the contribution thereof has been effectuated, operates a dissolution of the partnership with reference to all the partners.

The partnership is equally dissolved in all cases by the loss of the thing, when the enjoyment only has been put in common, and when the property thereof has continued in the hands of the partner.

But the partnership is not broken up by the loss of the thing of which the property has already been brought into partnership.

1868.

If it have been stipulated that in case of the death of one of the partners the partnership shall continue with his heir, or only between the surviving partners, such arrangements shall be followed : in the second case, the heir of the deceased has a right only to a distribution of the partnership, regard being had to the situation of such partnership at the time of the death, and he has no participation in any ulterior claims, except so far as they are a necessary consequence of what was done before the death of the partner whom he succeeds.

1869.

Dissolution of partnership by the desire of one of the parties applies only to partnerships of which the duration is unlimited, and is effected by a renunciation notified to all the partners, provided such renunciation be bona fide and not made at an unseasonable time.

1870.

The renunciation is not bona fide when the partner renounces in order to appropriate to himself alone a profit which the partners had proposed to draw in common.

It is made unseasonably when objects are no longer entire, and it imports the partnership that the dissolution should be deferred.

1871.

Dissolution of partnerships for a term cannot be demanded by one of the partners before the period agreed on, except so far as there shall be just grounds therefor, as when another partner fails in his engagements, or when habitual infirmity renders him inadequate to the business of the partnership, or other similar cases of which the lawfulness and importance are left to the determination of the judges.

1872.

The rules relating to the distribution of successions, the form of such distribution, and the obligations which resnlt therefrom between coheirs, are applicable to distributions between partners.

Disposition relative to Commercial Partnerships.

1873.

The dispositions of the present title only apply to commercial partnerships in the points which contain nothing contrary to the laws and usages of commerce.

TITLE X.

OF LOANS.

Decreed the 9*th of March,* 1804. *Promulgated the* 19*th of the same Month*

1874.

There are two kinds of loan:

That of things, which a party can use without destroying them;

And that of things, which are consumed by the use which is made thereof.

The first species is called *loan for use,* or *gratuitous lending;*

The second is termed *loan for consumption,* or simply *loan.*

CHAPTER I.

Of Loan for Use, or gratuitously.

SECTION I.

Of the Nature of Loan for Use.

1875.

Loan for use, or gratuitous lending, is a contract by which one of the parties gives up a thing to another in order to its employment, on condition by the borrower to restore it after having so employed it.

1876.

This loan is essentially gratuitous.

1877.

The lender remains proprietor of the thing lent.

1878.

Every thing which is of a commercial nature, and which does not consume by using, may be the object of this agreement.

1879.

Engagements which are formed by lending, pass to the heirs of him who lends, and also to the heirs of the borrower.

But if the party has lent only on account of the borrower, and to him personally, then his heirs cannot continue the enjoyment of the thing lent.

SECTION II.

Of the Engagements of the Borrower.

1880.

The borrower is bound to watch like a good father of a family over the security and preservation of the thing lent. He cannot make use of it except for the purpose determined by its nature, or by agreement, the whole on pain of damages, if there be ground.

1881.

If the borrower employ the thing for another use, or for a longer time than he ought, he shall be bound for any loss which happens even by accident.

65

1882.

If the thing lent perish by accident, against which the borrower would have been able to secure it, by employing his own property, or if, being able to preserve only one of the two, he prefer his own, he is bound for the loss of the other.

1883.

If the thing were estimated on lending it, the loss which happens, even by accident, falls upon the borrower, if there be no agreement to the contrary.

1884.

If the thing be deteriorated simply by the effect of the using for which it was borrowed, and without any fault on the part of the borrower, he is not bound for such deterioration.

1885.

The borrower cannot retain the thing by way of compensation for that which the lender owes him.

1886.

If, in order to use the thing, the borrower has been put to any expense, he cannot recover it.

1887.

If several persons have conjointly borrowed the same thing, they are jointly and severally responsible therefor to the lender.

SECTION III.

Of the Engagements of the Party who lends for Use.

1888.

The lender cannot withdraw the thing lent until after the term agreed on, or in default of agreement, until after it has been employed for the use for which it was borrowed.

1889.

Nevertheless, if during such interval, or before the necessity of the borrower has ceased, there occur to the lender a pressing and unlooked-for need of his property, the judge may, according to circumstances, compel the borrower to restore it to him.

1890.

If, during the continuance of the loan, the borrower has been compelled, for the preservation of the thing, to any expense, extraordinary, necessary, and to such a degree urgent, that he has not been able to advertise the lender thereof, the latter shall be bound to reimburse it to him.

1891.

When the thing lent has such defects that it may cause injury to the party who employs it, the lender is responsible, if he knew of such defects and did not inform the borrower thereof.

CHAPTER II.

Of Loan for Consumption, or simple Loan.

SECTION I.

Of the Nature of the Loan for Consumption.

1892.

The loan for consumption is a contract by which one of the parties delivers to the other a certain quantity of things which perish in using, on condition by the latter to return him so much of the same kind and goodness.

1893.

By the effect of such loan, the borrower becomes proprietor of the thing lent; and it is at his risk it perishes, in whatsoever manner such loss happens.

1894.

A party must not give, under title of loan for consumption, things which, though of the same species, differ individually, as animals: it is in that case a loan for use.

1895

The obligation which results from a loan in money, is always of that numerical sum only set forth in the contract.

If there have been an augmentation or diminution in the currency before the period of payment, the debtor must return the numerical sum lent, and is only bound to render such sum in the specie having currency at the time of payment.

1896.

The rule contained in the preceding article does not take place if the loan have been made in ingots.

1897.

If they were ingots or commodities which were lent, whatever be the augmentation or diminution of their price, the debtor must always restore the same quantity and quality, and need only restore that.

SECTION II.

Of the Obligations of the Lender.

1898.

In the loan for consumption, the lender is bound by the responsibility established by article 1891 for the loan for use.

1899.

The lender cannot demand again things lent, before the expiration of the term agreed on.

1900.

If a term for restitution have not been agreed on,

the judge may grant to the borrower a delay according to circumstances.

1901.

If it have been agreed only that the borrower shall pay when he can, or when he shall have means to do so, the judge shall fix a term of payment for him according to circumstances.

SECTION III.

Of the Engagements of the Borrower.

1902.

The borrower is bound to return the things lent in the same quantity and quality, and at the term agreed upon.

1903.

If he is under an impossibility of making satisfaction therein, he is bound to pay the value thereof, regard being had to the time and place at which the thing was to have been restored, according to the agreement.

If the time and place have not been regulated, the payment is made at the price of the time and place at which the borrowing took place.

1904.

If the borrower do not restore the things lent, or their value at the term agreed on, he owes interest thereon from the day of the demand in court.

CHAPTER III.

Of Loan on Interest.

1905.

It is lawful to stipulate for interest on simple loan either in money, or provisions, or other moveable things.

1906.

The borrower who has paid interest which was not stipulated, cannot either recover it or deduct it from the capital.

1907.

Interest is legal or conventional. Legal interest is that fixed by the law. Conventional interest may exceed that of the law in all cases where the law does not prohibit it.

The rate of conventional interest must be fixed in writing.

1908.

Acquittance of capital given without reservation of interest, raises presumption of the payment thereof, and operates as a discharge of it.

1909.

A party may agree on interest for capital which the lender binds himself not to demand.

In this case the loan takes the name of *annuity.*

1910.

Such annuity may be settled in two ways, in perpetuity or for life.

1911.

A perpetual annuity is essentially redeemable.

The parties can only agree that the redemption shall not be made within an interval not exceeding ten years, or without having advertised the grantee for the term before that they shall have determined.

1912.

The grantor of a perpetual annuity may be compelled to redemption,

1st. If he cease to fulfil his obligations during two years;

2d. If he fail in furnishing to the lender the securities promised by his contract.

1913.

The capital of a perpetual annuity becomes also demandable, in case of the bankruptcy or embarrassment of the grantor.

1914.

The rules concerning life annuities are established under the title "*Of aleatory Contracts.*"

TITLE XI.

OF DEPOSIT AND SEQUESTRATION.

Decreed the 14th of March, 1804. Promulgated the 24th of the same Month.

CHAPTER I.

Of Deposit in general and of its different Species.

1915.

Deposit in general is an act by which one party receives the property of another, on condition of keeping it safely, and restoring it in kind.

1916.

There are two descriptions of deposits: the deposit properly so called, and sequestration.

CHAPTER II.

Of Deposit properly so called.

SECTION I.

Of the Nature and Essence of the contract of Deposit.

1917.

Deposit properly so called is a contract essentially gratuitous.

1918.

It can only have for its object things moveable.

1919.

It is only perfected by the real or supposed delivery of the thing deposited.

Supposed delivery is sufficient when the depositary finds himself already possessed, by some other title, which the party consents to leave with him under the title of deposit.

1920.

Deposit is voluntary or necessary.

SECTION II.

Of voluntary Deposit.

1921.

Voluntary deposit is formed by the mutual consent of the person who makes the deposit, and of him who receives it.

1922.

Voluntary deposit cannot regularly be made except by the proprietor of the thing deposited, or with his consent express or implied.

1923.

Voluntary deposit must be proved by writing. Testimonial proof is not receivable for value exceeding one hundred and fifty francs.

1924.

When the deposit, being above one hundred and fifty francs, is not proved by writing, the party impleaded as depositary is believed thereon upon his declaration, either upon the fact itself of the deposit, or touching the thing which formed the object thereof, or upon the fact of its restitution.

1925.

Voluntary deposit can only take place between persons capable of contracting.

Nevertheless, if one person capable of contracting accepts a deposit from another incapable, he is bound by all the obligations of a bona fide depositary; he may be prosecuted by the guardian or administrator of the party who has made the deposit.

1926.

If a deposit have been made by one person capable with another who is not so, the person who has made the deposit has only his action for recovery of the thing deposited, so long as it remains in the hands of the depositary, or an action for restitution up to the amount of what has been the profit of the latter.

SECTION III.

Of the Obligations of the Depositary.

1927.

The depositary must employ on the custody of

the thing deposited the same care which he employs in the preservation of his own property.

1928.

The ordinance of the preceding article must be applied with more rigor:—1st, if the depositary has himself offered to receive the deposit; 2nd, if he has stipulated for wages for the custody of the deposit; 3d, if the deposit were made solely for the benefit of the depositary; 4th, if it has been expressly agreed that the depositary shall be responsible for every species of mischance.

1929.

The depositary is in no case bound for accidents proceeding from superior force, unless he has been guilty of delay in restoring the thing deposited.

1930.

He cannot make use of the thing deposited without the permission express or implied of the depositor.

1931.

He must not seek to know what articles have been deposited with him, if they were entrusted to him in a closed coffer or under a sealed cover.

1932.

The depositary must restore the thing identically the same as he received it.

Thus a deposit of sums coined must be restored

in the same currency as it was made, whether in case of augmentation, or in the case of diminution of value.

1933.

The depositary is only bound to restore the thing deposited in the state in which it is found at the moment of its restitution.

Deteriorations which have not occurred by his act, are at the charge of the depositor.

1934.

A depositary from whom the thing has been carried off by superior force, and who has received a price or some article in its place, must restore what he has obtained in exchange.

1935.

The heir of a depositary, who has sold bona fide the thing of whose deposit he was ignorant, is only bound to restore the price which he has received, or to cede his claim against the purchaser, if he has not obtained the price.

1936.

If the thing deposited have produced fruits which have been enjoyed by the depositary, he is obliged to restore them. He is not indebted in interest for money deposited, except from the day on which he was summoned to make restitution.

1937.

The depositary can only restore the thing deposited to the party who entrusted it to him, or to him in whose name the deposit was made, or to the party who has been appointed to receive it.

1938.

He cannot demand of the party who has made the deposit proof that he was the proprietor of the thing deposited.

Nevertheless, if he discover that the thing was stolen, and who was the veritable owner, he must announce to the latter the deposit which has been made with him, with a notice to claim it within a determinate and sufficient interval.

If the party to whom such announcement was made neglect to reclaim the deposit, the depositary is validly discharged by the delivery thereof which he makes to the party from whom he received it.

1939.

In case of the natural or civil death of the person who has made a deposit, the thing deposited can only be restored to his heir.

If there be several heirs, it must be restored to each of them as to his share and portion.

If the thing deposited is indivisible, the heirs must agree among themselves upon receiving it.

1940.

If the person who made the deposit has changed situation; for instance, if a woman, free at the moment at which the deposit was made, has been married subsequently and become subject to the authority of her husband; if one of full age at the time of the deposit has been put under restraint: in all these cases, and others of the same nature, the doposit can only be restored to the party who has the administration of the rights and property of the depositor.

1941.

If the deposit were made by a guardian, by a husband, or an administrator, in one of these characters, it can only be restored to the person whom such guardian, husband, or administrator represented, if their management or administration has closed.

1942.

If the contract of deposit points out the place in which the restitution is to be made, the depositary is bound to bring thither the deposit.

If there be expenses of conveyance, they are at the charge of the depositor.

1943.

If the contract do not point out the place of restitution, it must be made in the very place of the deposit.

1944.

The deposit must be returned to the depositor as soon as he claims it, even though the contract may have fixed a determinate interval for the restitution, unless there exist, in the hands of the depositor, an attachment or an opposition to the restitution and removal of the thing deposited.

1945.

An unfaithful depositary is not admitted to the benefit of cession.

1946.

All the obligations of the depositary cease, if he happens to discover and to prove that he is himself the proprietor of the thing deposited.

SECTION IV.

Of the Obligations of the Party by whom the Deposit was made.

1947.

The party who has made the deposit, is bound to reimburse to the depositary the expenses to which he has been put for the preservation of the thing deposited, and to indemnify him against all losses which the deposit may have occasioned him.

1948.

The depositary may retain the deposit until the complete settlement of what is due to him by reason of the deposit.

SECTION V.

Of necessary Deposit.

1949.

Necessary deposit is that which has been compelled by some accident; such as a fire, a ruin, pillage, shipwreck, or other unforeseen event.

1950.

Proof by witnesses may be received in regard to necessary deposit, even though question be of value exceeding one hundred and fifty francs.

1951.

Necessary deposit is moreover governed by all the rules previously set forth.

1952.

Keepers of inns and hotels are responsible, as depositaries, for property brought by the traveller who lodges in their house: the deposit of effects of this description must be regarded as a necessary deposit.

1953.

They are responsible for the stealing or damage of the property of the traveller, whether the robbery were committed or the damage were caused by the domestics and officers of the establishment, or by strangers going and coming within the inn.

1954.

They are not responsible for robberies committed with armed force, or any other superior force.

CHAPTER III.

Of Sequestration.

SECTION I.

Of the different Descriptions of Sequestration

1955.

Sequestration is either conventional or judicial.

SECTION II.

Of Conventional Sequestration.

1956.

Conventional sequestration is a deposit made by one or more persons of a thing in dispute, in the hands of a third person, who binds himself to restore it, after the litigation terminated, to the person to whom the right to obtain it shall be adjudged.

1957.

Sequestration cannot be gratuitous.

1958.

When it is gratuitous, it is subject to the rules of deposit properly so called, saving the distinctions hereafter declared.

1959.

Sequestration may have for its object, not only moveable effects, but even immoveables.

1960.

The depositary charged with sequestration, cannot be discharged, before the litigation terminated, except with the consent of all the parties interested, or for a cause adjudged lawful.

SECTION III.

Of Judicial Sequestration on Deposit.

1961.

The courts may order sequestration—

1st. Of moveables seized from a debtor;

2d. Of an immovable or of a moveable object of which the property or the possession is disputed between two or more persons;

3d. Of things which a debtor offers for his liberation.

1962.

The establishment of a judicial sequestration produces between the party whose goods are seized and him who is entrusted with them reciprocal obligations. The sequestrator must employ in the preservation of the effects seized the care of a good husbandman.

He must produce them, either in discharge of the party distraining for sale, or to the party against whom the execution was made, in case the distress is replevied.

The obligation of the party distraining consists in paying to the officer in possession the salary fixed by the law.

1963.

Judicial sequestration is given, either to a person on whom the parties interested have agreed among themselves, or to a person officially named by the judge.

In either case, the party to whom the thing has been entrusted, is subject to all the obligations which conventional sequestration imports.

TITLE XII.

OF ALEATORY CONTRACTS.

Decreed the 10*th of March*, 1804. *Promulgated the* 20*th of the same Month.*

1964.

An aleatory contract is a mutual agreement, of which the consequences, as regards advantages and losses, either for all the parties, or for one or more among them, depend on an uncertain event.

Such are

Contracts of assurance,

Loans on bottomry,

Play and betting,

Contracts for life annuities.

The two first are governed by maritime laws.

CHAPTER I.

Of Play and Betting.

1965.

The law does not allow an action for a debt at play or for the payment of a wager.

1966.

Games proper in the exercise of feats of arms, foot-races, horse or chariot-races, tennis and other sports of the same nature, which require address and agility of body, are excepted from the preceding ordinance.

Nevertheless the court may reject the demand, when the sum appears to it to be excessive.

1967.

In no case can the loser recover what he has voluntarily paid, unless there have been on the part of the winner foul play, fraud, or cheating.

CHAPTER II.

Of the Contract for Life Annuities.

SECTION I.

Of the Conditions requisite to the Validity of the Contract.

1968.

An annuity may be granted by chargeable title, for a sum of money, or for a moveable capable of being valued, or for an immoveable.

1969.

It may also be granted by gratuitous title purely, by donation during life, or by will. It must then be invested with the forms required by law.

1970.

In the case of the preceding article, the annuity is reducible, if it exceed that of which it is lawful to dispose: it is null if it is for the benefit of a person incapable of receiving it.

1971.

The annuity may be granted, either on the life of him who paid the price thereof, or upon the life of a third person who has no right to the enjoyment thereof.

1972.

It may be granted on one or more lives.

1973.

It may be granted for the benefit of a third person, although the price thereof be supplied by another person.

In the latter case, though it have the characteristics of a free gift, it is not subjected to the forms required for such donations; saving the cases of reduction and nullity set forth in article 1970.

1974.

Every contract for an annuity created on the life of a person who was dead at the time of the contract, is ineffectual.

1975.

It is the same with respect to the contract by which an annuity has been created on the life of a person attacked by a disorder of which he died within twenty days from the date of the contract.

1976.

The annuity may be granted at any rate on which it may please the contracting parties to fix.

SECTION II.

Of the Effects of the Contract between the contracting Parties.

1977.

The party for whose benefit the annuity has been granted for a price, may demand to have the contract rescinded, if the grantor do not give him the stipulated securities for its execution.

1978.

The single default in payment of the arrears of the annuity does not authorize the party in whose favor it was granted to demand the reimbursement of his capital, or to re-enter into the property aliened by him: he has only the right to seize and cause to be sold the goods of his debtor, and to cause him to order or consent, from the produce of the sale, the expending of a sum sufficient for the purposes of the arrears.

1979.

The grantor cannot disengage himself from the payment of the annuity by offering to reimburse the capital, and by renouncing his demand for the arrears paid; he is bound to satisfy the annuity during the whole life of the person or persons on whose lives the annuity has been granted, whatever be the duration of the lives of such persons, and however burthensome the payment of the annuity may become.

1980.

An annuity is only acquired to the proprietor in proportion to the number of days he has lived.

Nevertheless, if it were agreed that it should be paid in advance, the payment which ought to have been made, becomes due from the day on which the payment thereof ought to have been made.

1981.

The annuity cannot be stipulated as recoverable, except when it has been granted by gratuitous title.

1982.

The annuity is not extinguished by the civil death of the proprietor: the payment thereof must be continued during his natural life.

1983.

The proprietor of an annuity cannot demand the arrears thereof without proving his existence, or that of the person on whose life it has been granted.

TITLE XIII.

OF PROCURATION.

Decreed the 10*th of March,* 1804. *Promulgated the* 20*th of the same Month.*

CHAPTER I.

Of the Nature and Form of Procuration.

1984.

Procuration or commission is an act by which one person gives to another the power to do something for the constituent party, and in his name.

The contract is not binding without acceptance on the part of the agent.

1985.

The procuration may be given either by a public act, or by writing under private signature, even by letter. It may also be given verbally; but testimonial proof is only received thereon conformably to the title "*Of Contracts or Conventional Obligations in General.*"

The acceptance of procuration may be merely tacit, and result from the performance which has been given to it by the agent.

1986.

Procuration is gratuitous, if there be no contrary agreement.

1987.

It is either special and for one affair, or certain affairs only, or general and for all the affairs of the party giving it.

1988.

Procuration conceived in general terms embraces only acts of administration.

If the question be of alienating or mortgaging, or of some other act of ownership, the procuration must be express.

1989.

The agent can do nothing beyond what is contained in his commission : the power of transacting does not include that of compromising claims.

1990.

Women and minors emancipated may be chosen as agents ; but the principal has no action against his agent, a minor, except in conformity to the general rules relative to the obligations of minors, and against a married woman who has accepted a commission without the authority of her husband, only in conformity to the rules established under the title "*Of the Contract of Marriage, and of the respecting Rights of Married Persons.*"

CHAPTER II.

Of the Obligations of the Agent.

1991.

The agent is bound to accomplish the commission as far as he is charged therewith, and is answerable for the damages which may result from his non-performance.

He is in like manner bound to finish the thing begun, at the death of the principal, if there be hazard in the delay.

1992.

The agent is answerable not only for fraud, but also for mistakes which he commits in his management.

Nevertheless, the responsibility relative to mistakes is applied less rigorously to him whose commission is gratuitous than to him who receives a salary.

1993.

Every agent is bound to render an account of his conduct, and to make statement to his principal of all which he has received by virtue of his procuration, even though what he shall have received were not due to the principal.

1994.

The agent is answerable for the deputy employed by him in his management, 1st, when he has not received power to substitute any one for himself; 2d, when such power was conferred upon him without designation of a person, and when such person of whom he has made selection was notoriously incompetent or insolvent.

In all these cases, the principal may act directly against the person whom the agent has deputed.

1995.

When there are several attorneys or agents established by the same act, the obligation of each is only joint and several so far as it is expressed.

1996.

The agent is indebted in interest on sums which he has employed for his own use, dating from such employment; and on such in which he is debtor on the balance, computing from the day on which the balance became against him.

1997.

The agent who has given to the party with whom he contracts in this character, a sufficient knowledge of his powers, he is not bound by any warranty, for what has been done beyond them; unless he has personally subjected himself thereto.

CHAPTER III.

Of the Obligations of the Principal.

1998.

The principal is bound to execute engagements contracted by the agent, conformably to the power which has been given him.

He is not bound for what may have been done beyond them, except so far as he has expressly or tacitly ratified it.

1999.

The principal must reimburse to the agent advances and expenses which the latter has made in execution of the commission, and pay him his salary wherever a promise thereof has been made him.

If there be no fault imputable to the agent, the principal cannot relieve himself from making such reimbursement and payment, even though the affair shall not have succeeded, nor make reduction of such charges and advances under pretext that they might have been less.

2000.

The principal must also indemnify the agent against losses which the latter has sustained by reason of his management, where no imprudence is imputable to him.

2001.

Interest is claimable from the principal on advances made by the agent, computing from the day of verifying such advances.

2002.

Where an agent has been appointed by several persons for a joint business, each of them is bound jointly and severally towards him as to all effects of the commission.

CHAPTER IV.

Of the different Manners in which Commission is terminated.

2003.

Commission is put an end to,

By the revocation of the agent;

By the renunciation of the commission by the latter;

By the natural or civil death, the interdiction or embarrassment, either of the principal or of the agent.

2004.

The principal may recall his procuration whenever he thinks proper, and compel, if there be ground, the agent to remit to him, either the writing under private signature which contains it, or the original of the procuration, if it were delivered by public act, or a copy if he have kept a minute thereof.

2005.

Revocation notified to the agent alone, cannot be opposed to third persons, who have treated in ignorance of such revocation, saving to the principal his remedy against the agent.

2006.

The appointment of a new agent for the same business, is equivalent to a revocation of the first, computing from the day on which it has been notified to the latter.

2007.

The agent may renounce the commission, by notifying his renunciation to the principal.

Nevertheless, if such renunciation prejudice the principal, he must be indemnified therefor by the agent, unless the latter can prove himself under an utter incapacity of continuing the commission without thereby encountering considerable prejudice himself.

2008.

If the agent be ignorant of the death of his principal, or of any of the causes which put an end to the commission, what he has done in such ignorance is valid.

2009.

In the cases above, the bona fide engagements of the agent with third persons are to be executed.

2010.

In case of the death of the agent, his heirs must give advice thereof to his principal, and provide in the mean time according to circumstances for the interest of the latter.

TITLE XIV.

OF SECURITY.

Decreed the 14th February, 1804. Promulgated the 24th of the same Month.

CHAPTER I.

Of the Nature and Extent of Security.

2011.

He who becomes security for an obligation, subjects himself to the satisfaction of such obligation in respect of the creditor, if the debtor fails to satisfy it himself.

2012.

Security can only exist in a valid obligation. A party may, nevertheless, guarantee an obligation, although it may be annulled by an exception purely personal to the party bound, for example, in the case of minority.

2013.

The security must not exceed what is due from the debtor, nor be contracted under conditions more burthensome.

It may be contracted for a part of a debt only, and under conditions less burthensome.

The security which exceeds the debt, or which is contracted under conditions more burthensome, is not void: it is only reducible in proportion to the principal obligation.

2014.

A person may become security without the direction of the party for whom he binds himself, and even without his knowledge.

A person may also become security, not only for the principal debtor, but also for the party who has secured him.

2015.

Security cannot be presumed; it must be express, and the party cannot extend it beyond the limits within which it has been contracted.

2016.

The indefinite security of a principal obligation extends to all the appendages of the debt, even to the costs of the first demand, and to all those posterior to the declaration which is made thereof to the surety.

2017.

The engagements of sureties pass to their heirs, with the exception of personal arrest, if the engagement were such that the surety was compelled thereto.

2018.

A debtor compelled to furnish a security must produce one who has the capacity to contract, who has property sufficient to answer for the object of the obligation, and whose domicil is within the jurisdiction of the court of appeal where it is to be given.

2019.

The solvency of a surety is only estimated by having regard to his landed property, excepting in a commercial transaction, or where the debt is moderate.

No attention is paid to immoveables disputed, or respecting which inquiry would become too difficult by the distance of their situation.

2020.

When the surety accepted by a creditor, voluntarily or by act of law, afterwards becomes insolvent, another must be given him.

This rnle admits of exception in the case only where the security has merely been given by virtue of an agreement by which the creditor required one particular person as security.

CHAPTER II.

Of the Effect of Security.

SECTION I.

Of the Effect of Security between the Creditor and the Surety.

2021.

The surety is only bound towards the creditor to pay him on the debtor's default, whose property must previously be seised, unless the surety have renounced the benefit of such seisure, or unless he be bound jointly and severally with the debtor; in which case his engagement is regulated by the principles which have been established for joint and several debts.

2022.

The creditor is not obliged to seise the property

of the principal debtor, except when the surety requires it, on the first proceedings commenced against him.

2023.

The surety who requires the seisure must point out to the creditor the property of the principal debtor, and advance money sufficient to make such seisure.

He must not point out either property of the principal debtor, situated beyond the jurisdiction of the court of appeal of the place where the payment is to be made, or property in dispute, nor that pledged for a debt, and which is no longer in the possession of the debtor.

2024.

In all cases where the surety has pointed out property, as authorized by the preceding article, and has furnished a sufficient sum for the seisure and sale, the creditor is, up to the amount of the property pointed out, responsible, as regards the surety, for the insolvency of the principal debtor occurring through his neglect to proceed.

2025.

Where several persons have become sureties for the same debtor and the same debt, they are bound each for the whole of the debt.

2026.

Nevertheless, each of them may, unless he have

renounced the benefit of division, require that the creditor should previously divide his demand, and reduce it to the share and portion of each surety.

When, within the time at which one of the sureties has caused division to be pronounced, some have become insolvent, such surety is bound in his proportion for such insolvencies; but he can no longer be required on account of insolvencies occurring subsequently to the division.

2027.

If the creditor have voluntarily and of himself divided his action, he cannot contravene such division, although there were, even anterior to the time at which he consented to it, insolvent sureties.

SECTION II.

Of the Effect of Security between Debtor and Surety.

2028.

The surety who has made payment, has his remedy against the principal debtor, whether the security were given with or without the knowledge of the debtor.

This remedy takes place as well with regard to principal as to interest and expenses; nevertheless the surety has no remedy except for the expenses made by him after he has given notice to the principal debtor of the proceedings directed against himself.

He has also his remedy for damages, if there be ground.

2029.

The surety who has paid the debt, is invested with all the rights which the creditor had against the debtor.

2030.

Where there were many joint and several principal debtors for one and the same debt, the surety who has guaranteed them all has, against each of them, his remedy for the recovery of the whole of what he has paid.

2031.

The surety who has paid a first time has no remedy against the principal debtor who has paid a second time, when he has not advertised him of the payment which he has so made; saving his action for recovery against the creditor.

When the surety shall have paid without being proceeded against, and without having given notice to the principal debtor thereof, he shall not have a remedy against his debtor in the case where, at the moment of payment, such debtor shall have had means of making declaration of the extinction of his debt; saving his action for recovery against the creditor.

2032.

The surety, even before having paid, may implead his debtor in order to be indemnified by him,

1st. When he is proceeded against at law for the payment;

2d. When the debtor has become bankrupt, or is in embarrassment;

3d. When the debtor is obliged to send him his discharge within a certain time;

4th. When the debt is become due by the lapse of the term subject to which it was contracted;

5th. At the end of ten years, where the principal obligation has no fixed term of lapse; unless the principal obligation, such as a guardianship, should not be of a nature capable of being extinguished before a determinate period.

SECTION III.

Of the Effect of Security between Co-Sureties.

2033.

Where several persons have become security for the same person and for the same debt, the surety who has acquitted the debt, has his remedy against the other sureties, each for his share and portion;

But this remedy does not take place when the surety has paid in one of the cases set forth in the preceding article.

CHAPTER III.

Of the Extinction of Security.

2034.

The obligation which results from security, is extinguished by the same causes as other obligations.

2035.

The blending of interests which is effected in the person of the principal debtor and his surety, when they become heirs of each other, does not extinguish the action of the creditor against the party who has become security for the surety.

2036.

The surety may oppose to the creditor all the objections which appertain to the principal debtor, and which are inherent to the debt:

But he cannot oppose objections which are purely personal to the debtor.

2037.

The surety is discharged, when substitution into the rights, mortgages, and privileges of the creditor, can, in consequence of the act of such creditor, no longer operate in favor of the surety.

2038.

The voluntary acceptance which the creditor has made of an immoveable or of any effect whatsoever in payment of the principal debt, discharges the surety, although the creditor should hereafter be evicted therefrom.

2039.

The simple prolongation of the term allowed by the creditor to the principal debtor, does not discharge the surety, who may, in such case, sue the debtor in order to compel payment.

CHAPTER IV.

Of legal and judicial Security.

2040.

In all cases where a person is obliged, by the law or by a sentence, to provide a surety, the surety offered must fulfil the conditions prescribed by articles 2018 and 2019.

When jndicial security is in question, the surety must moreover be liable to personal arrest.

2041.

He who cannot find a surety is permitted to give in his place a sufficient pledge as security.

2042.

The judicial surety cannot demand seisure and sale of the goods of the principal debtor.

2043.

He who has simply become security for the judicial surety, cannot demand seisure and sale of the goods of the principal debtor and of the surety.

TITLE XV.

OF THE COMPOUNDING OF ACTIONS.

Decreed 15*th of March*, 1804. *Promulgated the* 25*th of the same Month.*

2044.

Compounding is a contract by which the parties terminate a litigation begun, or prevent a litigation about to commence.

This contract must be reduced to writing.

2045.

In order to compound, it is necessary to have the capacity of disposing of the objects comprised in the composition.

The guardian can only settle for the minor or interdicted person conformably to article 467, under the title "*Of Minority, Guardianship, and Emancipation;*" and he can only settle with the minor on his arriving at full age, on the accounts of his guardianship, conformably to article 472, in the same title.

The communes and public establishments cannot compound without the express authority of government.

2046.

A party may compound for the civil claims resulting from a wrong.

Such composition does not prevent the prosecution of the public ministry.

70

2047.

A party may add to his composition a stipulation for a penalty against him who shall fail to execute it.

2048.

Compositions are bounded by their object: the renunciation which is therein made of all claims, actions, and pretensions, imports only what relates to the dispute which has given rise to it.

2049.

Compositions only regulate the disputes which are therein comprised, whether the parties have manifested their intention by special or general expressions, or whether such intention can be understood as a necessary consequence of what is expressed.

2050.

If the party having compounded for a claim which he had in his own right, becomes afterwards possessed of a similar claim in right of another person, he is not bound by the anterior composition so far as regards the claim acquired.

2051.

Composition made by one of the interested parties does not bind others interested, and cannot be objected by them.

2052.

Compositions have, between the parties, the authority of a matter decided in the last resort.

They cannot be impeached on the ground of error in law, or on the ground of injury.

2053.

Nevertheless, a composition may be rescinded where there is mistake in the person, or in the object of the litigation.

It may be so in all cases where there is fraud or violence.

2054.

There is equal foundation for an action of annulment against a composition, when it was made in execution of a void title, unless the parties have expressly treated respecting such nullity.

2055.

Composition made upon documents which have subsequently been discovered to be false, is entirely null.

2056.

Composition on the ground of a suit terminated by a judgment given with the authority of a matter decided, of which the parties or one of them had no knowledge, is void.

If the judgment of which the parties had no knowledge were subject to appeal, the composition shall be valid.

2057.

Where parties have compounded generally upon all matters which they may have between them, documents which were then unknown to them, and which may have been subsequently discovered, are not a ground of rescission, unless they have been kept back by the act of one of the parties;

But the composition shall be null if it only relate to an object respecting which it shall be made manifest by documents subsequently discovered, that one of the parties had no claim.

2058.

Error in calculation in a composition must be rectified.

TITLE XVI.

OF PERSONAL ARREST IN A CIVIL MATTER.

Decreed 13th of February, 1804. Promulgated the 23d of the same Month.

2059.

Personal arrest takes place, in a civil matter, for *stellionate.*

Stellionate is,

Where a person sells or mortgages an immoveable, of which he knows himself not to be the owner;

Where a party offers as unencumbered, property mortgaged, or where he declares the mortgages as less than those with which such properties are actually charged.

2060.

Personal arrest takes place in like manner—

1st. For necessary deposit;

2d. In case of restitution, for abandonment of inheritance, ordered by the court, of an estate whereof the proprietor has been despoiled by force, for the recovery of the profits which have been received during the unlawful possession, and for the payment of damages adjudged to the proprietor;

3d. For the recovery of money entrusted to the hands of public persons appointed for that purpose;

4th. For the production of things deposited with sequestrators, commissaries, and other bailees;

5th. Against judicial sureties and against the sureties of persons liable to arrest, when they have been subjected to such arrest;

6th. Against all public officers for the production of their minutes, when it has been ordered;

7th. Against notaries, attornies, and officers, for the restoration of documents entrusted to them, and of money received by them for their clients, in the course of their duties.

2061.

Those who by a judgment given on petition, and passed with the authority of a matter decided, have been sentenced to quit an estate, and who refuse to obey, may by a second judgment be personally arrested, fifteen days after notice of the first judgment personally given or at the party's domicil.

If the estate or the inheritance be distant more than five myriameters from the domicil of the party sentenced, there shall be added to the fifteen days one day for five myriameters.

2062.

Personal arrest cannot be directed against farmers for the arrears of the rent of rural property, if it have not been formally stipulated in the act of lease.

Nevertheless, farmers and under-tenants may be personally arrested, on failure by them to produce, at the end of the lease, the beasts in *cheptel,* seeds, and agricultural instruments, which were entrusted to them, unless they can prove that the deficiency in such articles does not proceed from their act.

2063.

With the exception of the cases determined by the preceding articles, or which may be so hereafter by a formal law, it is forbidden to all judges to pronounce personal arrest, to all notaries and registrars to take acts in which it shall be stipulated, and to all Frenchmen to consent to such acts, although they should have been passed in a foreign country; the whole on pain of nullity, costs, and damages.

2064.

Even in the cases above set forth, personal arrest cannot be pronounced against minors.

2065.

It cannot be pronounced for a sum less than three hundred francs.

2066.

It cannot be pronounced against persons of seventy

years of age, against women and girls, except in case of *stellionate.*

It is sufficient that the seventieth year have begun in order to enjoy the indulgence granted to persons of seventy years.

Personal arrest on account of *stellionate* during marriage, does not take place except against women who have separate property, or when they have property of which they have reserved the free administration, and by reason of engagements which relate to such property.

Women, who having community shall have contracted obligations jointly and severally with their husbands, shall not on account of such contracts be reputed guilty of *stellionate.*

2067.

Personal arrest, even in cases authorized by law, cannot be put in force except by virtue of a judgment.

2068.

Appeal does not suspend the arrest pronounced by a judgment provisionally executory on giving security.

2069.

Exercise of personal arrest does not prevent or suspend prosecutions and executions against the goods.

2070.

No infringement is made of the particular laws which authorize personal arrest in matters of commerce, nor of the laws of correctional police, nor of those which relate to the administration of the public money.

TITLE XVII.

OF PLEDGING.

Decreed March 16*th*, 1804. *Promulgated* 26*th of the same month.*

2071.

Pledging is a contract by which a debtor places a thing in the hands of the creditor as security for his debt.

2072.

The pledging of a moveable is called pawning.

That of an immoveable is called antichresis.

CHAPTER I.

Of Pawning.

2073.

Pawning confers upon the creditor the right of paying himself out of the thing which is the object thereof, in preference to all other creditors.

2074.

This privilege only takes place where there is a public act or one under private signature, duly enrolled, containing a declaration of the sum due, as well as the description and nature of the things put in pledge, or a statement annexed of their quality, weight, and measure.

The reduction of the act to writing and its enrolment are nevertheless only prescribed in a matter exceeding the value of one hundred and fifty francs.

2075.

The privilege set forth in the preceding article is only established over moveables incorporeal, such as personal credits, by an act public or under private signature, also enrolled, and notified to the debtor of the credit assigned in pledge.

2076.

In all cases the privilege only subsists over the pledge were such pledge has been placed and has continued in the possession of the creditor, or of a third person agreed on between the parties.

2077.

The pledge may be given by a third person for the debtor.

2078.

The creditor cannot in default of payment dispose of the pledge ; saving to him the power of procuring an order of the court that such pledge shall continue with him in payment, and up to its due amount according to an estimate made by competent persons, or that it shall be sold by auction.

Every clause which shall authorize the creditor to

appropriate the pledge to himself, or to dispose thereof without the above-mentioned formalities, is void.

2079.

Until the deprivation of the debtor, if there be ground for it, he continues proprietor of the pledge, which is in the hands of the creditor, a deposit merely for the assurance of the preferable claim of the latter.

2080.

The creditor is answerable, according to the rules established under the title "*Of Conventional Obligations in General*," for the loss or deterioration of the pledge occurring through his negligence.

On the other hand, the debtor must settle with the creditor the useful and necessary expenses which the latter has been put to for the preservation of the pledge.

2081.

If a credit assigned in pledge be in question, and such credit carry interest, the creditor must deduct such interest from that which is due to himself.

If the debt for the security of which the credit has been assigned in pledge, does not itself carry interest, the deduction is made from the capital of the debt.

2082.

The debtor cannot claim the restitution of the pledge, unless the holder thereof abuse it, until he has made entire payment, as well in principal as interest and expenses, of the debt for the security of which the pledge was given.

If there exist on the part of the same debtor towards the same creditor another debt contracted subsequently to the handing over of the pledge, and which has become due before the payment of the first debt, the creditor shall not be liable to be disseized of his pledge before being entirely paid both debts, even though there should not have been any stipulation to bind the pledge for the payment of the second.

2083.

The pledge is indivisible notwithstanding the divisibility of the debt among the heirs of the debtor or those of the creditor.

The heir of the debtor who has paid his portion of the debt, cannot demand restitution of his portion of the pledge, so long as the debt is not entirely satisfied.

On the other hand, the heir of the creditor who has received his portion of the debt cannot return the pledge to the prejudice of those of his co-heirs who are not paid.

2084.

The dispositions above-mentioned are not applicable to subjects of commerce, nor to houses authorized to lend on pledge, and with regard to which the laws and regulations relative to them are to be followed.

CHAPTER II.

Of Antichresis.

2085.

Antichresis can only be established in writing.

The creditor only acquires by this contract the power of enjoying the fruits of the immoveable, on condition of deducting them annually from the interest, if any be due to him, and afterwards from the capital of his credit.

2086.

The creditor is bound, if it be not otherwise agreed thereon, to pay the contributions and annual charges of the immoveable which he holds in antichresis.

He must in like manner, under pain of damages, provide for the maintenance and useful and necessary reparations of the immoveable; saving a previous deduction from these fruits of all the expenses relative to these different objects.

2087.

The debtor cannot, before the entire acquittance of the debt, claim the enjoyment of the immoveable which he has placed in antichresis.

But the creditor who is desirous of discharging himself from the obligations expressed in the preceding article, may always, unless he have renounced such right, compel the debtor to resume the enjoyment of his immoveable.

2088.

The creditor does not become proprietor of the immoveable simply by default in payment at the term agreed on: every contrary clause is null: in such case, he may sue for the deprivation of his debtor by legal means.

2089.

Where the parties have stipulated that the fruits shall be balanced against the interest, either entirely or up to a certain amount, such agreement may be executed like every other which is not prohibited by the laws.

2090.

The dispositions of articles 2077 and 2083 are applicable as well to antichresis as to pawning.

2091.

Nothing which is decreed in the present chapter, can prejudice the rights which third persons may have over the immoveables placed in *antichresis.*

If the creditor, invested with such title, has moreover over the estate privileges and mortgages legally established and reserved, he may exercise them in their order, and in the same manner as every other creditor.

TITLE XVIII.

OF PRIVILEGES AND MORTGAGES.

Decreed the 19th March, 1804. Promulgated the 29th of the same Month.

CHAPTER I.

General Enactments.

2092.

Whosoever binds himself personally, is required to fulfil his engagement out of all his property moveable and immoveable, present and future.

2093.

The goods of the debtor are the common pledge of his creditors; and the value thereof is equally distributable among them, unless there exist among the creditors lawful causes of preference.

2094.

The lawful causes of preference are privileges and mortgages.

CHAPTER II.

Of Privileges.

2095.

Privilege is a right which the quality of his credit confers upon a creditor of being preferred to the others, though mortgage-creditors.

2096.

Between privileged creditors, the preference is regulated by the different qualities of the privileges.

2097.

Privileged creditors, who are in the same rank, are paid rateably.

2098.

Privilege arising from the claims of the public exchequer and the order in which it is exercised, are governed by the laws relating thereto.

Nevertheless the exchequer cannot obtain privilege to the prejudice of rights previously acquired by third persons.

2099.

Privileges may exist either over moveables or immoveables.

SECTION I.

Of Privileges over Moveables.

2100.

Privileges are either general, or peculiar to certain moveables.

§ I. Of general Privileges over Moveables.

2101.

Privileged creditors over moveables in general are those hereafter expressed, and are exercised in the following order:

1st. Law expenses;

2d. Funeral expenses;

3d. Expenses of whatever kind of the last sickness, concurrently among those to whom they are due;

4th. The salaries of persons in service, for the year elapsed, and what is due for the current year;

5th. Supplies afforded for the subsistence of the debtor and his family: that is to say, during the last six months, by retail shopkeepers, such as bakers, butchers, and others; and during the last year, by masters of boarding houses and wholesale dealers.

§ II. Of Privileges over certain Moveables.

2102.

Privileged credits over certain moveables are,

1st. The hire and rents of immoveables, on the fruits of the year's harvest, and on the value of all the stock and furniture of the house and farm, and of all that which serves to the cultivation of the farm; that is to say, to the amount of all which has accrued, or which may hereafter accrue, if the leases are authentic, or if, being under private signature, they have a certain date; and in both cases the other creditors have a right to under-let the house or farm for the remainder of the lease, and to make profit for themselves of the leases and rents, on condition however of paying to the proprietor all which shall still be due to him;

And in default of authentic leases, or when being under private signature they have not a certain date, for a year commencing from the expiration of the current year;

The same privilege takes place with regard to tenant's repairs, and with regard to all which relates to the execution of the lease;

Nevertheless, sums due for seed-corn or for the expenses of the harvest of the year, are paid from the value of the harvest, and those due for implements, from the value of the implements, with a preference to the proprietor in both cases;

The proprietor may seize the moveables which furnish his house or stock his farm when they have been removed without his consent, and he retains his privilege over them, provided he have laid claim to them; that is to say, in the case of moveables, stocking a farm, within an interval of forty days; and within one of fifteen, in the case of moveables furnishing a house;

2d. The credit upon a pledge of which the creditor has got possession;

3d. The expenses incurred by the preservation of the article;

4th. The price of moveable effects not paid for, if they are still in the possession of the debtor, whether he have purchased them for a term or not;

If the sale were made without a term, the seller may himself claim such effects as long as they are in the possession of the buyer, and prevent a resale thereof, provided the claim be made within eight days from the delivery, and that the effects are found in the same state in which such delivery was made;

The privilege of the seller is not exercised, however, until after that of the proprietor of the house or of the farm, unless it be proved that the proprietor had knowledge that the moveables and other objects furnishing his house or stocking his farm, did not belong to the occupier;

No innovation made upon the laws and usages of commerce with regard to claim;

5th. That which is furnished by an innkeeper, on the effects of the traveller which have been brought into his inn;

6th. Charges of carriage and additional expenses, on the thing conveyed;

7th. Credits resulting from want of integrity, and mistakes committed by public functionaries in the exercise of their functions, on the funds deposited as security, and on the interest which may be due thereon.

SECTION II.

Of Privileges over Immoveables.

2103.

Creditors having privileges over immoveables are,

1st. The seller, over the immoveables sold, for the payment of its price;

If there be several successive sales, of which the price is due in whole or in part, the first seller is preferred to the second, the second to the third, and so in order;

2d. Those who have supplied money for the acquisition of an immoveable, provided it be authentically verified, by the act of loan, that the sum was designed for such use, and by the acquittance of the seller, that such payment was made with money borrowed:

3d. Coheirs, over the immoveables of the succession, for the warranty of the distributions made among them, and for the surplus and balance of the lots;

4th. Architects, contractors, masons, and others employed in building, rebuilding, or repairing houses, canals, or any other works whatsoever, provided nevertheless that an estimate have been previously drawn up by a competent person officially nominated by the court of first instance within whose jurisdiction such buildings are situated, for the purpose of verifying the state of the places in relation to the works which the proprietor shall declare he has an intention to form, and that such works have been, within six months from their completion, admitted by a competent person likewise nominated officially;

But the amount of the privilege must not exceed the value set forth by the second statement, and it is reduced to the surplus value existing at the period of the alienation of the immoveable, and resulting from the works which have been done therein.

5th. Those who have lent money to pay or reimburse workmen enjoy the same privilege, provided such employment be authentically verified by the act of loan, and by the acquittance of the workmen, in the same manner as has been mentioned above with respect to those who have lent money for the acquisition of an immoveable.

SECTION III.

Of Privileges which extend over Moveables as well as Immoveables.

2104.

Privileges which extend over moveables and immoveables are those enumerated in article 2101.

2105.

When in default of moveables the privileges enumerated in the preceding article are presented for payment from the price of an immoveable in concurrence with creditors having privilege over an immoveable, the payments are made in manner following:

1st. The law expenses and others enumerated in article 2101;

2d. Credits pointed out in article 2103.

SECTION IV.

Of the Manner in which Privileges are preserved.

2106.

Among creditors, privileges produce no effect with regard to immoveables, except so far as they are made public by enrolment on the registers of the keeper of the mortgages, in the manner regulated by the law, and computing from the date of such enrolment, subject to those exceptions only which follow.

2107.

The credits enumerated in article 2101 are exempted from the formality of enrolment.

2108.

The seller having privilege preserves such privilege by the transcription of the title which has passed the property to the purchaser, and which verifies that the whole or part of the price is due to him: in consequence of which, the transcription of the contract made by the purchaser shall be equivalent to inscription on the part of the seller, and on that of the lender who shall have supplied the money paid, and who shall be substituted into the rights of the seller, by the same contract: the keeper of the mortgages shall nevertheless be bound, under pain of all damages towards third persons, to cause an official insertion on his register, of credits resulting from the act conveying the property, as well in favor of the seller as in favor of the lenders, who may also cause to be made, if it have not been already done, a transcription of the contract of sale, for the purpose of acquiring the enrolment of what is due to them from the price.

2109.

The coheir or the coparcener retains his privilege over the property of each lot or over the property put up to auction, for the surplus and balance of the lots, or for the price of the auction, by enrolment made at his instance, within sixty days, to be dated from the act of partition or of purchase by auction; during which time no mortgage can take place respecting the property charged with such balance or adjudged by auction, to the prejudice of the creditor of the balance or of the price.

2110.

Architects, contractors, masons, and other workmen employed in building, rebuilding, or repairing edifices, canals, or other works, and those who, in order to pay and reimburse them, have lent money, of which the employment has been verified, retain, by the double enrolment made 1st of the statement which verifies the condition of the premises ; 2d of the statement of allowance, their privilege at the date of the enrolment of the first statement.

2111.

The creditors and legatees who demand a separation of the patrimony of the defunct, conformably to article 878, under the title "*Of Successions*," retain, with regard to the creditors of the heirs or representatives of the defunct, their privilege over the immoveables of the succession, by the enrolments made respecting each of such goods, within six months, to be computed from the opening of the succession.

Before the expiration of this interval, no mortgage can effectually be established over such property by the heirs and representatives, to the prejudice of those creditors or legatees.

2112.

The assignees of these different privileged credits may all exercise the same rights as the parties making cession, in their place and stead.

2113.

All privileged credits subjected to the formality of enrolment, in regard to which the conditions above prescribed for retaining privilege have not been complied with, nevertheless do not cease to be hypothecary; but the mortgage takes date with respect to third persons, only from the period of the enrolments which ought to have been made, as shall be hereafter explained.

CHAPTER III.

Of Mortgages.

2114.

Mortgage is a real right over immoveables charged with the acquittance of an obligation.

It is in its nature indivisible, and subsists in entirety over all the immoveables affected by it, over each and over every portion of such immoveables.

It pursues them into whatever hands they may pass.

2115.

Mortgage takes place only in the cases and according to the forms authorized by law.

2116.

It is either legal, or judicial, or conventional.

2117.

Legal mortgage is that resulting from the law.

Judicial mortgage is the result of judgments or judicial acts.

Conventional mortgage is that which depends on covenants, and on the external form of acts and contracts.

2118.

The following only are susceptible of mortgage:

1st. Immoveable goods which relate to commerce, and their appendages reputed immoveable;

2d. The usufruct of the same goods and appendages during the time of its continuance.

2119.

Moveables have no liability to mortgage.

2120.

No innovation is made by the present code upon the regulations of the maritime laws concerning ships and other vessels.

SECTION I.

Of legal Mortgages.

2121.

The rights and credits to which legal mortgage is applicable, are,

Those of married women, upon the goods of their husbands;

Those of minors and interdicted persons, upon the goods of their guardians;

Those of the nation, of communes, and public establishments, upon the property of receivers, and accountable administrators.

2122.

The creditor, who has a legal mortgage, may exercise his right over all the immoveables belonging to his debtor, and over those which may belong to him hereafter, under the modifications which shall be hereafter expressed.

SECTION II.

Of judicial Mortgages.

2123.

The judicial mortgage is the result of judgments, either upon a hearing, or by default, final or provisional, in favor of the party who has obtained them. It is the result of acknowledgments or verifications made in the judgment, of signatures affixed to an obligatory act under private signature.

It may be exercised over the existing immoveables of the debtor, and over those which he may acquire, saving also the modifications which shall be hereafter expressed.

Judgments on arbitration do not import mortgage, except so far as they are invested with a judicial order for their execution.

Mortgage in like manner is the result of judgments given in a foreign country, only so far as they have been declared executory by a French court; without prejudice to contrary regulations in political laws, or in treaties.

SECTION III.

Of conventional Mortgages.

2124.

Those only are permitted to assent to conventional mortgages who have the capacity of alienating the immoveables which they subject thereto.

2125.

Those who only possess over an immoveable a right suspended by a condition, or voidable in certain cases, or subject to annulment, can only consent to a mortgage subject to the same conditions, or to the same annulment.

2126.

The property of minors, of interdicted persons, and that of absentees, so long as the possession thereof is only provisionally conferred, cannot be pledged except for the causes and in the forms established by the law, or by virtue of judgments.

2127.

Conventional mortgage can only be consented to by an act passed in authentic form before two notaries, or before one notary and two witnesses.

2128.

Contracts made in a foreign country cannot give

a mortgage upon property in France, unless there be stipulations contrary to this principle in the political laws, or in treaties.

2129.

No conventional mortgage is valid, except that which, either in the authentic document constituting the credit, or in a subsequent authentic act, declares specially the nature and situation of each of the immoveables actually belonging to the debtor, over which he grants the mortgage of the credit. Every article of his present personal property may be by name subjected to mortgage.

Future property cannot be mortgaged.

2130.

Nevertheless, if the present and unencumbered goods of the debtor are insufficient for the security of the debt, he may, on expressing such insufficiency, consent that the whole of the property which he may hereafter acquire, shall continue charged as soon as acquired.

2131.

In like manner, in case the present immoveable or immoveables, subjected to mortgage, have perished, or sustained deterioration, in such manner that they have become insufficient for the security of the creditor, the latter shall be permitted either to sue immediately for repayment, or to obtain an additional mortgage.

2132.

Conventional mortgage is not valid except so far as the sum for which it is granted is certain and determined by the act: if the credit resulting from the obligation is conditional as to its existence, or indeterminate as to its value, the creditor shall not be permitted to require the enrolment of which mention shall be made hereafter, except to the amount of an estimated value expressly declared by him, and of which the debtor shall have a right to make reduction if there be ground.

2133.

A mortgage acquired extends to all the improvements which may occur in the immoveable mortgaged.

SECTION IV.

Of the Order of Mortgages with Regard to each other.

2134.

Among ceditors, the mortgage, whether legal, or judicial, or conventional, takes order only from the day of the enrolment made by the creditor with the keeper of the registers, in the form and in the manner prescribed by the law, saving the exceptions contained in the following article.

2135.

Mortgage exists, independently of every enrolment,

1st. For the benefit of minors and interdicted persons, over the immoveables belonging to their guardian, in the proportion of his administration, from the day of his acceptance of the guardianship ;

2d. For the benefit of women, by reason of their dowry and matrimonial covenants over the immoveables of their husbands, and computing from the day of marriage.

The wife has no mortgage for sums in dowry arising from successions fallen to her, or from donations made to her during marriage, except computing from the opening of the successions, or from the day on which the donations have taken place.

She has no mortgage as indemnity for debts which she has contracted with her husband and for compensation for her property alienated, except computing from the day of the obligation or of the sale.

In no case, shall the regulation of the present article prejudice rights acquired by third persons before the publication of the present title.

2136.

Nevertheless, husbands and guardians are bound to make public the mortgages with which their property is encumbered ; and for this purpose, they are to require without any delay, at the offices established for them, enrolment against the immoveables belonging to them as well as those which may belong to them hereafter.

Husbands and guardians, who, having failed to

require and cause to be made the enrolments directed by the present article, shall have granted or suffered to be taken privileges or mortgages over their immoveables, without declaring expressly that the said immoveables were charged with the legal mortgage of their wives or wards, shall be deemed guilty of stellionate, and as such liable to arrest.

2137.

Supplementary guardians shall be bound, under their personal responsibility, and under pain of damages, to take care that the enrolments be made without delay touching the goods of the guardian, by reason of his administration, even to cause the said enrolments to be made.

2138.

On default by the husbands, guardians, and supplementary guardians, in causing the enrolments directed by the preceding articles to be made, they shall be demanded by the commissioner of government in the civil court at the domicil of the husbands and guardians, or at the place where the property is situated.

2139.

The relations, either of the husband or of the wife, and the relations of the minor, or in default of relations, their friends, may require the said enrolments ; they may also be demanded by the wife and by minors.

2140.

Where, in the contract of marriage, the parties being of age shall have covenanted that enrolment shall not be made except over one or certain immoveables of the husband, the immoveables which shall not be indicated for enrolment shall remain free and unencumbered by mortgage for the dowry of the wife, and for her claims and matrimonial stipulations. It cannot be covenanted that no enrolment shall take place.

2141.

The same rule shall apply to the immoveables of the guardian when the relations, in a family-council, shall have resolved that the enrolment shall only be made touching certain immoveables.

2142.

In the case of the two preceding articles, the husband, the guardian, and the supplementary guardian, shall not be bound to require enrolment, except of the immoveables pointed out.

2143.

Where the mortgage shall not have been restricted by the act nominating the guardian, the latter may, in the case in which the general mortgage upon his immoveables shall manifestly exceed the security sufficient for his administration, demand a restriction of the mortgage to immoveables sufficient to effect a full guaranty in favor of the minor.

The demand shall be made against the supplementary guardian, and it ought to be preceded by a resolution of the family.

2144.

The husband also in like manner, with the consent of his wife, and after having taken the advice of her four nearest relations in an assembly of the family, may demand that the general mortgage upon the whole of his immoveables, by reason of dower, first claims, and matrimonial covenants, shall be restricted to immoveables sufficient for the entire preservation of the rights of the wife.

2145.

Judgments, on the petitions of the husbands and guardians, shall not be given without having heard the commissioner of government, and the parties interested.

In the case in which the court shall pronounce reduction of the mortgage to certain immoveables, the enrolments made, with regard to all the others, shall be cancelled.

CHAPTER IV.

Of the Mode of Enrolment of Privileges and Mortgages.

2146.

The enrolments are made at the office for preserving the mortgages, within the jurisdiction of which is situated the property subjected to privilege or to mortgage. They do not produce any effect if they are taken within the interval during which acts made previously to the opening of bankruptcies are declared null.

It is the same between the creditors of a succession, if the enrolment were not made by one of them until subsequently to the opening, and in the case in which the succession is accepted only with benefit of inventory.

2147.

All the creditors inscribed the same day exercise in concurrence a mortgage of the same date, without distinction of an enrolment of the morning and that of the evening, although such difference shall be marked by the keeper.

2148.

In order to effect enrolment, the creditor must produce, either by himself, or by a third person, to the keeper of the mortgages, the original or an authentic copy of the judgment, or of the act which gives rise to the privilege or to the mortgage.

Added thereto are two accounts upon stamped paper, of which one may be upon the copy of the document; they must contain,

1st. The name, Christian name, domicil of the creditor, his profession if he have one, and the election of a domicil for him in any place whatsoever within the jurisdiction of the office;

2d. The name, Christian name, domicil of the debtor, his profession, if he have one known, or an individual and special designation, such as that the keeper may recognise and distinguish in all cases the individual encumbered with mortgage;

3d. The date and nature of the document;

4th. The amount of the capital of the credits expressed in the document, or estimated by the party making enrolment, for rents or sums lent, or for rights eventual, conditional, or indeterminate, in the cases in which such estimate is directed; as also the amount of the appendages of such capital sums, and the period of their becoming due;

5th. The indication of the description and situation of the property over which he intends to preserve his privilege or his mortgage.

This last regulation is not imperative in the case of legal or judicial mortgages: in default of agreement, a single enrolment for such mortgages, affects all the immoveables comprehended within the jurisdiction of the office.

2149.

Enrolments to be made touching the property of a party deceased, may be made under the simple designation of the defunct, as was mentioned in number 2 of the preceding article.

2150.

The keeper makes mention, upon his register, of the contents of the accounts, and returns to the petitioner as well the document or copy of the document, as one of the accounts, at the foot of which he certifies having made enrolment.

2151.

The creditor enrolled for a capital producing interest or arrears has a right to be placed for two years only, and for the current year, in the same order of mortgage as for his capital; without prejudice to particular enrolments to be taken, importing mortgage to be computed from their date, for other arrears than those reserved by the first emolument.

2152.

It is lawful for the party who has demanded enrolment, as well as for his representatives or assignees, by authentic act, to change upon the register of mortgages the domicil elected by him, on condition of choosing and pointing out another within the same jurisdiction.

2153.

The right of a mortgage purely legal belonging to the nation, to communes, and to public establishments upon the property of parties accountable, those of minors and interdicted persons upon their guardians, married women upon their husbands, shall be enrolled, on the production of two lists, containing only,

1st. The Christian and surname, profession and real domicil of the creditor, and the domicil which shall be elected by him or for him, within the jurisdiction;

2d. The Christian and surname, profession, domicil, or precise designation of the debtor;

3d. The nature of the rights to be preserved, and the amount of their value as relates to determinate objects, without being bound to fix it as to those which are conditional, eventual, or indeterminate.

2154.

Enrolments keep alive mortgage and privilege during ten years, computing from the day of their date: their effect ceases, if such enrolments have not been renewed before the expiration of such interval.

2155.

The expenses of the enrolment are charged upon the debtor if there be no stipulation to the contrary; they are advanced by the party making enrolment, except in the case of legal mortgages, for the enrolment of which the keeper has his remedy against the debtor. The charges of the transcription, which may be required by the seller, are laid upon the purchaser.

2156.

The actions to which the enrolments may give rise against creditors shall be brought before the competent tribunal, by summons given personally or at the last domicil elected on the register; and this, notwithstanding the decease either of creditors, or of those at whose houses they shall have made election of domicil.

CHAPTER V.

Of Cancelling and Reducing Enrolments.

2157.

Enrolments are cancelled by the consent of the parties interested, and who have the requisite power for this end, or by virtue of a judgment in the last resort or passed with the force of a matter decided.

2158.

In either case, they who require cancellation deposit in the office of the keeper a copy of the authentic act containing consent, or that of the judgment.

2159.

Cancellation not consented to is to be demanded in the court within whose jurisdiction the enrolment has been made, unless such enrolment have taken place for the security of an eventual or indeterminate sentence, touching the execution or liquidation of which the debtor and pretended creditor are in litigation, or are to be judged in another court; in which case the demand for cancellation must be brought there or remitted thither.

Nevertheless, an agreement made between the creditor and the debtor to bring, in case of dispute, a petition before a court determined on by themselves, shall be executed by them.

2160.

Cancellation may be directed by the courts, when the enrolment has been made without being founded either in law, or on a title, or when it has been so by virtue of a title, either irregular, or extinguished or discharged, or when the rights of privilege or of mortgage are destroyed by legal means.

2161.

Whenever enrolments made by a creditor, who, according to law, would have had right to make them upon the present and future property of the debtor, without a covenant of restriction, shall be made over a greater portion of different estates than is necessary for the security of the debts, an action is permitted to the debtor for reduction of the enrolments, or for the cancellation of that part which shall exceed the due proportion. The rules concerning jurisdiction are to be followed as established in article 2159.

The enactment of the present article does not apply to conventional mortgages.

2162.

Those enrolments are deemed excessive which extend over several domains, when the value of one alone or of some of them exceeds by more than one third in unencumbered property the amount of the claims in capital and legal charges.

2163.

Those enrolments also are reducible as excessive which are made according to an estimate by the creditor, of claims, which, so far as concerns the mortgage to be established for securing them, have not been regulated by agreement, and which in their nature are conditional, eventual, or indeterminate.

2164.

The excess in this case is determined by the judges, according to circumstances, the probabilities of contingencies and presumptions of fact in such a manner as to reconcile the probable rights of the creditor with the interest of the reasonable credit to be preserved to the debtor; without prejudice to new enrolments to be made with right of mortgage from the day of their date, when the event shall have raised uncertain credits to a larger sum.

2165.

The value of immoveables of which a comparison is to be made with that of credits and one third beyond, is determined by fifteen times the value of the revenue declared by the standard of the returns to the land-tax, or indicated by the quota of contribution upon such return, according to the proportion which exists in the communes of the situation between such standard, or such quota and revenue, for immoveables not liable to perish, and ten times such value for those which are subject thereto. The judges, nevertheless, may avail themselves, moreover, of discoveries which may be drawn from unsuspected leases, from statements of valuation which may have been drawn up previously to the arrival of such periods, and from other similar acts, and value the revenue at an average rate derived from the results of such different information.

CHAPTER VI.

Of the Effect of Privileges and Mortgages against third Persons in wrongful Possession.

2166.

Creditors having privilege or mortgage enrolled over an immoveable may follow it into whatever hands it passes, in order to be arranged and paid according to the order of their credits or enrolments.

2167.

If the third person in wrongful possession do not comply with the formalities which shall be hereafter established, in order to clear his title, he remains, by the single operation of enrolment, bound as wrongful possessor for all mortgage debts, and enjoys the same terms and delays allowed to the original debtor.

2168.

A third person in wrongful possession is bound, in the same case, either to pay interest and capital sums due to whatever amount they may reach, or to abandon the immoveable subjected to mortgage, without any reservation.

2169.

In default by the third person wrongfully possessed to satisfy fully each of these obligations, every mortgage creditor has a right to cause the immoveable mortgaged to be sold, thirty days after notice to the original debtor, and summons given to the wrongful detainer to pay the debt due or abandon possession.

2170.

Nevertheless the wrongful possessor, who is not personally bound for the debt, may oppose the sale of the mortgaged estate conveyed to him, if other immoveables mortgaged for the same debt remain in the possession of the principal debtor or debtors, and may require the previous seizure and sale of them according to the form regulated under the title "*Of Security:*" pending such seizure, the sale of the estate mortgaged is postponed.

2171.

Exception to seizure and sale cannot be made to a creditor privileged or having a special mortgage upon an immoveable.

2172.

As respects abandonment by mortgage, it may be made by all third parties wrongfully possessed who are not personally bound for the debt, and who have power of alienation.

2173.

It may be so even after the third party in wrongful possession has acknowledged the obligation or incurred sentence in this character only: abandonment does not, up to adjudication, prevent the third party in wrongful possession from regaining the immoveable on paying the whole debt and costs.

2174.

The abandonment by mortgage is made at the record-office of the court where such property is situated, and an act thereof is granted by such court.

On the petition of the more diligent of the interested parties, there is created for the immoveable abandoned a curator against whom the sale of the immoveable is sued for in the forms prescribed for ejectments.

2175.

Deteriorations proceeding from the act or the negligence of third parties in wrongful possession to the prejudice of mortgage or privileged creditors, afford ground for an action of indemnity against them: but they cannot recover sums expended and improvements, except to the amount of the additional value resulting from such improvement.

2176.

The fruits of the immoveable mortgaged are only

due from the third party in wrongful possession computing from the day of the summons to pay or to abandon it, and if the proceedings commenced have been discontinued during three years, computing from the making of a new summons.

2177.

Servitudes and real claims which a third party in wrongful possession had upon it before such possession, revive after abandonment or adjudication made against him.

His personal creditors, after all those who are enrolled against previous proprietors, exercise their mortgage in their turn, over the property abandoned or adjudicated.

2178.

A third party in wrongful possession who has paid the mortgage debt, or abandoned the immoveable mortgaged, or been subject to ejectment from such immoveable, has his remedy for warranty, as of right against the principal debtor.

2179.

A third party in wrongful possession who is desirous of clearing his title by paying the sum, must observe the formalities which are established in the 8th chapter of the present title.

CHAPTER VII.

Of the Extinction of Privileges and Mortgages.

2180.

Privileges and mortgages are extinguished,

1st. By the extinction of the principal obligation;

2d. By the renunciation of the mortgage by the creditor;

3d. By compliance with the formalities and conditions prescribed to third persons in wrongful possession for the purpose of clearing property acquired by them;

4th. By prescription.

Prescription is acquired by the debtor, with regard to property in his hands, by the time fixed for the prescription of actions which confer mortgage or privilege.

As regards property in the hands of a third person wrongfully possessed, it is acquired in his favor by the time regulated for the prescription of property for his benefit: in the case in which prescription supposes a title, it only begins to run from the day on which it has been transcribed on the registers of the keeper.

Enrolments made by the creditor do not interrupt the course of prescription established by the law in favor of the debtor or of a third party in wrongful possession.

CHAPTER VIII.

Of the Mode of clearing Property of Privileges and Mortgages.

2181.

Contracts conveying right of ownership in immoveables, or real rights over immoveables, which third persons in wrongful possession shall wish to clear of privileges and mortgages, shall be transcribed throughout by the keeper of the mortgages within the jurisdiction in which the property is situated.

Such transcription shall be made upon a roll destined for this purpose, and the keeper shall be bound to give an acknowledgment thereof to the party requiring it.

2182.

The simple transcription of deeds conveying property upon the register of the keeper, does not exonerate from mortgages and privileges established over the immoveable.

The seller transfers to the purchaser that property and those rights only which he had himself over the thing sold : he transfers them subject to the same encumbrances of privilege and mortgage with which he was charged.

2183.

If the new proprietor is desirous of protecting himself from the effect of the proceedings authorized in the 6th chapter of the present title, he is bound, either previously to such proceedings, or within a month at the latest, computing from the day on which the first summons was given, to notify to the creditors, at the domicils by them chosen in their enrolments,

1st. An extract from his title, containing only the date and quality of the act, the name and precise designation of the seller or donor, the nature and situation of the thing sold or given ; and if a quantity of goods be in question, the general denomination only of the domain and of the circlès within which they are situated, the price and the charges forming part of the price of the sale, or the estimate of the thing if it were the subject of donation ;

2d. An extract from the transcription of the act of sale ;

3d. A table of three columns, of which the first shall contain the date of the mortgages and that of the enrolments ; the second, the names of the creditors ; the third, the amount of the credits enrolled.

2184.

The purchaser or donee shall declare, by the same act, that he is ready to satisfy immediately the debts and encumbrances by mortgage, up to the amount of the price only, without distinction of debts due or not due.

2185.

Where the new proprietor has made such notification within the interval fixed, every creditor whose title is enrolled, may require the immoveable to be put up to public auction and sold to the highest bidder; on condition,

1st. That such requisition shall be signified to the new proprietor within forty days, at the latest, from the notification made at the instance of the latter; adding thereto two days for the distance of five myriameters between the domicil elected and the real domicil of each creditor making requisition;

2d. That it shall contain the proposal of such creditor to raise the price or cause it to be raised to one-tenth above that which shall have been stipulated in the contract, or declared by the new proprietor;

3d. That the same notification shall be made within the same interval to the preceding proprietor, the principal debtor;

4th. That the original and the copies of these instruments shall be signed by the creditor making requisition, or by his attorney expressly appointed, who in such case is bound to produce a copy of his warrant;

5th. That he shall offer to give security up to the amount of the price and the charges.

The whole on pain of nullity.

2186.

In default by the creditors of requiring the auction within the interval and in the forms prescribed, the value of the immoveable becomes finally fixed at the price stipulated in the contract, or declared by the new proprietor, who is in consequence exonerated from every privilege and mortgage, on paying the said price to the creditors who are authorized to receive it, or on depositing the same.

2187.

In case of re-sale by auction, it shall take place according to the forms established for forcible ejectments, at the instance either of the creditor who shall have required it, or of the new proprietor.

The prosecutor shall announce in the bills the price stipulated in the contract, or declared, and the additional sum to which the creditor has bound himself to raise it or cause it to be raised.

2188.

The highest bidder is bound, beyond the price he bid, to repay to the purchaser or to the donee dispossessed, the charges and lawful costs of his contract, those of transcription upon the register of the keeper, those of notification, and those made by him for the purposes of re-sale.

2189.

The purchaser or donee who retains the immoveable put up to auction by becoming highest bidder, is not bound to cause the judgment of adjudication to be transcribed.

2190.

The creditor who has required the sale by auction, cannot by desisting therefrom, even though he should pay the amount of his proposal, prevent the public adjudication, except with the express consent of all the other mortgage creditors.

2191.

The purchaser who shall become highest bidder shall have his remedy as of right against the seller, for the reimbursement of that which exceeds the price stipulated in his contract, and for interest on such excess, computing from the day of each payment.

2192.

In the case in which the title of the new proprietor shall comprehend some immoveables, and some moveables, or several immoveables, some mortgaged, others not mortgaged, situated within the same or within different official jurisdictions, alienated for one and the same price, or for separate and distinct prices, subject or not to the same execution, the price of each immoveable affected by particular and separate enrolments shall be declared in the notification of the new proprietor, by valuation, if there be ground, of the total price expressed in the title.

The creditor being highest bidder cannot in any case be compelled to extend his proposal either to moveable property, or to any other immoveables than those which are mortgaged for his credit, and situated within the same circle; saving the remedy of the new proprietor against his principals, for indemnity, from the damage which he would sustain, either from the division of the objects of his purchase, or from that of the execution.

CHAPTER IX.

Of the Mode of exonerating from Mortgages, where no Enrolment exists, over the Property of Husbands and Guardians.

2193.

Purchasers of immoveables belonging to husbands or to guardians, when there shall be no enrolment over the said immoveables by reason of the administration of the guardian, or by reason of dower, the preferable claims and matrimonial covenants of the wife, may clear off the mortgages which may exist upon property acquired by them.

2194.

For this purpose, they shall deposit a copy, duly examined, of the contract conveying the property, among the rolls of the civil court of the place where such property is situated, and they shall certify, by an act notified, as well to the wife or supplementary guardian, as to the civil commissioner in the court, the deposit by them made. An abstract of such contract, containing its date, the christian and surnames, professions and domicils of the contracting parties, a detail of the nature and situation of the property, the price and other charges of the sale, shall be and remain publicly affixed during two months in the hall of the court; during which time the wives, husbands, guardians or supplementary guardians, minors, interdicted persons, relations or friends, and the commissioner of government, shall be permitted to require, if there be ground, and to cause to be made at the office of the keeper of the mortgages, the enrolments upon the immoveable alienated, which shall have the same effect as if they had been made on the day of the marriage-contract, or on the day on which the guardian entered upon his administration; without prejudice to proceedings which may take place against husbands and guardians, as was mentioned above, with regard to mortgages consented to by them for the benefit of third persons, without having declared to them that the immoveables were already encumbered with mortgages, by reason of marriage or guardianship.

2195.

If, in the course of two months from the exposition of the contract, enrolment have not been made on the part of married women, minors, or interdicted persons, over the immoveables sold, they pass to the purchaser without any charge on account of the dowry, the matrimonial claims and covenants of the wife, or by reason of the administration of the guardian, and saving the remedy, if there be ground, against the husband and guardian.

If enrolments have been made in right of the said married women, minors, or interdicted persons, and if there are anterior creditors who absorb the whole or part of the price, the purchaser is exonerated from the price or from the portion of the price paid by him to creditors arranged in the order to which they are entitled; and the enrolments in right of such married women, minors, and interdicted persons, shall be cancelled, either entirely, or up to the due amount.

If the enrolments on the part of the married women, minors, and interdicted persons, are the more ancient, the purchaser shall not be at liberty to make any payment of the price to the prejudice of the said enrolments, which shall always, as was mentioned above, bear the date of the contract of marriage, or of the entry upon administration by the guardian: and in this case, the enrolments of the other creditors who do not come in beneficial order shall be cancelled.

CHAPTER X.

Of the Publicity of the Registers, and of the Responsibility of the Keepers.

2196.

The keepers of the mortgages are bound to deliver to all those who require it, a copy of the acts transcribed upon their registers as well as of enrolments existing, or a certificate that none exist.

2197.

They are responsible for injury resulting,

1st. From omission in their registers of the transcription of acts of transfer, and of enrolments demanded in their offices;

2d. For failure in mentioning in their certificates the existence of one or more enrolments, unless in the latter case the error has proceeded from insufficient instructions which cannot be charged upon them.

2198.

The immoveable with regard to which the keeper shall have omitted in his certificates one or more charges enrolled, remains, saving the responsibility of the keeper, disencumbered thereof in the hands of the new purchaser, provided he have demanded the certificate subsequently to the transcription of his title; without prejudice nevertheless to the right of creditors to cause themselves to be arranged according to the order which belongs to them, as long as the price has not been paid by the purchaser, or so long as the order made among the creditors has not been allowed.

2199.

In no case can the keepers refuse or delay the transcription of the acts of transfer, the enrolment of mortgage rights, or the delivery of certificates demanded, under pain of damages to the parties; for the effecting of which, statements of refusal or delay shall, at the instance of the parties requiring them, be drawn up forthwith, either by a justice of the peace or by the clerk of the court, or by another officer or a notary, in the presence of two witnesses.

2200.

Nevertheless, the keepers shall be bound to have a register on which they shall inscribe, day by day, and in numerical order, deliveries which shall be made to them of acts of transfer for the purpose of being transcribed, or of the lists to be enrolled; they shall give, on request, an acknowledgment on stamped paper, which shall set forth the number of the register on which the enrolment shall have been made, and they shall not be at liberty to transcribe the acts of transfer, or to enrol the abstracts upon the registers designed for this purpose, except at the date and in the order of the deliveries thereof which shall be made to them.

2201.

All the registers of the keepers must be on stamped paper, endorsed, and signed on each page, from first to last, by one of the judges of the court within whose jurisdiction the office is established. The registers shall be bound up every day like those used in the enrolment of acts.

2202.

The keepers are bound in the exercise of their functions to conform to all the regulations of the present chapter, on pain of a fine from 200 to 1000 francs for the first infringement, and of deprivation for the second; over and above damages to the parties, which shall be paid before the fine.

2203.

The mention of deposits, enrolments, and transcriptions, are made upon the registers, in order, without any blank or interlineation, on pain of a fine of from 1000 to 2000 francs against the keeper, and damages to the parties, payable also previously to the fine.

TITLE XIX.

OF FORCIBLE EJECTMENT, AND OF THE ORDER AMONG CREDITORS.

Decreed the 19th of March, 1804. Promulgated the 29th of the same Month.

CHAPTER I.

Of forcible Ejectment.

2204.

The creditor may sue for ejectment, 1st, from property immoveable and appendages thereto deemed immoveable belonging to his debtor as proprietor thereof; 2d, from the usufruct of property of the same nature appertaining to his debtor.

2205.

Nevertheless the undivided portion of a coheir in the immoveables of a succession cannot be put up to sale by his personal creditors, before the partition or auction which they may demand if they judge it convenient, or with which they have the right to interfere conformably to article 882, under the title "*Of Successions.*"

2206.

The immoveables of a minor, even emancipated, or of an interdicted person, cannot be exposed to sale before the sale of the moveables.

2207.

The sale of moveables is not required before ejectment from immoveables held indivisibly between one of full age, and a minor or interdicted person, if the debt is common to them, nor in the case where the proceedings have been begun against an adult, or before interdiction.

2208.

Ejectment from immoveables which form part of the community, is sued for against the husband alone, although the wife be bound for the debt.

That from immoveables of the wife which have not entered into community, is sued for against the husband and wife who, upon the refusal of her husband to carry on proceedings with her, or in case her husband is a minor, may be authorized by the court.

In case of the minority of the husband and of the wife, or of the wife only, if her husband being adult refuse to carry on proceedings with her, a guardian is nominated for the wife by the court, against whom the suit is to be carried on.

2209.

The creditor can only sue for the sale of immoveables which are not mortgaged to him, in case of the insufficiency of the property which is mortgaged to him.

2210.

A compulsory sale of property situated in different circles can only be claimed successively, unless they form part of one single estate.

It is sued for in the court within whose jurisdiction the principal part of the estate lies, or in default thereof, that part of the property which produces the greatest revenue according to the rent-roll.

2211.

If property mortgaged to the creditor, and property not mortgaged, or property situated in different circles, form part of one and the same estate, the sale of both is pursued together, if the debtor require it; and an estimate is made of the price of the adjudication, if there be ground.

2212.

If the debtor prove, by authentic leases, that the net and unencumbered revenue of his immoveables during one year, is sufficient for the payment of the debt in capital, interest, and expenses, and if he offer to transfer such sum to the creditor, the suit may be suspended by the judges, saving a right to resume it if any opposition or obstacle occur to the payment.

2213.

Compulsory sale of immoveables can only be sued for by virtue of an authentic and executory title, for a debt certain and determined. If the debt consist of coin the value of which is not ascertained, the suit is valid; but the adjudication cannot be made until after computation.

2214.

The assignee of an executory title cannot sue for ejectment until after notification of the conveyance has been made to the debtor.

2215.

The suit may take place by virtue of a provisional or final judgment, executory by provision, notwithstanding appeal; but the adjudication cannot be made until a final judgment in the last resort, or one passed with the force of a matter decided.

The suit cannot be carried on by virtue of judgments given on default during the interval of opposition.

2216.

The suit cannot be annulled under pretext that

the creditor should have commenced it for a larger sum than that which is due to him.

2217.

Every suit for ejectment from immoveables must be preceded by a summons to pay, made, at the instance of the creditor, personally to the debtor or at his domicil by the means of an officer.

The forms of the summons and those of the suit in ejectment are regulated by the laws relating to that procedure.

CHAPTER II.

Of the Order and Distribution of the Price among the Creditors.

2218.

The order and the distribution of the price of immoveables, and the manner of proceeding therein, are regulated by the laws upon that procedure.

TITLE XX.

OF PRESCRIPTION.

Decreed the 15th of March, 1804. Promulgated the 25th of the same Month.

CHAPTER I.

General Ordinances.

2219.

Prescription is a means of acquisition or of exoneration by a certain lapse of time, and subject to conditions determined by the law.

2220.

Prescription cannot be renounced by anticipation; prescription acquired may be renounced.

2221.

Renunciation of prescription is express or tacit: tacit renunciation results from an act which presumes abandonment of a right acquired.

2222.

He who is incapable of alienating, cannot renounce prescription acquired.

2223.

Judges cannot supply officially the argument resulting from prescription.

2224.

Prescription may be objected in every stage of the cause, even before the court of appeal, unless the party who shall not have urged the objection of prescription can, from circumstances, be presumed to have renounced it.

2225.

Creditors or any other person having an interest in establishing prescription, may object it, although the debtor or the proprietor renounce it.

2226.

Prescription cannot be set up against the property in things which are not the objects of commerce.

2227.

The nation, public establishments, and communes, are subjected to prescription equally with private persons, and may plead it in like manner.

CHAPTER II.

Of Possession.

2228.

Possession is the retention or enjoyment of a thing or a right which we hold or which we exercise by ourselves, or by another who holds it or who exercises it in our name.

2229.

In order to be able to prescribe, there is required possession continual and uninterrupted, peaceable, public, unequivocal, and under the title of proprietor.

2230.

A party is always presumed to possess for himself, and under the title of proprietor, unless it be proved that he commenced his possession for another.

2231.

Where a person has commenced his possession in right of others, he is always presumed to possess by the same title, if there be no contrary proof.

2232.

Acts of pure license and simple toleration can lay no foundation either for possession or prescription.

2233.

Acts of violence can lay no better ground for a possession capable of operating prescription.

Useful possession does not commence until violence has ceased.

2234.

The actual possessor who proves his possession at an antecedent period, is presumed to have possessed in the intermediate time; saving proof to the contrary.

2235.

In order to complete prescription, the party may join to his own possession that of his predecessor, in whatsoever manner he may have succeeded to him, whether by universal or particular title, or by lucrative or chargeable title.

CHAPTER III.

Of the Causes which prevent Prescription.

2236.

They who possess in right of others can never prescribe by any lapse of time whatsoever.

Thus the farmer, the depositary, the usufructuary, and all others who hold by precarious title the property of the proprietor, are incapable of prescribing for it.

2237.

The heirs of those who held the thing by any one of the titles designated in the preceding article, are also incapable of prescribing.

2238.

Nevertheless, the persons enumerated in articles 2236 and 2237 may prescribe, if the title of their possession be overthrown, either by a cause proceeding from a third person, or by the opposition which they may have made to the claim of the proprietor.

2239.

Those to whom farmers, depositaries, and other precarious holders, have transmitted the thing by a title conveying ownership may prescribe.

2240.

A man cannot prescribe against his own title, in this sense that he cannot change upon himself the cause and principal of his possession.

2241.

A man may prescribe against his own title, in this sense that he may prescribe for exoneration from an obligation which he has contracted.

CHAPTER IV.

Of the Causes which interrupt, or which suspend the Course of Prescription.

SECTION I.

Of the Causes which interrupt Prescription.

2242.

Prescription may be interrupted either naturally or civilly.

2243.

There is a natural interruption, when the possessor is deprived, during more than a year, of the enjoyment of the thing, whether by the ancient proprietor, or even by a third person.

2244.

A citation in court, a peremptory demand, or a seizure notified to the party whom it is desired to impede in prescription, form a civil interruption.

2245.

A summons for reconciliation before the office of the peace, interrupts prescription from the day of its date, when it is followed by a citation from the court given within legal intervals.

2246.

Citation in court given, even before an unauthorized judge, interrupts prescription.

2247.

If the summons be null for defect in form;
If the plantiff discontinue his demand;
If he fail to prosecute his suit;
Or if his petition be rejected,
The interruption is considered as not having occurred.

2248.

Prescription is interrupted by the acknowledgment which the debtor or the possessor makes of the right of the party against whom he was prescribing.

2249.

A demand made, conformably to the articles above, to one of the joint and several debtors, or his acknowledgment, interrupts prescription against all the rest, and even against their heirs.

A demand made on one of the heirs of a joint and several debtor, or the acknowledgment of such heir, does not interrupt prescription with regard to the other coheirs, even though the debt should be a mortgage one, if the obligation is indivisible.

Such demand or such acknowledgment does no interrupt prescription, with regard to the other joint debtors, except for that portion in which such heir is bound.

In order to interrupt prescription entirely, with regard to the other joint-debtors, there must be a demand made to all the heirs of the deceased debtor, or an acknowledgment by the whole of such heirs.

2250.

Demand made upon the principal debtor, or his acknowledgment, interrupts prescription against the security.

SECTION II.

Of the Causes which suspend the Course of Prescription.

2251.

Prescription runs against all persons, unless they are within some exception established by a law.

2252.

Prescription does not run against minors and interdicted persons, saving what is said in article 2278, and with the exception of the other cases determined by the law.

2253.

It does not run between married persons.

2254.

Prescription runs against a married woman, although she be not separated by the contract of marriage, or by the law, with regard to property of which her husband has the administration, saving her remedy against her husband.

2255.

Nevertheless, it does not run, during marriage, with regard to the alienation of an estate settled according to the regulations of dower, conformably to article 1561, under the title "*Of the Contract of Marriage, and of the respective Rights of Married Persons.*"

2256.

Prescription is in like manner suspended during marriage,

1st. In the case where the action of the wife cannot be brought until after an election to be made touching the acceptance or renunciation of community;

2d. In the case in which the husband, having sold property belonging to the wife without her consent, is guarantee for the sale, and in all other cases in which the action by the wife shall lie against the husband.

2257.

Prescription does not run,

With regard to a debt which depends on a contingency, until such contingency occur;

With regard to an action for warranty, until eviction have taken place;

With regard to a debt at a fixed day, until such day have arrived.

2258.

Prescription does not run against the beneficiary heir, with regard to demands which he has against the succession.

It runs against a vacant succession, although not provided with a curator.

2259.

It runs also during the three months for making inventory, and the forty days for deliberation.

CHAPTER V.

Of the Time required in order to prescribe.

SECTION I.

General Ordinances.

2260.

Prescription is computed by days, and not by hours. It is acquired when the last day of the term is accomplished.

2261.

In prescriptions which are accomplished within a certain number of days, the supplementary days are reckoned.

In those which are accomplished by months that of Fructidor comprehends the supplementary days.

SECTION II.

Of a thirty Years' Prescription.

2262.

All actions, as well real as personal, are prescribed by thirty years, without compelling the party who alleges it to produce a document thereon, or without permitting an objection to be opposed to him derived from bad faith.

2263.

After twenty-eight years from the date of the last title, the grantor of an annuity may be compelled to furnish at his own charge a new title to his creditor or to his assigns.

2264.

The rules of prescription on other subjects than those mentioned in the present title, are explained in the titles peculiar to them.

SECTION III.

Of Prescription by ten and twenty Years.

2265.

The party who acquires an immoveable bona fide, and by just title, prescribes for property therein in ten years, if the true proprietor lives within the jurisdiction of the court of appeal within the compass of which the immoveable is situated; and in twenty years, if he is domiciled beyond the said jurisdiction.

2266.

If the real proprietor have had his domicil at different times, within and without the jurisdiction, it is necessary, in order to complete prescription, to add to the deficiency from ten years of presence therein, a number of years of absence therefrom double of such deficiency, in order to complete the ten years of presence.

2267.

A title void by defect in form cannot serve as the basis of prescription by ten and twenty years.

2268.

Good faith is always presumed, and it lies with the party who alleges bad faith to prove it.

2269.

It suffices that good faith existed at the moment of acquisition.

2270.

After ten years, architects and contractors are discharged from the warranty of workmanship performed or directed by them by estimate.

SECTION IV.

Of some particular Prescriptions.

2271.

The actions of masters and instructors in sciences and arts, which they give by the month;

That by keepers of inns and taverns, on account of lodging and board which they supply;

That by artisans and work-people, for the payment of their daily labor, provisions, and salaries,

Are prescribed in six months.

2272.

The action by physicians, surgeons, and apothecaries for their visits, operations, and medicine;

That by officers of the court, for compensation for acts notified by them, and for commissions which they execute;

That by merchants, for commodities sold by them to private persons not merchants;

That by keepers of boarding-houses, for the price of the board of their pupils; and by other masters for the price of apprenticeship;

That by servants who are hired by the year for the payment of their wages,

Are prescribed after a year.

2273.

The action by attornies, for the payment of their costs and charges, is prescribed after two years, computing from the judgment on the process, or from the settlement by the parties, or from the revocation of the said attornies. With regard to affairs not terminated, they cannot make demands for their costs and charges which shall extend more than five years backward.

2274.

Prescription takes place, in the cases above, although there has been a continuation of supplies, deliveries of goods, services, and works.

It only ceases to run when there has been an account balanced, a schedule or obligation, and a legal citation not annulled.

2275.

Nevertheless, those to whom such prescriptions are objected, may tender an oath to the parties objecting them, for the purpose of ascertaining this question whether payment has really been made.

The oath may be tendered to widows and heirs, or to the guardians of the latter, if they be minors, in order that they may declare whether they know the demand to be just.

2276.

Judges and attornies are discharged as to documents five years after judgment on the proceedings.

Officers of the court, after two years from the execution of the commission, or from the notification of the acts with which they were intrusted, are in like manner discharged therefrom.

2277.

The arrears of perpetual and life annuities;

Those of alimentary pensions;

The rents of houses, and the price of a lease of rural property;

Interest on sums lent, and generally every thing which is payable by the year, or at shorter periodical intervals;

Are prescribed after five years.

2278.

Prescriptions which form the subject of the articles of the present section run against minors and interdicted persons, saving their remedy against their guardians.

2279.

In the case of moveables, possession is equivalent to a title.

Nevertheless, the party who has lost any thing, or from whom it has been stolen, may reclaim it within three years computing from the day of the loss or robbery, against the party in whose hands he finds it; saving to the latter his remedy against the person from whom he obtained it.

2280.

If the actual possessor of the thing stolen, or lost,

has purchased it in a fair, or in a market, or at a public sale, or from a merchant who sells similar articles, the original proprietor can only procure it to be restored to him on repaying to the possessor the price which it cost him.

2281.

Prescriptions commenced at the period of the publication of the present title, shall be regulated conformably to the ancient laws.

Nevertheless, prescriptions at that time commenced, and for which there was still requisite, according to the ancient laws, more than thirty years computing from the same date, shall be accomplished by such lapse of thirty years.

(Signed) BONAPARTE, First Consul.

(Countersigned) The Secretary of State,
HUGHES B. MARET,
And sealed with the Seal of State.

Seen, the Chief Judge, Minister of Justice,
(Signed REGNIER.

Certified, the Grand Judge, Minister of Justice,
REGNIER.

HE END.

Printed in the United States
74496LV00002B/198